Survival Guide

DAVID SOLOMON

CB

CONTEMPORARY BOOKS

Library of Congress Cataloging-in-Publication Data

Solomon, David.
    Nutz & boltz automotive survival guide / David Solomon.
       p.   cm.
    ISBN 0-8092-3059-3
    1. Automobiles—Maintenance and repair—Amateurs' manuals.
  I. Title.
TL152.S64543   1997
629.28'72—dc21   97-36121
                                              CIP

Cover design by Scott Rattray
Interior design by Mary Lockwood

Published by Contemporary Books
An imprint of NTC/Contemporary Publishing Company
4255 West Touhy Avenue, Lincolnwood (Chicago), Illinois 60646-1975 U.S.A.
Copyright © 1997 by David Solomon
Printed in the United States of America
International Standard Book Number: 0-8092-3059-3
17   16   15   14   13   12   11   10   9   8   7   6   5   4   3   2   1

To my children, Sky and Sparky
To my right hand and friend, Catherine

To all the hard-working automotive mechanics
who deserve more respect than the world gives them

Contents

Introduction

This guide is designed to give you, the driver, an upper hand in just about any automotive situation, from maintenance to repairs to full-blown emergency situations. If you like cars and you like knowing how to keep them running smoothly, how to get problems fixed when they occur, and how to avoid common problems and mistakes that many car owners make, you have picked up the right book. If you aren't all that familiar with (or, frankly, even interested in) your car, the way it works, and what can go wrong with it, you have definitely picked up the right book, and it belongs in your glove compartment right now. Why? Because inside this book you'll find a wealth of expert tips and advice that will save you money, time, energy—maybe even your life.

Got a flat tire? Car won't start? Overheating? Did the kids spill ice cream on the upholstery? Is the steering pulling? No brakes? This book will take you, step-by-step, through pinpointing and fixing these problems and answering hundreds of other questions, including:

- How do I get out of this mud?

- When was I supposed to have the oil changed?

- What is that weird sound?

- I forget—do jumper cables go on positive to positive, or positive to negative?

- How did that green puddle get under my car?

- Why is my mechanic always so happy to see me?

- Do you smell something funny?

Whether you have a simple question or a real auto emergency, this book will tell you what you need to know and show you how to handle it—in clear, nontechnical language and easy-to-follow directions that don't require a master technician's degree to understand. You'll learn how to keep your car out of the breakdown lane, and you'll learn mechanics' tricks for making your automobile give you better fuel mileage, run more smoothly, and last longer.

Flip through this book. Become familiar with the contents. If you want to read the whole thing now, by all means, feel free. You'll find dozens of great tips that can help you take care of your car right now. If you'd rather wait until a problem rears its head, well, that's your choice too. But whatever you do, don't let this book collect dust on a shelf in your living room. Keep it in your glove compartment. You never know when you'll face a car question, problem, or crisis. With this book in hand, however, you will be prepared.

Safety Reminder

Always keep safety in mind when working on your car. Remove all jewelry and scarves and tie back long hair before you begin. Do not smoke in or near your car while you are working on it. Wear safety goggles or glasses to protect your eyes, and avoid wearing loose-fitting clothing that could get caught in something or catch fire. Make sure the area you're working in is well lighted and ventilated, and always work with an assistant or buddy. Avoid carelessness at all times. If you are not certain you understand or are able to safely perform a task or procedure described in this book, see a qualified auto mechanic for assistance and diagnosis.

Fluids and Filters

In these days of self-serve gas stations, you need to know how to properly check and service the area under the hood of your car. Also, you can save big bucks by handling many maintenance items yourself. This chapter will help you do the maintenance properly, without cutting corners and without using shoddy procedures. You'll also learn some of my best tricks and tips for working under the hood of your car.

Fill-Up Procedures

Filling the gas tank is a part of everyday life. Most people learn from watching Dad or Mom, but many don't get proper lessons on fueling a vehicle. The fact is, there's more to fueling your car than just pumping and paying. This section gives you some tips for tanking up right.

Gas Cap Capers

First, memorize the gas cap's location. If you park on the wrong side of the pump and have to drag the hose over the car, you may damage your paint.

After you remove the gas cap, don't put it on top of the gas pump. Most gas stations have a big box full of gas caps that people have left behind. Instead, check to see whether the cover flap is equipped with a handy notch or holder for the gas cap. If not, put the cap on the fender directly above the filler hole or somewhere in plain sight so that you won't forget it when you finish.

Filling the Whole Tank Properly

When pumping fuel, remember to stand upwind of the nozzle. Gasoline fumes are extremely hazardous to your health; avoid breathing them in at all costs. Here are the steps for getting a perfect fill-up without damaging your car:

Static electricity can create a spark when you remove the gas cap and may ignite the fumes! In dry, cool weather, when a great deal of static is in the air, always lean against the vehicle with one hand and unscrew the cap with the other to prevent this from happening.

1 *Carefully* **lower the gas nozzle into the filler neck.** Care is necessary because the last person may have left fuel in the nozzle, and this fuel may spill onto your paint.

2 **Insert the nozzle as far as possible into the filler neck.** This reduces the chance of the fuel "burping" out of the filler neck and onto your car and your shoes. If the car doesn't take fuel well without making the nozzle click off, try inserting the nozzle upside down or even sideways.

3 **Shut off the pump at the second click.** *Do not* overfill the tank. If you are in the habit of filling the tank right to the top, you are wasting fuel, damaging the emission system, and hurting the environment. Overfilling causes excess gas to either run out on the ground or be drawn into the car's evaporative emission canister, ruining it. The canister is designed to store gas *fumes*, not liquid gas. If it becomes saturated with gasoline, its activated charcoal (used to store gas fumes) will be worthless, and the car will start to smell like gas after sitting in the sun on a hot day.

4 **Before removing the nozzle from the filler neck, make sure that all the fuel has drained out of it.** If you pull the nozzle out too soon, you will spill gas on the car, the ground, and you.

If you do spill gas on your car, wash it off immediately with water. Wipe the area with some of your favorite auto polish as soon as possible to avoid gas stains. Do not use the windshield wash squeegee to wash off the gas—you'll contaminate the water bucket for the next user.

5 **Don't drain the fuel hose.** If the next person prepays a precise amount, the pump will shut off at the nozzle and keep that person from draining the hose like you did. The customer pays for the gas it took to refill the hose but doesn't get to use it.

Debunking the High-Test Myth

Here are some commonly asked questions about gasoline.

Do not fill metal gas cans that are in plastic pickup truck liners. This combination generates electricity and may ignite the fumes as the nozzle is removed. Always fill gas cans on the ground.

"Does my car need high-test fuel? What about all the advertising that says that it needs high-test to run properly? How do you know if using high-test really makes a difference? What if I want to treat my car to the very best? Is using high-test bad for any reason?"

Unless your engine is turbocharged, supercharged, or a multivalve, high-performance engine, you are probably wasting money if you use high-test fuel. One of the best ways to find out your engine's minimum fuel octane requirement is to check your owner's manual. If you can't find that information, check the area near the gas cap for a decal advising you of the vehicle's fuel requirements.

"What happens if I use higher-octane fuel than required?"

Some carmakers say that using high-test can cause drivability problems. High-octane fuels burn more slowly than regular fuels. If your engine is not designed to ignite the fuel early enough, the fuel won't have time to burn completely and will be wasted. The unburned portion of the fuel goes into the exhaust system, where it continues burning. This wasted energy goes right out the tailpipe, along with the money you spent on something your car didn't need. In some cases, using high-test can make your car hard to start or cause stalling, hesitation, or engine surging.

"Does it hurt to use regular when premium is recommended?"

Yes. If you constantly hear engine ping or knock, stop using regular-octane gas. Constant engine pinging destroys the tops of the pistons and leads to the early demise of your engine. It can also lower gas mileage.

"What if my engine is supposed to use regular but knocks and pings unless I use premium?"

Have your mechanic repair the problem causing the knock. Likely candidates are lean air–fuel mixture, carbon buildup in the combustion chamber, or a faulty EGR (exhaust gas recirculation) system.

Some modern engines are equipped with knock sensors that prevent the engine from pinging. These engines can fool you into thinking that it's OK to use regular gas because engine timing is automatically retarded by the engine computer when the knock

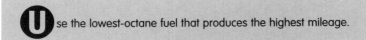
Use the lowest-octane fuel that produces the highest mileage.

sensor detects ping. But the engine will perform with less power and achieve less gas mileage. In the long run, you pay more for gas and get poorer performance than if you had used higher-octane fuel.

Fuel Economy

The way you use your car and take care of it will have a tremendous impact on fuel economy. It will also increase your enjoyment of the car and reduce your cost of operation. Here are 16 fuel-saving tips:

- Keep your tires inflated at the correct pressure. Underinflation causes tire wear and wastes fuel.

- Don't carry unneeded weight in your vehicle. Excess weight puts a heavier load on the engine, causing greater fuel consumption.

- Avoid lengthy warm-up idling. Once the engine is running smoothly, begin driving—but gently. Remember, however, that on cold winter days it may take a little longer to warm up.

- Accelerate slowly and smoothly. Avoid jackrabbit starts. Get into high gear as quickly as possible.

- Avoid long engine idling. If you have a long wait and you're not in traffic, it's better to turn off the engine and start again later.

- Avoid engine lug or overrevving. Use a gear range suitable for the road you are traveling.

- Use your air conditioner only when absolutely necessary. The air conditioner puts an extra load on the engine, increasing fuel consumption.

- Avoid continuously speeding up and slowing down. Stop-and-go driving wastes fuel.

- Avoid unnecessary stopping and braking. Maintain a steady pace. Try to time the traffic signals so you have to stop as little as possible, or take through streets to avoid traffic lights.

- Keep enough distance from other vehicles to avoid sudden braking. This will also reduce wear on your brakes.

- Avoid heavy traffic or traffic jams whenever possible.

Octane Explained

Back in 1927, Graham Edgar proposed the idea of measuring fuel octane based on an arbitrary number scale. It became known as the **research method**. For this purpose, Edgar used two hydrocarbons—isooctane and heptane—as reference points based on their resistance to engine knock. Isooctane has a very high resistance to knock and was assigned a primary value of 100. Heptane has a low resistance to knock and was assigned a value of zero. The octane value became the volume percentage of the two ingredients.

In 1932, the American Society for Testing Materials (ASTM) got into the act and established its method for rating gasoline octane because Edgar's octane testing methods were showing poor correlation with what was happening in cars. ASTM wanted a test condition that better reflected the results in actual real-world motors, not just lab motors.

The ASTM test was done at a higher fuel–air mixture temperature and engine speed than Edgar's research method. ASTM's corresponding numbers were called the motor octane number (MON) and research octane number (RON). This new procedure became known as the **motor method for octane labeling**.

Today's octane formula is expressed as the gas **antiknock index** (AKI) rating. The AKI is the measure of a fuel's capability to burn slowly or resist knock (ping)—a measure of its octane quality. The AKI is the **average** of the RON and the MON. That is, $AKI = (R + M) \div 2$. This equation is displayed on a black-and-yellow decal on all gas pumps.

While you never know the actual numbers used to get at the final octane number posted on the pump, you do pick and choose octane levels. It's important to know that there are big differences in fuel quality of the same octane based on how the fuel is blended. Just because one fuel is 93 octane may not mean it is the same as another brand that lists 93 octane on the pump. The posted octane could have been created by using different levels of ingredients.

Two different brands with the same octane may perform differently in your engine. That's why it's important to try different brands of fuel until you find one that you and your engine like. Which one produces the best fuel mileage and pep and the least knock or ping?

- Don't rest your foot on the clutch or brake pedal. This causes needless wear, overheating, and poor fuel economy.

- Maintain a moderate speed on highways. The faster you drive, the greater the fuel consumption. By reducing your speed, you will cut down on fuel consumption.

- Keep the front wheels in proper alignment. Avoid hitting curbs and slow down on rough roads. Improper alignment not only causes faster tire wear but also puts an extra load on the engine, which wastes fuel.

- Keep the bottom of your vehicle free from mud, snow, and the like. This not only lessens weight but also helps prevent corrosion.

- Keep your vehicle tuned up and in top shape. A dirty air cleaner, improper valve clearance, dirty plugs, dirty oil and grease, brakes that need adjusting, and other problems all lower engine performance and contribute to poor fuel economy. For longer life of all parts and lower operating costs, do all maintenance work on schedule. If you often drive under severe conditions, see that your vehicle receives more frequent maintenance.

Electric Fuel Pumps

There is a science to the care and feeding of your car's electric fuel pump. Follow this advice and you will save the pump—not to mention hundreds of dollars in repair costs.

- **First and foremost, keep the tank full.** If you typically wait until the empty light comes on before refueling, you are inviting trouble in two ways:

  1 Condensation will form in the tank. Water is the enemy of your fuel system. It is heavier than gasoline, so it settles at the bottom of the tank. There it starts to attack the tank lining, causing flaky rust. Your fuel pump picks up the rust particles and is ruined. The best defense in this case is to keep the tank full, especially if you don't drive very often.

  2 The fuel pump will "starve." Modern electric fuel pumps depend on fuel for internal cooling and lubrication. Without fuel, the pump can be ruined in seconds. To avoid this problem, try to keep the tank at least one-quarter full at all times.

- **Be careful with gas additives**. Don't use additives that contain xylene, toluene, acetone, or methanol (methyl alcohol). These can damage the rubber fuel hoses and fuel tank lining. The contamination caused by the attack damages the rollers in the fuel pump and plugs the fuel filter.

- **Forget the moisture.** Modern gasoline already contains enough alcohol to absorb the moisture from the tank. Additional gas-drying additives make a potent cocktail out of the water in the tank, actually pulling alcohol from the fuel where it is held in suspension. Then the fuel pump gets a big hit of water and additive all at once. In general, don't use gas-drying additives unless you know there is water in the tank. When in doubt, it's better to drain the tank to be sure.

- **Buy gas carefully.** Don't buy gas from pumps that are seldom used and off the beaten path. You are more likely to get fuel that is contaminated or laced with water. Try to frequent a filling station that pumps a great deal of fuel, like one located at a busy intersection. They usually have better prices, too!

- **Change the fuel filter.** Changing the filter is your best protection against fuel problems. Fuel filters not only remove solid particulates, but they also absorb some moisture from the system. Larger filters can hold three to four ounces of water. Some cars have *two* fuel filters; both should be changed.

Fuel Filter Testing

Fuel filters do the silent job of protecting the intimate parts of your car's fuel system. Many carmakers don't list change intervals in the owner's manuals, even though fuel filters should be changed every two years or 30,000 miles. A partially plugged fuel filter restricts the flow through the pump and causes it to wear prematurely. Replacing electric fuel pumps is costly, so changing the fuel filter is cheap insurance.

A partially plugged fuel filter also causes fuel starvation when the engine needs fuel the most—on heavy acceleration and at high engine speeds. For fuel-injected cars, a partially plugged filter is bad for the electric fuel pump because the pump needs fresh fuel to cool and lubricate its internal moving parts. Once the filter plugs completely, the engine will not run at all.

Save the old fuel filter, if possible. It is a great diagnostic tool. If you don't service your own car, ask your mechanic to save the fuel filter for you in a clean, clear glass jar that you provide. Once you get the old filter, here's the drill:

1 Find the arrow on the filter indicating the direction of fuel flow.

2 Blow into the filter in the *opposite* direction so that the contents of the filter go into the jar. (**Caution: *Do not* put your mouth in direct contact with the filter. Gasoline is poisonous, a potential carcinogen.**)

If you can't blow through the filter, this indicates a plugged filter and serious fuel contamination problems. Instead, use an air nozzle to blow through the filter.

3 Examine the contents of the filter for potential fuel system problems, described in the following sections.

4 Let the contents of the jar sit for about 20 minutes to see what settles to the bottom.

Read on to discover possible signs of trouble.

Black Fuel

The black color comes from deteriorating fuel hoses, indicating prolonged exposure of the hoses to alcohol, xylene, toluene, or acetone. These chemicals are found in cheap fuel and some brands of gas additives. Mechanics following improper fuel-injection cleaning techniques can also allow power-injector cleaning solvents to return to the fuel tank and damage the hoses.

Water

If you see small, clear "bubbles" that stay on the bottom of the jar, you have water in your fuel tank. Infrequent use of the vehicle can cause moisture to condense in the fuel tank, or rainwater can enter the tank through a cracked gas-cap seal. No matter the reason, water leads to a rusted fuel tank, corrosion in the fuel rail, or damaged metal parts in the fuel system.

Make sure you have a full tank of gasoline when having your injectors cleaned. If some of the injector cleaner chemicals are allowed to return to the tank, the full tank will dilute them.

Gray Deposits

Fuel or fuel additives containing methanol or methyl alcohol cause the fuel tank lining to dissolve, causing gray deposits in the jar. Soon, the tank rusts. (Modern fuel tanks are now being made of plastic to avoid problems with rust and additive corrosion.)

Rust-Colored Fuel

The rust comes from prolonged exposure to water. The gas tank should be replaced or recoated with an approved gas tank sealer. Rust particles are the enemy of electric fuel pumps and fuel injectors.

Metal Particles

Metal particles are usually a sign that the fuel pump is about to fail. Some types of high-pressure fuel pumps use metal rollers that pressurize the fuel. Tiny slivers of metal come from disintegration of the plating on the outside of these rollers, which indicates impending pump failure.

Changing Filters

When it comes to changing filters on your vehicle (a very important service), it's not always the best idea to have someone else do it for you. If you do it yourself, you can perform several extra procedures that are beneficial for your vehicle. Most mechanics are in a hurry and don't want to bother with additional steps even though they know they're important. If you do it yourself, you can do it right—every time!

Oil Filters

Always change your oil filter when you change the oil. Not all filters are alike. Factory filters are of excellent quality, as are some brand names (Hastings, Wix, and Bosch, for example). Call the dealer and ask for a price break on a case. Filters used at some "el cheapo" places are substandard, don't filter oil adequately, and leave the engine unprotected against harmful contamination. If you frequent chain stores or quick-change shops, take your own filter with you.

Air Filters

Typically, air filters are replaced unnecessarily. While the owner's manual is a good guide, take a look at the filter before routinely changing it.

You should service your own air filter, checking to see if it's so dirty that you can't see light through it. Twice a year, tap it against the ground to dislodge dirt. Also, rinsing it with a garden hose can extend its life two to three times. Air filters get dirty faster where there is sand, dust, or other airborne debris. Beware of cheap filters, which don't fit well and allow dirt to enter.

Fuel Filters

Some carmakers don't recommend fuel filter changes. They don't want the cost of this important service to be considered when their vehicle is rated against competitors' vehicles in terms of maintenance costs. But changing the fuel filter regularly can prevent costly fuel-system problems. To save money, change it as part of your regular tune-up.

Oil Change Procedures

There are many ways to change motor oil. Follow these steps to make the procedure as faultless as possible:

1 **Make sure that the engine is** *hot.* **(Take precautions to avoid being burned.)** Oil has dispersants in its additive package. These chemicals are there to keep dirt in suspension in the oil so that dirt leaves the engine when the oil is drained. Ideally, the oil should be hot so that the dispersants can do their job. Run the engine for at least 20 minutes at highway speeds to ensure the oil is hot.

2 **Raise or park the vehicle in such a way that the drain plug is at the lowest point of the oil pan.** This may require making one wheel higher than the other. Chock the wheels, set the parking brake, and place the transmission in gear (manual transmission) or in Park (automatic transmission).

3 **Open the hood and pull the dipstick out of the dipstick tube.** Pull the dipstick out far enough to make it easy to spot. This step is important because the protruding dipstick will remind you that the oil is being changed and that there is no oil in the motor. It can also serve as a reminder to secure the drain plug before adding oil.

4 **Remove the oil filter** *before* **draining the oil.** Some cars have an air lock that holds several ounces of dirty oil in the oil filter housing, channels, and ducts. This trapped oil will drain out with the dirty oil if you remove the filter first.

Be sure the drain pan is ready to catch oil from the filter. If the filter is mounted straight up, use an ice pick and punch a hole in it to drain the filter before you remove it. This helps to prevent a mess.

5 **Remove the drain plug.** The drain pan should be positioned so that it can catch the stream of oil. Use a box-end wrench or a closed wrench to avoid stripping the plug. A socket wrench works well, too. The drain pan should be positioned so that it will catch any drips of oil from both the drain hole and the oil filter.

Be sure that the oil filter seal comes off with the filter can. If not, be sure to remove it from the engine before installing the new filter. Sometimes the sealing washer sticks to the engine block and remains there after the old filter is removed. If it is allowed to remain in place and the new filter is screwed on top of it, you might not notice it, but this "double gasket" will quickly destroy your engine! The extra sealing gasket pops out and creates a leak when the engine is running at higher rpms (revolutions per minute), probably when you are on the highway. Suddenly all the engine oil gushes out of the leak, and, by the time the oil pressure warning light comes on, you have lost an engine from running without oil pressure.

6 **Examine the drain plug for the presence of a sealing washer.** Some carmakers (for example, Toyota, Mercedes-Benz, and Isuzu) require that the drain plug sealing washer be replaced at every oil change. When in doubt, find out what the local dealership recommends. Take the following precautions:

- Check for poor centering of the drain plug washer, which can cause oil leaks at the plug.

- Tighten the drain plug by hand until the washer contacts the oil pan squarely. This helps to center the sealing washer. Then tighten it with the box wrench.

- Be careful if the drain plug seal has a raised portion. The plug will leak if the raised portion is not placed securely against the oil pan.

- Be sure to remove all traces of the old drain plug gasket or sealing washer before installing the new one. If any pieces of the old gasket remain, the new gasket won't seal and you will have a new leak.

7 **Install the oil filter.** If the filter mounts with the threaded end upward, fill the filter with fresh oil before installing it. Wipe the engine mounting flange (the round place against which the filter mounts) clean and wipe the filter rubber sealing ring with fresh oil. Follow the directions on the filter about hand-tightening torque. In general, the filter should be tight enough to seal properly but not so tight that the metal filter canister comes into contact with the mounting flange.

8 **Add the right amount of oil to the motor.** Most engines take either four or five quarts of oil. It is generally safe to start with four quarts and add the last quart if needed. Check the owner's manual for recommended fill amounts.

9 **Prime the motor before starting it.** This step requires cranking the engine over several times without allowing it to start. Observe the proper procedure for your car:

- Carbureted vehicles: Unplug the ignition coil or disconnect and ground the high-tension coil wire to disable the ignition. After the oil-pressure light on the dash goes out, enable the ignition and start the motor.

- Most fuel-injected cars: Crank the engine over (as if you're trying to get it to start) while holding the gas pedal to the floor. This puts the motor in clear flood mode, and the computer shuts off fuel to the injectors, preventing the engine from starting. After the oil-pressure light goes out, release the pedal to let the motor start and idle.

10 **While the motor is idling, look underneath for oil leaks.
Turn off the motor, reinsert the dipstick, and check the
oil level.** Some oil will "hang up" in the engine for as long as
20 minutes, so the dipstick may read slightly low. Keep this
in mind before deciding to top off the oil level to make the
dipstick read totally full. Put a sticker on the door post or
under the hood indicating the mileage at the oil change.

Motor Oil: Engine Lifeblood

Should you add fresh oil to dirty oil if the car's oil level is low?
Probably not. If the oil level is down a quart or more, it is usually
a good indication that the useful life of the oil is over and it's time
for an oil change. However, if your car is a leaker, keep adding oil
as needed to prevent it from dropping below a quart low.

If there are over 2,000 miles on the oil or more than three
months have passed since your last oil change and the level is down
a quart or more, have the oil changed right away. Adding fresh oil
to old, burned oil does not help the engine because the remaining
oil is practically useless anyway. If the oil level in your engine is
low, here's what may happen:

• **Oil breakdown:** One of the most important jobs of motor oil
is to help cool the engine. A certain amount of oil is needed to
carry heat away from the hot internal parts of the engine. When
the oil level drops, the remaining oil becomes hotter and begins
to break down. The oil molecules form long chains of hydrocarbons, causing some of the oil to turn into tar and stick to the
bottom of the engine—becoming useless. Without a good supply of cool oil, engine wear is accelerated.

• **Heat loss:** When motor oil becomes hot, it loses its ability to
lubricate the hot parts of the engine. Just like hot oil in a hot
frying pan, the oil forms into beads and runs off the hot metal
where it is needed the most. Without oil on the sliding surfaces
inside the engine, engine wear is accelerated.

• **Additive losses:** When the oil level drops, the remaining oil
does not have enough detergent additives to keep the inside of
the engine clean. A low oil level causes sludge to form inside
the engine, clogging up oil passages and starving critical parts
of much-needed oil.

• **Driveway spots:** Pay attention to your parking spot. Does your
vehicle leave suspicious stains on the ground? These stains can
be tip-offs to problems.

Lay a flattened-out cardboard box in your parking place, and
after driving some distance, park your car over it. ***Important:***
Make sure the cardboard is flat and not near a hot muffler.

The next day, move the car and examine the cardboard for spots. If you see any, make a mental note of where on the car the spot came from. Cut out the soiled piece of cardboard and take it to your mechanic for further diagnosis.

> **I**f you get stuck in traffic for any length of time in really hot weather, consider how your motor oil is affected. A couple of bad cases of gridlock and your oil could really be fried.

What to Do with No Oil Pressure

You're driving merrily along one fine day and suddenly your red oil-pressure or engine light comes on. You don't hear any knocking and have no idea what can possibly be causing the problem. Do you:

A Drive to the next exit, pull into a service station, and have the oil level checked?

B Drive to your destination and have the problem checked at your convenience?

C Reach under the dash and remove the offending bulb?

D Immediately pull off the road, check your oil level, and add oil as necessary?

Surprising as it may seem, the answer is D (though a significant number of people choose answer A, which can ruin an engine).

Usually, the oil light comes on when there is a leak and the engine oil level is low. But what if the engine is full of oil and the light comes on? There are several possible reasons for the oil-pressure light to come on:

- **You are low on oil.** For whatever reason, you should get more oil in the engine and get the oil loss problem checked. When the light comes on, it means no oil will show on the dipstick. The engine is at least two quarts low.

- **There has been a catastrophic loss of oil pressure.** When this happens, the engine usually begins to knock and rattle within a few minutes of the light coming on. (Technically speaking, as the lifters are deprived of oil pressure and bleed down, they start to go clickety-click. The rod bearings begin to make low-end knocking noises as they lose oil pressure.) This cacophony of horrible engine noises increases in amplitude until the engine either seizes up or throws a connecting rod through the side of the block. In either case, the end result is the total demise of your engine.

If you think that the engine has lost oil pressure, don't try to tough it out unless you are hell-bent on replacing the engine. If you are in a tight spot and really have to get farther down the road, add a couple of extra quarts of oil to the engine. Drive as if you have an egg under your foot, giving the engine as little gas as possible. Keep the engine rpm as low as you possibly can and don't go over 35 miles per hour.

- **The hole leading into the oil pressure switch has been plugged, fooling it into believing that there is no oil pressure.** If you don't hear noises and the engine purrs just as nicely as always, there is a chance that you have nothing immediate to worry about. Nonetheless, be sure to have the oil pressure checked as soon as possible.

   If your engine has enough sludge to plug up the switch, you have a serious sludge problem. Sludge can also prevent oil from lubricating important parts inside the engine and, in extreme cases, can starve the engine of oil.

- **The oil pressure sending unit has failed.** Technically speaking, the sending unit is nothing more than a switch that completes a ground for the oil light. When the engine develops enough oil pressure, the resistance of a spring opens the switch. It is possible for the switch to short internally. Even though there is oil pressure, the switch remains grounded. In other words, the switch is defective.

- **The wire connecting the sending unit to the dash gauge has somehow been grounded** (shorted to ground or shorted out). If you suspect this to be the case, unplug the oil-pressure sender. If the light stays on, the wire is grounded. If the light goes out, there may still be a problem with the sending unit.

If the oil light comes on at idle or low speeds and then goes off at higher engine rpms, there is almost always a loss of oil pressure. This loss is not bad enough to cause the engine to seize up and destroy itself, but you are living on borrowed time, and engine replacement looms in your immediate future.

People employ several tricks of the trade to borrow a little more time before the engine goes out to lunch:

- **Dump the oil and use 100 percent synthetic oil.** I personally have used this tactic on my own 1980 Chrysler 225 engine. The engine had been knocking for a long time, yet it was still going strong after 400,000 miles, when I junked it. Synthetic oil does such a good job of lubricating the bearings that it pretty much eliminates further wear.

- **Add two or three cans of STP oil treatment to the engine or change the oil to straight 50-weight oil.** The thicker oil temporarily causes the oil light to stay off but buys only a little time before you face inevitable engine failure. (**Note:** This used-car-lot trick has been around for many years and is used to thicken the oil just enough to keep the warning light from coming on.)

- **Replace the oil pump.** Because the pump generates oil pressure, this fix can actually last for a while. However, the pump usually wears out with the engine bearings. Replacing the pump helps to restore the pressure, but rest assured that the bearings will soon fail.

- **Remove the oil pan and replace the worn-out bearings.** Since the crankshaft is probably ruined (it has been worn out-of-round and can't be repaired), the bearings won't last long. Remove the crankshaft and replace it along with all the bearings. One trick is to remove the oil pan and replace the worn-out bearing shells.

Some used-car-lot salespeople actually install pieces of leather in place of bearings. This fix is good only for a few minutes. One fellow installed leather in place of a spun bearing and towed the car to within a few blocks of a used-car lot. He started the car and drove it onto the lot. Then he traded it in for another used car, making a killing on the deal. By the time the car lot discovered the ruse, the sly customer was long gone. This time someone actually pulled a reverse scam on a used-car lot!

Determining Oil Pressure

How do you know whether you have enough oil pressure? What if your car came equipped with an oil-pressure gauge? Can you trust it? When do you start making plans for a new engine or a new car? Can your oil pressure tell you when things are about to start coming apart inside your engine? Is there such a thing as too much oil pressure? Is too much oil pressure harmful? These are some commonly asked questions.

Before making oil-pressure readings, change the engine oil. The oil may be diluted with gasoline, throwing off the readings. Also, used oil may have lost its foam inhibitors. Foam also causes low readings.

Next, thoroughly heat up the oil. The oil on the dipstick should be almost too hot to touch. This takes 20 minutes or more, depending on the ambient temperature. Failure to allow oil to reach operating temperature results in artificially high pressure readings!

Rule of thumb: There should be one pound per square inch (1 psi) of oil pressure for every 100 rpm of engine speed. If the engine is idling at 650 rpm, for example, there should be at least 6.5 pounds of oil pressure. At 3,000 rpm, there should be at least 30 psi of oil pressure.

Most oil-pressure sending units are set to close their internal contacts and illuminate the oil-pressure warning light at 3 to 5 psi of oil pressure. This is considered the minimum amount of oil pressure for an engine at idle.

If your engine is running at the minimum level of pressure, it is time to think about a rebuilt engine or another vehicle. Usually the oil light will start coming on at idle after you drive for some distance. This means the oil has heated up and thinned out—and the pump cannot make enough pressure to turn off the oil-pressure switch.

Most oil pumps have internal pressure relief valves that limit engine oil pressure to no more than 70–80 psi. When an engine is cold and the oil is thick, the pressure can easily reach that high. If the oil-pressure relief valve doesn't open and bleed off the excess oil pressure, the oil filter may rupture. The oil pump can easily produce more than 100 psi of oil pressure if the pressure relief valve sticks shut.

While good oil filters are made to withstand this kind of pressure, cheap ones are not. For example, a Hastings oil filter is rated to hold 300 psi of oil pressure. An off-brand filter can handle only 60–80 psi of pressure before the can splits open at the seam or separates from the base.

To accurately determine engine oil pressure, fit a mechanical gauge to the engine oil-pressure port. Usually the oil-pressure sending unit is removed and an analog gauge is plumbed into the passageway. This type of gauge doesn't rely on the electrical circuitry used by the engine sending unit and dash gauge cluster. Dash gauges are not accurate and should be used only to monitor changes in the pressure in relation to your typical readings.

Be a Dipstick Detective

When was the last time you considered your oil level dipstick a diagnostic tool? As simple as it seems, a thorough examination of your dipstick can give you valuable information about the health of your engine. Everyone who checks his or her own oil should become familiar with the trouble signs that can show up on the end of a dipstick.

The Automotive Panic Button

BE A DIPSTICK DETECTIVE

EGAD,
HOLMES!

Pull the dipstick and carefully examine the oil on the end. Do so *before* changing the oil, or you will miss the story. If you wait until the oil is clean, all the evidence will be gone.

Goopy Scuzz

If the end of the dipstick looks as if it was used to stir a chocolate milk shake, you have problems. Here are several possible causes:

- **Short-distance driving:** People who don't drive very far never warm their oil enough to boil off any contaminants. (Short trips are 10 miles or less per trip per direction.) This causes moisture buildup inside the engine, resulting in a whitish film on the dipstick. When you see such a film, it is time for an oil change. Short-distance drivers should change their oil more often than the recommended intervals.

- **Bad thermostat:** Sometimes cooling system thermostats fail to close completely and the engine never gets hot. The results are the same as in the preceding situation, even for long-distance drivers.

- **Blown seal:** Commonly resulting from a blown head gasket, this kind of dipstick goop signals the need for some expensive repairs. If you detect it in time, you are in for a head gasket replacement with some additional machine shop costs. If not, the scuzz will neutralize the oil on the cylinder walls, and the piston rings will scrape the walls without lubricating oil. Then you'll need a new engine.

Slimy Sand

Now grab a bit of the stuff right off the end of the stick and squeeze it between your fingers. **Take care to avoid being burned—let**

the oil cool before you touch it. This is not a job for the faint of heart; that oil can be slimy and gross. Does it seem gritty? If so, your engine is in danger from the sandman. Fine grit or sand is getting in somehow and is about to cost you a motor. Sand quickly infiltrates and destroys engine bearings unless you take immediate steps. The time to start is right now.

Begin by checking for every possible source that would allow sand to leak into the engine. Don't stop until you have fixed the leak. Also, change the oil, oil filter, and air filter immediately. Possible "sand doors" include the following:

- Poor air-filter seal or air-filter canister seal, including possible holes in the air ductwork and seals connecting the filter to the throttle body

- Leaking crankcase ventilation system, grommets, PCV valve hoses, or vent filter

- Leaking oil-filler cap seal, gasket, or rubber sealing grommet

- Leaking valve-cover gasket or valve-cover end seals

- Leaking front or rear engine seals

> **U**sed oil can cause cancer if left on your skin for prolonged periods. Be sure to clean it off completely with warm soap and water.

Smelly Stew

Let your nose play detective. Sniff the end of the oil dipstick. If it smells something like old turpentine, the oil is polluted with unburned gasoline. After smelling enough oil, you can easily identify this condition with your nose.

Another test is to place a drop of the suspicious oil on a piece of white copy paper. Watch how the oil soaks in and spreads. If it soaks right into the paper and quickly spreads into a big stain, it is contaminated with gas. If you still aren't sure, try testing oil from several other cars, as well as some fresh oil.

If the oil is contaminated, your engine is leaking fuel into the oil, and your duty is to track down the source. It is important to check this out because you have a fire hazard under the hood. If you don't find the fuel leak, the engine can catch fire. Furthermore, the piston rings and cylinder walls may become damaged if you don't do something.

Start by checking for the following:

• Leaking carburetors or injectors allow fuel to run into the oil pan when the engine is not running.

• Leaking rubber diaphragm on the fuel pump (carbureted vehicles) or fuel-pressure regulator (fuel-injected vehicles) may be contaminating the oil.

• The charcoal evaporative emission canister may not be doing its job. If the activated charcoal can't hold gas fumes from the fuel tank because the charcoal is deactivated, the engine will be filled with gas fumes. Also, be suspicious of the plumbing and valves to the canister. On occasion, the canister venting system allows fuel from an overfilled gas tank to be routed into the intake manifold, filling the engine.

Black Blot

If the dipstick is so dark that you can't even see the metal marks under the blackened oil, you are overdue for a change. While engine oil normally blackens with age, it should not resemble molasses tar.

After changing the oil, keep checking the dipstick. If the oil seems to darken quickly, be suspicious. Blackened oil usually means that the oil contains burned carbon particles (soot). Soot is getting into your engine, and the oil is suffering because soot causes the detergents to break down and the oil to thicken. (**Note:** Diesel engines are an exception because their oil is normally black.)

The oil should be changed immediately, and you should figure out how it got contaminated in the first place. Here are some of the more common causes:

• Oil change intervals may be too far apart for your driving conditions. You are probably running the engine hard, revving it too high, or otherwise stressing it.

• Your engine is running too hot due to malfunction of one or more other systems. Anything that causes engine overheating can cause the oil to burn and darken quickly.

• Combustion by-products are polluting the oil. Sources of combustion by-products in the oil include worn piston rings and excessive blowby caused by poor crankcase ventilation when the engine is under load.

• Using the wrong grade of oil can cause oil breakdown. Oils marked 5W-30 and 10W-40 are likely culprits when they are pushed past their limits. These thinner oils don't hold up to sustained high-speed driving or hot weather operation.

With practice, you will be able to diagnose most major problems with a glance, a sniff, a touch, and some hand soap. Avoid a lot of wasted time, money, and grief by regularly inspecting your dipstick.

Zen Dipsticks: Easy Everyday Maintenance

Your car owner's manual plainly details the factory-recommended service intervals for your automobile. But what about the in-between times? Do you simply leave the hood closed between required service visits? This section gives you some tips on what you can do to maintain your car with minimal effort. For the sake of preventive maintenance, it is a good idea to get involved with your vehicle.

Zen is the practice of doing a great deal with little effort. It also refers to carrying out a duty without needing to think about it. Think of this as an exercise in Zen: A little effort to carry out the necessary steps for maintaining your car produces benefits of huge proportions, especially in saving money. The idea is to achieve maximum results by doing the bare minimum, just as in Zen.

When? Most people purchase fuel every week. While this may seem an ideal time to check your vehicle, the liquid levels in the engine cooling system and oil are best checked when the engine is cold, before you run it. A weekly check, perhaps one morning, is generally the best.

Where? If you have no idea what the oil level should be or where the dipstick or fill indicator mark is, consult your owner's manual or stop by the shop and find out where to look.

Why bother? Because you want to develop a relationship with your car, like a Zen master and student. Don't be intimidated. You are your car's master; it is in your charge. You must monitor its progress as it gets old, or you run the risk of surprise repairs down the road. You can avoid many repairs if you follow a good preventive maintenance program. You have to put a little bit of energy into the relationship to gain the benefits of a trouble-free car.

Who? Face it—somebody has to do it. Who do you trust: the corner gas station attendant or yourself? Yes, you are the best person to carefully monitor the situation under your hood. By using the methods outlined in Chapter 4 and getting a little practice, you can learn a lot about your engine.

Batteries and Brakes

Without the battery in your car, you have nothing! No lights, no radio, and even more important, no starting power. When was the last time you took a look at your battery or gave it some care? This chapter passes on some tips that will make you a battery expert—or at least a more knowledgeable battery owner. Also, I'll explain some ways to tackle a battery that appears dead and bring it back from the great beyond. Finally, you'll learn how to spot and deal with your brakes' failure to release and how to break in new brakes so that they will last much longer.

Making Your Battery Last

You must begin with the right battery. Select one with a minimum cold-cranking amp (CCA) capacity of at least 1 CCA per cubic inch of engine displacement, 1.5 CCA per cubic inch for reliable sub-zero starting, or 2 CCA per cubic inch for diesel engines.

Always wear protective eyewear when working with batteries.

The life span of your battery depends on you. Proper attention can extend its life, and poor treatment can shorten it. This section gives you some practical advice to help you get the most from your battery.

Heat is harmful to batteries as well. Modern cars have hotter engine compartments because of downsizing. In addition, smaller front grilles and lower hoodlines allow less air into the engine area. As a result, engines run hotter than ever. Air space around a battery is important, and the engine area should have a cooling duct directing air flow toward the battery. Heat can cause the internal

Tap water is poisonous to batteries. If you have a battery that allows water to be added, do not let garage mechanics add tap water; it contains minerals that are harmful to the battery. Always use distilled water in your battery.

battery plates to warp. Warped plates can touch, shorting out the battery, so do not remove the battery cooling duct or case.

Make sure the battery is mounted securely. Vibration shakes off the chemical coating on the battery plates inside, ruining the battery. Pounding on a battery clamp with a hammer has the same effect and can also break the battery case. A loosely secured battery can be jarred hard enough to hit the hood and short out. Also, vibration damage from road shocks can cause separations between plates, resulting in dead cells and premature battery failure.

Keep in mind that improper handling can cause permanent damage to internal battery connections. Do not lift the battery by the posts. Also, use caution when connecting battery cables, and don't overtighten the connections because the terminals may break away.

Clean the battery and its tray regularly, especially in areas where road salt is used. The accumulation of dirt and grime on the battery top will cause it to discharge itself in short order. This accumulation makes the alternator work harder, too.

Recognizing Signs of Impending Battery Doom

Winter plays havoc with batteries, especially in the snowbelt. Even loose or corroded battery connecting terminals and cables can cause a no-start condition. Batteries don't quit suddenly. If your battery dies one cold, dark morning, the truth is that it has been terminally ill for some time.

By the time your battery shows symptoms of a problem, it's usually beyond help. You may have to buy another one, pay tow charges, and possibly shell out for a new alternator. While there is little or nothing you can do to repair a battery, it is possible to predict its imminent failure. Here are some telltale signs of trouble:

Wet on top: This usually means the battery system is overcharging, but it may also mean the battery is incapable of accepting a charge. As the internal plates wear out, their ability to accept and retain a charge diminishes. The remaining active portion of the battery plates does all the work but is overcharged by the alternator. The overheated portion of the plates boils the battery acid electrolyte, making the battery wet on top.

Thirsty: Does the battery level keep going down? Are you constantly adding water? The battery electrolyte level drops, and the cells require additional water as a result. After the battery starts to use water, it is almost certain to fail within 12 months. Refilling the battery with tap water hastens its death.

Fuzzy terminals: When the battery heats up and gases are released, acid from the electrolyte is carried out the vents and attacks the terminals and battery posts. The terminals become covered with corrosion. A healthy battery doesn't need to have the terminals cleaned.

One fuzzy terminal: This is the sign of a cracked battery case. The crack may be invisible to the eye, but it's there. Usually it's near the edge where the metal post meets the battery top. Movement of the vehicle causes the electrolyte to splash onto the post, where it enters the underside of the battery top. The acid wicks up the post to the terminal, causing the terminal to corrode and creating excessive resistance in the battery circuit.

Excessive resistance makes the alternator work harder to keep the battery charged. This condition quickly ruins the alternator as it overworks to charge the battery through a corroded terminal. Acid may also leak onto the battery tray, ruining it and any other nearby electrical connections.

Bulge: A bulging battery case means that the end is near. Excessive internal heat buildup caused by an aging battery makes the metal plates expand and push outward on the battery case. Conversely, a battery case may bulge if it is frozen. The electrolyte turns to ice, expands, and pushes outward on the battery.

Meter reader: The dash ammeter shows that the battery is charging constantly. If your car has an ammeter, it should show a charge condition (positive or higher readings) only after you start the car and while you are using the lights and accessories. Otherwise, the battery is weak and the alternator is working overtime to keep it charged. If the meter registers full charge immediately after you start the vehicle, the battery is very weak.

Allowed to continue, this condition may cause the alternator to quit before the battery dies, making it seem as though the alternator is at fault. Your mechanic will probably replace the alternator and charge the battery, which will then weaken the new alternator, and so on. The battery will finally refuse to accept a charge and will be replaced. But by then it may have destroyed several alternators.

(For a full-size poster of "Jump Start Procedures," send $2 to Nutz & Boltz, P.O. Box 123, Butler, MD 21023.)

Beating the Battery Blues

Nothing ruins a day like getting into your car or truck, turning the key, and . . . nothing. Don't let the battery blues get you down. Know your battery's enemies and how to fight them off so that you don't get left in the dark.

Undercharging

Average battery life is about 48 months, depending on type, size, and internal construction. Many batteries fail earlier because of deep discharging or chronic undercharging.

Excessively cranking over the engine or leaving the lights on completely discharges the battery. Letting the car sit for long periods without using it also discharges the battery. As a result, *sulfation* occurs: sulfur permanently attaches to the metal plates in the battery, preventing it from fully recovering when recharged. Sulfur on the plates slows the chemical reaction that produces electrical current.

Chronic undercharging can be caused by too many short trips, excessive cranking, a defective voltage regulator, a weak alternator, a slipping fan belt, or undetected excessive voltage drain resulting from an electrical short or trunk light that stays on. It takes about 30 minutes of driving to restore the current used in just two minutes of cranking.

In general, a sulfated battery is junk and must be replaced. However, you can easily and cheaply employ several tricks that will sometimes bring a dead, sulfated battery back from the boneyard.

Restoring Sulfated Batteries

Slow charging at 6–8 amps for up to 24 hours may bring a dead battery back to life. If a battery does not accept a "trickle charge" (1–2 amps) after two hours, it's probably beyond hope. Use a trickle charger or the battery charger set on the lowest setting.

Note: Some battery chargers are specifically designed to break through the sulfate layer by applying a higher charging amperage.

> **I**f a dead battery will not accept a charge, connect the dead battery in parallel (positive to positive, negative to negative) with a good battery and then connect both batteries to a charger.

Overcharging

If your alternator is overcharging your battery, your battery can fail from plate damage or loss of electrolyte. A low electrolyte level (low liquid level inside the battery) or frequent lightbulb replacement is a symptom of an alternator that is overcharging. Have a shop test your alternator's output and compare your results with the specifications. If output is high, first check the voltage regulator connections and its ground, which are likely sources of alternator overcharging problems.

Reviving a Really Dead Battery

If you go away for a while, leave your car lights on, and run the battery dead flat, is it possible to revive it? Long sitting without charging also runs down the battery. Can it be revived when you come back and want to use it? The answer is *sometimes*—it is worth the effort to try. When a battery goes totally flat, the acid goes into the lead plates, leaving the electrolyte composed of mostly water. This is why a battery that is low on charge can freeze in cold weather. A charged battery contains a liquid that is mostly acid. A dead one contains water that will easily freeze and crack the battery case.

> **D**o not attempt to charge a battery that is low on electrolyte. It might overheat and explode! Also, be sure to add only distilled water.

Before attempting to revive a dead battery, check the condition of the battery posts. If they are loose, the battery is junk. Now, gently pry off the top of the battery. Look inside and see whether the liquid electrolyte is up to the top of the filler hole liquid-level mark. If the top is sealed, inspect it closely. In many cases, the seal can be cut open so that the cover can be removed.

Sometimes the battery is so dead that it needs a very high initial charge to shock it back to life. Your mechanic can use a boost charger placed on the highest setting (at least 30 amps) to give the battery a boost for about 30 minutes to get the charge started. Now the battery is ready for a lower charge for at least eight hours.

If the battery has been discharged too many times, some of the sulfuric acid becomes permanently bonded to the lead plates. This sulfation can result in a charging voltage of more than 16 volts because the cells are taking only a very surface charge. Even after a two-day charge, a sulfated battery may come to only 60 to 80 percent of capacity.

Sometimes a mildly sulfated battery can be cycled and brought back to near 100 percent capacity. To do this, the battery needs to be discharged to about a 50 percent state of charge and recharged through several charging and discharging cycles. If the battery fails to come up on subsequent charges, it is junk. Remember, a slightly sulfated battery will cause the vehicle's alternator to run all the time—costing gas mileage and eventually killing the alternator!

A battery below 11.6 volts is considered to be heavily sulfated and in a low state of charge. It needs special charging and should be placed on a very long, slow state of charge for at least two days, preferably three to four days. (Because the sulfuric acid is tied up and stratified into the plates, the acid needs a sufficient overcharge to get back into solution.)

Even after the battery comes up to a full state of charge, it is a good idea to give it an additional 1 amp charge for another day to "freshen it up." Do this after a one-day cooling-off period.

Batteries showing from 11.6 to 12.1 volts also need extra time to reach full charging capacity. They too can use freshening up with a 1 amp charge for another day. With any low-voltage battery, it is always wise to give it a second charge after letting it cool down for a day.

Looking for Internal Shorts in the Battery

Checking a battery's specific gravity is a good way to tell whether it has internal problems. Use a quality hydrometer ($5 to $15). Avoid using one whose floating balls have been saturated with battery acid; it may be inaccurate. If there is any question, compare your hydrometer with a known good one. Also, beware of bubbles sticking to the float(s) and compensate for ambient temperature as shown on the hydrometer. If the hydrometer doesn't have a built-in temperature chart, consult a battery charging chart or ask a battery store for the correct number for the ambient temperature in your area.

Batteries with specific gravity readings between cells differing more than 30 points are suspect and may harbor potential problems down the road. Batteries showing more than 50 points' difference between cells in gravity are junk. Ditto for two or more nonfloating balls when using a hydrometer.

When checking the voltage levels on the battery, first check the voltage with the battery connected to the charger and then check it again after the battery has been at rest for about an hour. A sulfated battery shows very high initial voltage, which drops off as soon as the charger is turned off.

Beware of a battery that is below 11.6 volts and is shorted between the lead plates. Lead sulfate in the separator will form a

Always wear safety goggles when working around batteries, and never make a spark in the region of the battery when it is charging or after it has been charged. Treat it with respect. A sulfated or shorted battery can explode without warning while being charged! Sulfuric acid causes severe skin burns, damages the car's paint, and corrodes metal parts. **Always protect your hands and eyes when handling a battery.**

shunt across the positive and negative plates, and the battery will self-discharge quickly. Also, if a standard charger is used with a maximum voltage of 14.8 volts, beware of a battery that gets really hot to the touch when charging. This is another sign of internal shorts.

Blasting Batteries

Imagine the force of an explosion from a quarter of a stick of dynamite. The hydrogen in your car battery would have that much force if it exploded. Heed the following advice to avoid a blasted battery:

- Never charge a battery while it is connected to the car.

- Make sure that the vent caps are tight. Cover them with a damp cloth if possible.

- Never disconnect a car battery while the car is running or while the ignition is on.

- Be sure to turn off all accessories before charging or jump-starting, especially car phones, radios, and stereos.

- Leaving the blower motor on high when jump-starting will put a damper on dangerous voltage spikes—which will help protect the computer and all other on-board, solid-state devices.

- Always connect the negative jumper cable clamp last and disconnect it first. Never connect to fuel-line tubing or moving parts. Don't allow the positive clamps to touch any metal other than the battery cables.

- Always fully recharge any battery before installing it. Installing a dead battery or jump-starting a car with a dead battery and letting the alternator charge it may overtax the alternator, causing system failure and an unexpected breakdown.

- Never use a 24-volt truck charger on a 12-volt automotive system. Doing so can damage sensitive components, which may fail later.

- Never attempt to jump-start or recharge a frozen battery or a battery with a low electrolyte level.

- Always wear safety glasses and stand back before starting the disabled car.

Slaying "Dragon Brakes"

One common cause of poor fuel mileage is dragging brakes. They also cause car owners to replace brake pads or shoes frequently. Many vehicles have this problem, and the owners have no idea that something is wrong. It's like driving with one foot on the gas and the other pushing the brake pedal. Your car is trying to go and stop at the same time. What a waste of gas and brake material!

Spotting Dragon Brakes

One of the simplest ways to determine whether your brakes are dragging is to do a coast test. Simply put the gear selector in neutral and see how far the car will coast. Does it feel as if the vehicle is freewheeling, or does it seem as if the brakes are slowing you down? This type of brake drag is especially noticeable just before the vehicle comes to a rest.

An easy tip-off is the smell of burning friction material. To some people, this smells like burning plastic or Bakelite. If you have ever left a pot on the stove and burned the Bakelite handles, you know the smell. Get out of the car and give each wheel a sniff. Smell hot? Now, carefully do the touch test to find the hot one.

Dragging brakes also generate friction and heat up the brake assembly, including the wheel. One way to catch a dragging brake is to feel the hub of the wheel carefully. If you have driven for some distance and coast to a stop, the hub should be cool to the touch. If it is hot, the brakes are dragging. **Careful! The hub can be really hot and burn your hand.**

As the brake friction material heats up, mechanics say in technical jargon that "its coefficient of friction will change." In other words, as the friction material and rotor (drum) get hot, they become more grabby. At some point, the friction material gets so hot that it loses its coefficient of friction and stops working. Overheated brakes will either stick or react poorly when you press the pedal, causing the brakes to fade.

Why Is It Happening?

The list of reasons for brake drag is a long one. Start at the top of the list and work your way down. The causes are generally written in most likely to least likely order.

A typical reason for brake drag is linkage binding. Another common cause is poor adjustment of the brake-light/pedal switch. Sometimes pulling up on the brake pedal provides temporary relief, but the brake-light switch is usually faulty. A weak brake pedal return spring could also be at fault.

Lubricating the brakes with WD-40 oil may be all that is necessary to cure binding linkage. But the brake-light switch, mounted at the top of the brake pedal arm, usually must be replaced or at least repositioned. The spring, also located at the top of the brake pedal, must be replaced if it is too weak.

Another common cause for brake drag is a restricted hydraulic line (hoses that act as check valves) where the inside of the hose lining comes loose and you can't see it. When mechanics do brake

Testing the Mechanical Way

Here are some neat, quick tests to determine the mechanical cause of dragging brakes:

Bleed and squirt. If you suspect that a certain wheel is not releasing fully, break open the bleeder on that wheel. If opening the bleeder screw results in a healthy squirt of brake fluid, that wheel's brakes are being held under brake-fluid pressure.

This test works even better when the wheels are off the ground. If the wheel is hard to turn before you open the bleeder and turns freely afterward, there is a fluid restriction somewhere upstream.

Crack and drip. Crack the master cylinder connecting lines (where the lines come out from the vehicle and join to the master cylinder) about one-half turn. If the master cylinder is fully released, the fluid will be able to seep past the internal seals and drip out of the loosened fittings. If there is pressure on the master cylinder pushrod, the internal seals will cover up the fluid reservoir, preventing fluid from dripping out.

If there are no drips, pull up on the brake pedal and see whether the fluid starts dripping. Sometimes you may have to unbolt the master cylinder from the mount to make it drip. These conditions mean that the master cylinder pushrod is being held in a slightly applied position by a binding brake pedal, stop lamp switch, or faulty power booster.

Turn and rock. In rare cases, loose wheel bearings or suspension components allow the brakes to drag. To find this kind of problem, remove the cover from the master cylinder. Turn the wheel completely from lock to lock and watch for a spurt of liquid on the surface of the master cylinder as you reach the end of the turn in each direction. Repeat the test while pushing and pulling on the front end, rocking it from side to side. If there is a spurt, the wheel bearing is loose, allowing the brake rotor to move against the brake pad.

Pump and squirt. If air is trapped in the brake system, the brakes may drag when the air expands as it is heated by the brake fluid. To quickly identify trapped air, pump the brakes vigorously several times. Remove the master cylinder cover and quickly release the brake pedal. If air is trapped, there will be a **huge** squirt of fluid from the reservoir when the air pushes back against the fluid. Be careful not to allow the fluid to get on the paint or in your eyes!

Mechanical test. A mechanical device that uses hydraulic pressure and a very high-reading pressure gauge actually measures the amount of force on the pad. The device can be used to measure residual pressure on each brake caliper. These devices are not common, so you may have to ask a professional to do this for you. Using this device will unfailingly pinpoint a sticking brake component.

work, they often use brake hose pliers (or Vise-Grips) to pinch off brake lines. The internal walls of the hose may become damaged and come loose. The brake fluid is forced into the brake wheel caliper or cylinder but can't get back to the master cylinder when the brake is released. This is because the hose lets the fluid come from the master cylinder but acts like a check valve and doesn't let it return. The end result is that the brakes are held applied by the fluid pressure buildup.

Corrosion of brake hardware can cause brake drag. Most common is corrosion of the brake caliper slides, mounts, and other sliding hardware.

Parking brake cable corrosion, linkage, or adjusting hardware causes rapid rear-brake wear because the parking brake cable attaches to the rear wheels. When it binds, only the rear brakes drag.

Corroded caliper slides are typically the cause of one front brake wearing out faster than the other.

Dirty work habits can cause premature brake failure. Machining brake drums and rotors is a normal part of every brake job. The components are mounted in a lathe and machined until they are *trued*, or flat, again. Then the metal shavings should be cleaned out of the rotor or brake drum with hot, soapy water. Most mechanics don't bother cleaning the part, leaving fine metal dust impregnated in the friction surface. These metal shavings are caught up by the brake friction material and become abrasive, causing the brake pad material to wear out quickly. There is really nothing you can do about this practice unless you do your own brake work. In this case, you can clean the drums and/or rotors yourself before you install them.

Why does one brake job seem to last twice as long as another? Why do the original brakes that came with the car last so much longer than the replacement brake linings? Where does the brake pad and brake shoe friction material go? How long a brake job lasts depends on the type of lining chosen for the replacement brake shoes and/or pads. The friction material goes into the dust alongside the highway (as well as all over your wheels).

If the wrong grade or type of friction material or cheap brake linings are chosen by the mechanic for your particular brake job, the pads or shoes won't last long. (For example, semimetallic material may be the standard equipment, but cheaper organic material is used instead.) Brake lining friction material is graded to show the coefficient of friction. The grade AA is very soft, and the FF is very hard. If the friction material is supposed to be FF and the mechanic uses EE, it will be too soft. You'll be back for another brake job in record time!

If the brake friction material chosen is too hard, you will have difficulty pressing the brake pedal (excessive effort) and the brakes will squeal like a stuck pig every time you use them (very annoying and embarrassing). If you want to determine the correct coefficient grade for your vehicle, stop by the dealer parts department and examine the edge code on a new set of linings.

Faulty shoe adjustment is responsible for the rear shoes not doing their share in stopping the vehicle. The fronts have to do all the work and quickly wear out. Improper rear shoe/pad adjustment is typically caused by your not using reverse gear or the parking brake often enough.

> **U**sing the reverse gear and/or the parking brake automatically adjusts the rear brakes.

Two-footed drivers are another common cause of excessive brake wear. Have you ever driven behind someone who keeps pressing the brake? The brake lights flash on and off as the driver goes along. Most people who rest their left foot on the brake pedal don't realize it. They merrily press on the brakes as they simultaneously press on the gas pedal. You can't stop and go at the same time! The brakes really take a beating when you drive with two feet.

Other less likely causes of brake wear include a rough, corroded master cylinder; swollen rubber cups in the system; loose or worn front-wheel bearings; bent linings; loose or distorted backing plate; weak or broken shoe return springs; faulty power brake booster (leaky valves, weak reaction springs binding); overfilled master cylinder (with a diaphragm-type cover gasket); defective master cylinder quick-take-up valve; or aftermarket wheels or wheel covers that cause the brakes to overheat.

Breaking in New Brakes

The world's biggest automaker recently published a new procedure for breaking in new brakes. The procedure was published in a technical service bulletin for GM technicians to follow when replacing brake pads and applies to all brands of brakes on all types of vehicles. Following GM, several aftermarket companies have come out with their versions of the procedure.

If you are a technician, you probably don't have time to leave your repair bay and drive the vehicle for half an hour in order to break in (burnish) the new brake pads. Make a copy of the procedure and give it to your customers to follow. If you are not a mechanic and you get a new set of brake pads installed, consider following this procedure to get the best results from your brakes.

When a new set of pads is installed in a disc brake system, the pads must form a proper seat against the brake rotor. It takes a number of stops before the friction material grinds down enough to conform to the surface of the brake rotor. Until this happens, only a small part of the brake pad is able to make contact with the spinning brake rotor.

This process is called *burnishing the pads*. If the brake pads are not properly burnished, the friction material can be subjected to a great deal of excessive heat while the pads are seating themselves. This heat causes the brake bonding resins in the brake pad to crystallize, turning the friction material into a very hard substance.

Crystallized pads cause poor brake performance, a hard brake pedal, and brake noise. Brake pads that are crystallized and too hard squeal, grind, or groan when you apply the brakes. The rotors also suffer from excessive scoring and accelerated wear by the pads.

While it is not necessary to go out and do the burnish procedure in a parking lot, you can carry it out by paying attention to your braking and making sure that you don't overheat the brakes. In fact, it may take you days or even weeks to complete the procedure on your own. Here's the burnish procedure:

1 **From 40 mph, take 6 seconds to stop.** Keep rotors cool by driving half a mile between stops.

2-11 **From 50 mph, take 5 seconds to stop.** In other words, for the next 10 stops, take 5 seconds to stop. Remember to drive half a mile between stops to cool the rotors.

12 **From 40 mph, take 6 seconds to stop.**

13 **Finally, cool the brakes by driving three or four miles without braking.**

Tires and Other Important Parts

Why should you rotate your tires? What can you do to get the most from your tires? What is the proper way to change spark plugs? How can you get rid of squeaks, and what are the best ways to loosen rusty nuts and bolts? How do you make those noisy wiper blades shut up? What is vapor lock, and how do you deal with it when it attacks your engine? This chapter answers all these questions and more.

Tire Rotation Pros and Cons

To rotate or not to rotate, that is the question—and a controversial one at that. To some, it is simply a matter of economics. To others, it is a safety concern. One way of looking at it involves only short-term considerations; the other takes into account the big picture. One school of thought says never rotate tires, just replace them as they wear out. The other side says that tire rotation makes all four tires wear evenly and you should install a set of four new tires all at once.

The debate gets hotter. Because of a fleet management magazine article on how to avoid overmaintaining vehicles, fleet managers believe that rotating tires is a waste of time and money. The article describes the tire rotating procedures for several thousand leased Buick Century cars. The findings were that tire rotation did nothing to improve tire life and was only an expense. Instead of rotating the tires, this fleet manager replaced the front tires at about 30,000 miles. The rears were left in place until the cars were turned in after three years of use or 60,000 miles, whichever came first. Because the cars were used by traveling salespeople, mileage was the deciding factor. The vehicles usually racked up the mileage in about two years.

The article's author claims to have saved $204,000 by not replacing the rear tires. This article made the rounds in the automotive maintenance trade circles, and now the advocates for not rotating are jubilant.

Arguments Against Rotation

The "nonrotators" give the following reasons for leaving the tires alone:

- When you replace tires in pairs, two tires on the car are always in fairly good shape. Rotating the tires means the four tires have dangerously low tread patterns just before they are replaced.

- The cost of having the tires removed and reinstalled outweighs any value gained by rotation.

What about it? Good idea? Actually, the issue is much more involved. The following section rebuts this theory.

Arguments for Rotation

Rotating the tires allows the mechanic to make a visual check of the tires and brake system for wear of the brake pads and tire wear abnormalities. Spotting a thin brake pad can save the life of a brake rotor, and uncovering an alignment problem by recognizing uneven tire wear patterns can save the life of a perfectly good tire.

Vehicle designers engineer the suspension, steering, and brake system around four matched tires, all with equal tread. Operating a car with two of the tires always worn more or less than the other two creates a dangerous imbalance in the vehicle's handling characteristics. The front or rear will have more aggressive tire treads, which can contribute to loss of control in a panic situation or in inclement weather. On the other hand, if all four tires are rotated regularly, their traction capabilities are always comparable.

Replacing all four tires doesn't mean the tread patterns are dangerously low. The U.S. Department of Transportation (DOT) requires all tiremakers to put built-in wear indicators (called *wear bars*) on all tires sold in the United States. When the first tire shows a wear bar, it has only enough tread to go a short while longer before it becomes unsafe. The other three usually are replaced as a matter of course, even though their wear bars aren't showing. According to the DOT, all tires are safe right down to the wear bar, leaving $1/32''$ tread depth for a safety margin.

Front-wheel-drive cars have vastly different wear patterns. The front tires tend to wear on the shoulders (the part on the side where the tire curves). The rear tires tend to wear in the centers. Rotating them tends to even out those wear patterns, producing maximum tire life from all four. Instead of 30,000 miles on the front tires, rotation can make them last 40,000–60,000 miles.

Racking up a lot of miles on a vehicle in a short time may result in only the front tires wearing enough to require replacement. The cost savings comes out of the pocket of the next owner, who usually has to replace all four. When someone buys a car and half the tires are worn, the typical response is to get rid of all the tires because nothing is known about their history. And it is human nature to want to start out with four "known-good" tires.

Failure to rotate the rear tires makes for a very noisy ride. Anyone who drives rental cars often knows the howling sound of cupped rear tires. (Cupped tires have scalloped places in the tread area, as if someone took a knife and carved out parts of the tread all around the tire.) A fleet manager may be able to force all the drivers to live with this noise because the car is provided as part of the job. But most car owners find the sound of poorly maintained rear tires unacceptable and replace them long before the wear indicators show up.

If you are a fleet manager and are trying to squeeze the maintenance dollar as hard as you can, tire rotation is not for you. But if you want the maximum safety and comfort from your tires and are unwilling to put up with tire noise, read the next section to learn the proper method for rotating tires.

Maintaining Maximum Tire Life

Don't rob your tires of a long life. You can achieve the minimum life for your set of tires by following the P-R-A-B rule: pressure, rotation, alignment, and balance.

Pressure

Incorrect tire pressure is one of the main causes of premature tire wear and is the easiest to correct. The less pressure a tire has, the hotter it runs. Heat is the enemy of tire rubber. Low pressure also costs in fuel economy and handling. But too much air pressure causes the middle of the tire to contact the road more than the sides do, resulting in poor traction and reduced ability to avoid emergencies. Overinflation also causes a harsh ride. Both over- and underinflation cause uneven tire wear.

Check tire pressure when the tires are cold, before you drive that day. If necessary, wait at least two hours after use for the tires to cool before checking pressure. Use your own gauge; the ones on the air hoses at gas stations are grossly inaccurate. Check your tires every month, or at least when the seasons change.

Changes in temperature can result in low tire pressure. One pound of pressure is lost for every 10 degrees of temperature drop. Tires with perfect air pressure in the summer can easily lose 10 pounds of air pressure when the thermometer drops. Conversely, tires correctly inflated in the winter months can become grossly overinflated in the summer.

Using a Tire Gauge

First, purchase an accurate gauge. Never use one that is attached to an air hose because these gauges are terribly inaccurate. Find the label on the glove box or door post telling you the correct air pressure for your car. If you can't find the label, stop by a tire store that sells your brand of tires and ask about the correct pressure for your car. The local dealer should also have this information. Press the tire gauge firmly against the valve stem until the tire gauge gets a good reading of the tire pressure.

Rotation

The front and rear tires wear differently. The drive axle of the car always wears more evenly than the nondrive axle. This means that the rear tires of a front-wheel-drive car wear unevenly; for a rear-wheel-drive car, the front tires wear unevenly.

The general rule of thumb is to rotate the tires every 7,500 miles. Stop-and-go city driving calls for more frequent rotation. If you drive long distances and seldom stop along the way, rotate the tires less often. **Note:** Rotate unidirectional tires only front to rear.

Alignment

Poor alignment costs in two ways: premature tire failure and poor gas mileage. Poor alignment can also rob your car of steering and handling capability. Alignments should be done only by a shop with modern equipment, using the latest technology to measure *thrust angle*, which determines whether all four wheels are going in the same direction. Just measuring the front wheels is not adequate for modern cars, especially front- and four-wheel-drive cars.

Front-wheel alignment problems are usually easy to spot. If your car has a problem with rear-end alignment, however, you may not even know it unless someone tells you that your car is "dog-tracking."

Balance

Unbalanced tires wear unevenly and make your vehicle shake. In the process of balancing, tire technicians add small weights to the edges of the wheels. If you feel vibration through the steering wheel, check your wheels for missing weights. (Look for a clean spot where the weight used to be. If you have any doubt, have the tires rechecked for proper balance.) To prolong the life of your tires and suspension, have your tire balance checked every 30,000 miles, more frequently if you're a stop-and-go driver.

Rules for Rotating

The rotation procedure rule is this: Swap the tires front to rear and rear to front. Now switch the tires side to side on the drive axle (the axle that powers the wheels). On a front-wheel-drive car the drive axle is the front axle; for a rear-wheel-drive car, it's the rear axle. The old rule for radial tires, "Never cross radials," is no longer true.

Four-wheel-drive exception: Do not cross the tires from one side to the other unless you see directional wear of the tire, called **heel-toe wear**. Using the palm of your hand, feel around the circumference of the tire. If it feels rough in one direction and smooth in the other, there is heel-toe wear. In this case, cross the tires.

Measuring Tread Depth

Use a tread-depth measuring gauge to keep track of tread loss. Uneven tread depth means that you need to rotate the tires. Purchase a tread-depth gauge (under $10) and measure the tread in the center and sides of the tire. Keep a record to pinpoint uneven wear.

Installing New Spark Plugs

Modern tune-ups require little more than the replacement of spark plugs. Many people elect to do this job themselves. Some techniques make the job easier—others lead to the early demise of the replacement plug. Here are spark plug installation techniques and mistakes to avoid.

Getting the Plug Torque Correct

Proper tightening specifications are especially important for today's engines. Too much *torque*, or tightening, can result in the following problems:

- The electrode spreads farther apart, increasing the plug gap and required firing voltage.

- The plug shell becomes distorted and damages the seal, causing the center electrode to blow out.

- The threads seize in place and damage the cylinder head.

  Too little torque can result in the following problems:

- The plug comes loose and leaks compression, allowing the threads to fill with carbon and compression blowby.

- The plug runs hot, causing engine ping.

- The center electrode overheats and melts.

  Generally, you achieve proper plug torque by using an inch/pound torque wrench. In reality, many mechanics use air ratchets or impact tools to install spark plugs and do not heed proper torque specifications.

  As an alternative, you can tighten plugs by using the "angle method." There are two types of spark plug designs: the older gasket seal type and the tapered seat design. (When you remove the old plugs, you can see what type you have. When you purchase new ones, the type should be apparent when you look at them.) Here are the procedures for each type:

- **Gasketed plugs:** Tighten a quarter to a half turn after the gasket meets the cylinder head, depending on application. New engines require a half turn. Older engines require less, assuming you're using a new sealing gasket.

- **Tapered plugs:** Tighten one-sixteenth turn after the seat touches the head.

Doing It Right

A new set of plugs may be the most important service your engine receives. How you install the plugs can make a terrific difference in their life and the life of the engine. Here are some tips:

- Wait for the engine to cool completely before you remove the plugs. If you don't, the plug threads are more likely to seize and strip out the threads.

- Don't yank on the spark plug wires. This mistake can be an expensive one. Instead, rotate the spark plug boot (the part that covers the spark plug), gently twisting and pulling until it comes free. The plug boots have a tendency to stick to the spark plugs and will tear if you yank on the wire. Gently turning and twisting the boot helps to free it up so that it doesn't tear.

- Before you remove the old plugs, remove any traces of dirt lodged in the spark plug area. When the plugs are removed, that crud can fall into the engine and damage the piston rings. Use compressed air or spray solvent to clean the area before you remove the plugs.

- Unscrew the plugs by using a hand ratchet, not an air impact tool. If a plug starts to seize, *stop*. Spray some penetrating oil into the plug thread area and let it soak for a few minutes. Gently screw the plug into the cylinder head and back out again several times while soaking the threads with penetrating oil.

- Compare the part number and the physical size and shape of the old plug with a new one. Be sure to check with the dealer for any updates on part numbers. Ongoing changes in technology can sometimes provide a new spark plug to solve some types of drivability concerns.

- *Lightly* coat the threads with antiseize compound. Don't overdo it! Too much can make the compound leak onto the electrode and cause a short.

- Always start screwing in the plugs by hand. This step is very important because you can cross-thread the plug if you aren't careful. If the spark plug threads go into the engine threads wrong, the spark plug will not screw in all the way and the threads will be mucked up. Screw in the plug as far as you can to feel for burrs or damaged threads. If the plugs don't screw in properly, chase the threads with a tap.

- If you do damage the threads and they don't clean up with a spark plug thread tap, you can always fix the plug hole with new threads. Repair kits are available that allow you to install new threads in the engine plug hole.

Modern engines equipped with platinum spark plugs can easily go 100,000 miles between spark plug changes.

Squashing Squeaks

Few automotive problems are as pesky and irritating as a persistent squeak inside your car. Modern cars are generally very quiet due to aerodynamics advances, better assembly techniques, and new sound absorption materials, which makes the occasional "car cricket" even more bothersome.

Squeaks are generally caused by two materials rubbing against each other. Usually they are two different materials, such as plastic and steel or other materials with different coefficients of friction. As the two surfaces alternately catch and let go, the energy released causes the high-pitched vibration that I call a squeak. This is known as the *slip-stick effect.*

To correct a squeak, you must first locate it. Car interiors reflect sound because of all the glass, so finding the squeak may not be as simple as it seems. To safely pinpoint the spot, have a friend drive down a bumpy road while you listen for sounds. Confirm that you've found the offending area by pressing down on the spot to see whether the sound is interrupted. Still having trouble finding the squeak? Put one end of a small piece of rubber hose to your ear and use the other end as a stethoscope.

After you've cornered the gremlin, you can use any of several

Fire-Retardant Squeakproofing

Avoid treating squeaky ashtray cover springs or hinges with penetrating oils. Because the lighter is usually nearby, the electricity and heat can ignite the flammable oils and cause a fire. Instead, try using one of the following substances:

Drylubes: Powdered graphite is excellent for friction reduction, coats the surface well, lasts a long time, and will not ignite. It can be messy to use, so place a cloth or newspaper to catch any overspray. Sprays with lithium, Teflon, or moly compounds are also effective antisqueak agents. Because the aerosol uses an oil-based carrier, be careful around electrical connections and upholstery. It may be safer to disconnect the battery's ground cable until after the carrier evaporates and leaves a dry film.

Lithium grease: This surface lubricant is often overlooked but very effective. Lithium grease is slippery and provides a tenacious, long-lasting fix. This aerosol is easy to use, especially with the thin tube plastic extension usually provided. Be careful not to overspray onto fabrics because lithium lubes are hard to remove. Take the same precautions you would for any combustible. Lithium grease is great for panels, springs, lock cylinders, and hinges.

Talcum: This substance is similar to graphite in its properties, especially for coating large areas. Talcum works great for quieting sounds from the leather or rubber boot covering the gear shift lever on manual transmission cars or anywhere leather, vinyl, or rubber touches other materials.

techniques. First, make sure that the squeak is not from a loose fastener. Even new cars can have loose fasteners; vibrations inherent in driving often cause screws to back off. When dealing with a dashboard squeak, you can use a piece of polyurethane foam to separate the panels. Poly foam is preferable to a metal shim or a penny because metal can fall into a fan motor or short across two electrical connectors.

If separating the surfaces is not appropriate, try a silicone spray. Although effective, it often does not provide a lasting fix. After the lubricant dries up, the surfaces will squeak again.

Squawking Sway-Bar Bushings

One of the most common complaints in the colder winter months is noisy sway-bar bushings. The rubber becomes hard and brittle and makes lots of noise when going over bumps. Lubricating the rubber bushings is futile and can even make things worse, as the lubricant attacks the rubber.

- First find out if the manufacturer has made updated versions of the sway-bar bushings. Some have issued Teflon-coated bushings.

- If there is no updated bushing, you may want to replace the old ones anyway, especially if they are cracked or worn.

- If all else fails, try lubricating the rubber part of the bushing with a grease containing a solid lubricant, such as graphite, molybdenum, lithium, or Teflon. Be sure to clean the surface of the roll bar thoroughly until the metal is rust free and perfectly smooth. If the bar is pitted, it may need to be replaced for a lasting fix.

Squeaky Dashboards

One of the most vexing problems with modern cars is a squeaky dashboard. Somewhere down in the guts of the console or dash hides the elusive squeak gremlin. Just how do you catch it?

- While someone else drives the car, push and pull on various parts of the dash until you isolate the noise.

- If the source of the noise is impossible to isolate, remove the dash pad and dash front fascia one at a time. If removing the pad or fascia makes the noise go away, insulate the offending part and use one of the trick cures that follow.

- Removing the fascia and pad gives you access to the innards of the dash. Have someone drive the car once again and try to isolate the noise.

Try one of the following tricks to get rid of the noise:

- Remove the sheet-metal screws and coat the threads with silicone RTV. The RTV will set in a few hours and help to stop the vibration.

- If the sheet-metal screws are too small, replace them with larger screws.

- Insulate the dash or fascia plate by using mechanic's "dum-dum," which is equivalent to air conditioning insulation compound.

- Whittle small wood wedges and jam them into the spaces where the noise is occurring.

Squeaky Body Parts

Does your seat squeak? Is an elusive squeak gremlin loose somewhere inside the car? Is a body panel or piece of sheet metal full of chirping birds? Here are some tips for locating and curing those annoying noises:

- Have someone else drive the vehicle over bumpy roads while you ride in the back seat or trunk or even on the hood. Doing so will help you isolate the part of the car where the noise is coming from.

- Put a sandbag on the fender and drive. Then put the sandbag, in turn, on the hood, trunk, and bumper. Does the noise stop? If so, try tightening the mounting bolts. If the bolts are tight, try spraying one of the "trick cure" substances into the offending area.

- Use a long piece of hose to find the source of the noise. Tape the hose onto the body and leave the end terminating at the suspected source. Do you hear the noise when you put the other end to your ear?

- Use a solid particulate lubricating spray on the various areas where the squeak is occurring.

One of the following trick cures may help to get rid of that annoying chirp:

- Graphite powder or spray gets into tight spots well. The powder can be puffed into tight spots and will work into the squeak, making it go away after a little while. As the graphite works into the squeak, it coats the surface and gradually kills the squeak.

- Teflon-based sprays are excellent for lubricating squeaking rubber and plastic panels. Teflon is a great sliding surface lubricant.

- Lithium-based sprays are great for spraying into squeaking hinges, sliding surfaces, and any metal-to-metal assembly. (Lithium is also known as "white grease.")

- Baby powder is great for interior squeaks and chirps. Liberally coat the area until the noise goes away, and repeat as necessary. Talcum powder also works well.

Wind Noise

Noise made by the wind passing over, around, and through various body panels of your car can drive you crazy. Here are some tips to cure those ghostly moans, screeches, and howls:

- Have someone else drive the vehicle while you hang out the window. Listen to the sound from the outside the car. Is it coming from the front, top, or rear of the vehicle?

- Place large pieces of masking tape over the windshield trim. Cover only one side at a time until you hit the spot that makes the noise go away. After you locate the source of the noise, remove and reinstall the windshield trim, using butyl rubber sealer to fill the cracks and stop the noise.

- Place large pieces of masking tape over the front and side trim. Cover only one side at a time until the noise goes away. After you locate the source of the noise, remove and reinstall the trim, using butyl rubber sealer to fill the cracks and stop the noise.

- If the roof-mounted rack is the source of the noise, remove the rack when you're not using it.

- If you can't fill the cracks, try deflecting the wind by installing a hood-mounted wind deflector. A front-end body bra is another possible cure.

Recipe for Rusty Nuts

Here are some of the time-honored concoctions, chemicals, and elixirs that have proven invaluable in curing a multitude of vehicular ills. If you don't have any penetrating oil handy, you can use any of the following items to help free up a rusty fastener:

- Use oil of wintergreen from a drugstore as a penetrating oil.

- Remove the dipstick and use it to apply some engine oil on the stuck part. Add a drop or two of gasoline to make it penetrate. Use a crayon, candle, or even better, beeswax as a lubricant. Heat the frozen part with a propane torch and let the wax flow between the threads.

- Shake things loose with a sharp rap with the ball end of a ballpeen hammer. If possible, use a pneumatic chisel to vibrate the fastener loose.

- Slowly tighten the fastener just a smidgen and then slightly loosen it. Keep up the back-and-forth movement, all the while soaking the part with oil.

- Use the heat wrench. An oxyacetylene torch is a great tool for removing stuck parts. If necessary, use dry ice to cool off the part in the middle after heating the part on the outside.

- Use a reverse-fluted drill. These twist drills have counterclockwise flutes. When you use them in a reverse drill, the force of the drill bit turning counterclockwise will back out the frozen bolt.

Windshield Wiper First Aid

Do your windshield wipers wipe out your nerves? Do they screech like fingernails on a chalkboard? Have hope! You can cure your car of the wiper woes.

First, thoroughly clean your windshield. Get the glass really clean. A grease-free windshield cures most problems. Squeaks are usually caused by oil and grease buildup on the windshield and wiper blades. Follow these steps for a squeaky-clean, but screechless, windshield:

1 Clean the windshield with ammonia and wadded-up newspapers.

2 Clean the wiper blades with rubbing alcohol or straight windshield washer fluid.

3 If steps 1 and 2 fail to cure the problem, replace the wiper blades.

The rubber wiper insert is supposed to flip freely back and forth as the wiper goes across the glass. After time, the rubber stays flipped to the side where it always stops.

Imagine a push broom for a moment. The bristles are angled, or set in the direction the broom is supposed to go. When you push the broom, it glides smoothly across the floor, but when you pull back on the handle, it hops back toward you. This is exactly what happens with your wiper blades when they take a set, and that's why replacing them can cure the problem. After the blades are permanently bent to one side or another, they are not repairable or cleanable. Just like an old push broom with the bristles permanently bent in one direction, the rubber is permanently bent and will not recover.

Wiper Mortis

What can you do if it's pouring rain, your windshield-wiper motor is broken, and you absolutely **must** drive? Cut an onion in half and rub the juice on the outside of the windshield. The oil in the onion juice will cause rain to roll off the glass in beads, usually improving vision enough to safely drive your car—preferably to a repair shop!

Notice! I am not advocating driving without your wipers! This is only for emergency situations.

Have you seen those ads for "lifetime" wiper blades, so tough that they never wear out? Don't fall for it! When you buy those expensive wipers, you have to pay a hefty shipping and handling charge to exchange them. And they still wear out—maybe not as fast as normal wiper blades, but by the time you pay for the wipers, shipping, handling, and postage to return them, you are better off buying name-brand replacement blades from your local parts store.

Be careful when you change wiper blades! After you remove the blade from the spring-loaded arm, don't leave the arm standing out away from the windshield. It can snap back with enough force to crack the glass. After you remove the blade, return the arm gently against the glass while you replace the blade insert.

OK, you cleaned the glass and replaced the blades. Still got a problem? Here's the fix for those really stubborn cases:

1 Turn on the ignition and turn on the wipers.

2 Turn off the ignition when the wiper is halfway across the windshield.

3 Carefully lift the wiper off the windshield and slowly lower it back onto the windshield. Observe the edge of the wiper blade when you do so. The wiper blade should contact the glass at a 90-degree angle. If the blade is tilted to either side, you must bend the wiper arm.

4 Look at the blade and determine which way the arm needs to be bent.

5 Using a pair of pliers, carefully bend the wiper arm a small amount in the direction that will make the blade perpendicular to the glass.

If this procedure still doesn't cure the problem, consider replacing the wiper arms, which contain a spring that is calibrated for your windshield. As the wiper arm gets old, the spring loses its tension, causing the blade to skip across the glass or make noise.

Unlocking Vapor Lock

Many owners of carbureted cars experience problems with vapor lock. The problem usually manifests itself as hard starting after the car has been driven and shut off. The car has to cool for a time ranging from a few minutes to a few hours. Fuel-injected cars are less prone to vapor lock, but they can suffer from the problem.

Vapor lock is often caused by high fuel volatility, which is measured by *Reid vapor pressure*. Reid vapor pressure refers to the expandable (volatile) capacity of gasoline when exposed to increased temperatures. In general, high-octane fuel is more volatile than regular grades.

High-Volatility Fuel Problems

Fuel volatility is the fuel's ability to turn from a liquid to a vapor while inside the engine. The problem is that winter-grade fuels are sometimes too volatile and summer grades are not volatile enough. This situation causes a plethora of drivability conditions that are difficult to understand and impossible to fix. Sometimes just changing brands of fuel cures hard-starting or hesitation problems—something a tune-up cannot address.

Carburetor Flooding

When fuel in the carburetor float bowl evaporates after shutdown, hot soak of the engine compartment occurs.

Hot soak can cause excessively long cranking times, even after the car has been sitting overnight. Does your engine crank and crank before catching and firing up? The reason could be that the carburetor is dry and has to be filled with gas before the car will

Hot Soak Defined

Hot soak happens when an engine is shut off after reaching operating temperature. Latent heat from the combustion chamber and exhaust manifold continues to heat the engine block. Under-hood temperatures soar. The engine block actually boils the coolant in critical passages in the cylinder head. All the fuel in the engine compartment is hot soaked and tends to boil, creating vapor lock.

start. Modern fuel is often too volatile, which causes carburetors to empty themselves of fuel and makes starting difficult.

Charcoal Canister Saturation
The charcoal inside the canister holds fuel vapors from the fuel tank and carburetor. If the fuel is too volatile, it foams out of the fuel tank and saturates the activated charcoal, deactivating the charcoal. The canister ceases to store fuel vapors and routes the fumes right into the carburetor, flooding the engine.

Flying Gas Caps
Excessive pressure buildup in the gas tank can cause the gas cap to pop out of your hand when you loosen it.

Vehicle Fires

Saturated charcoal canisters can dump fuel into the engine compartment. Combine this condition with one small spark from the alternator, and your car has an engine fire.

Fuel Dribbling
Hot soak can cause expansion in the fuel line between the fuel pump and the carburetor, resulting in high pressure at the needle and seat of the carburetor. This condition can make the needle unseat and additional fuel enter the float bowl, causing flooding.

Using winterized fuel blends during warm weather can cause problems. Winter fuel is blended to be more volatile so that it ignites easily in freezing weather. If the car still has winterized fuel during a warm snap, the fuel may boil and create a vapor-lock problem.

Mechanical Causes

Hot air problems: If you have a stuck heat riser or thermal air door, remove the top of the air cleaner. Does the problem go away? If so, the thermally heated air intake system (called Thermac or EFE) may be working overtime. This system is supposed to route warm air into the intake of the throttle housing only when the temperature drops below 60°F. Problem: Hot air at other times can cause the fuel to superheat. Removing the air cleaner will pinpoint the problem because it allows the engine to draw in unheated fresh air.

Carburetor base gasket or spacer problems: The omission of the insulator under the carburetor, or an old, hardened spacer, can allow the carburetor to overheat when the engine is shut down. Some manufacturers incorporate metal or phenolic spacers under the carburetor to insulate it from heat transmission through the intake manifold. Two carmakers use phenolic resin float bowls to lower fuel temperature on high-heat applications.

Thermostat problems: If the engine runs too hot, try running a cooler thermostat in the system. Cooling system scale can prevent engine heat from radiating into the cooling system and can cause hot soak problems. Too much coolant mixed with too little water can also cause overheating.

Exhaust leak problems: Hot exhaust gas leaking under the hood can cause the under-hood temperatures to soar. Also, exhaust gas leaks can dilute the air charge into the engine and cause lean mixtures, which make the engine run even hotter.

Simple Solutions

Change fuel brands. Not all fuels have the same Reid vapor pressure. In general, the more alcohol in the fuel, the more it tends to boil. Try different brands and compare their drivability. **Note:** Oxygenated fuel can contain more alcohol and can be much more volatile. Ditto for premium grades.

Pop the hood. On excessively hot days, pop open the hood and let out the heat before it has a chance to boil the fuel.

Cool the fuel. For carbureted cars, place a wet wash rag on the mechanical fuel pump to cool it. For fuel-injected cars, cool the entire fuel system with a garden hose.

Insulate the fuel line. Be sure the fuel line is away from all heat sources. Wrap suspect hoses or pipes located near hot engine parts with fiberglass insulation, aluminum foil, or silver duct tape. Do not substitute rubber hose for metal line, or you might cause vapor lock.

Install an underhood fan. An underhood fan can cool things a bit. Purchase the kind that mounts on the radiator and pushes extra air into the engine compartment. Be sure to get an adjustable thermostatic control so that you can set the temperature so the fan will run for a few minutes after shutdown to cool the under-hood area. Installing a fan to blow directly on the carburetor can also help.

Complex Solutions

Cool the air ducts. Installing an auxiliary air duct from the front of the car to the carburetor will help keep it cool. You can rig up an add-on air duct to bring cool fresh air into the area of the carburetor or fuel injectors.

Make pressure modifications. Because fuel under pressure resists boiling, raising pressure from the tank to the carburetor can help. Install an electric fuel pump as close to the tank as possible. Install a pressure regulator as close to the carburetor as possible. The fuel pump will raise the pressure to about 6 psi and the regulator will lower it back to about 2 psi. Follow the instructions that come with the pump for installation help.

Insulate the fuel tank. Install heat shields between the muffler/exhaust system and the gas tank to keep the exhaust heat from boiling the fuel in the tank. A muffler shop will be helpful here.

Insulate the carburetor. Adding an asbestos plate or layer of fiberglass between the manifold and carburetor can help keep the carburetor cool. Consult a local carburetor specialist for help here.

Make design changes. Later fuel system designs allow fuel to return to the tank, preventing excessive pressure from developing in the fuel lines. Internal bleeds in the fuel pump or an additional metering port on the filter or pump will let high pressure and vapors escape back to the fuel tank. This keeps the fuel cool by constantly circulating it between the fuel tank and pump. Retrofitting these systems (known as a *three-line fuel filter* or *three-line fuel pump*) requires fitting a return line back to the fuel tank. This solution is complex and may require the assistance of a mechanic.

4

Preventive Maintenance

How many times have you heard, "You can pay me now or pay me *much more* later"? Can you beat the game by maintaining your own car? Do dealers provide the best service? What about chain stores and quick-lube places? Is there any reason why you should go one place and not another?

When it comes to maintaining your car, *you* are the one who decides what should be done. Which repair shop you pick can make a big difference in the outcome. Some people spend money needlessly, paying for work that's not necessary or is done prematurely. Most people want to do the bare minimum in order to stretch their dollars. How can you do the least yet make the most of your car?

Routine preventive maintenance can add years to the life of your car. Follow these guidelines, and I guarantee that your car will run more smoothly and spend much less time at the repair shop.

Now it's time to dive in under the hood and get started. Remember, preventive maintenance is the best way to save money on your car repairs.

Checking Fluid Levels

It is best to check your oil level every week before you start the car for the first time in the morning. It takes only a moment. You

---

One big money-saving tip is to find a shop that will do several maintenance items at the same time. This is called doing **overlapping repairs**. For example, when having the hoses changed, get the coolant flushed. When changing the timing belt, replace the water pump. If the shop doesn't want to overlap repairs, go somewhere else.

don't even need to wipe off the dipstick. This one basic preventive maintenance measure is fundamental to long engine life. The most important liquid in your vehicle is the oil in your engine and drivetrain (which includes the transmission, transaxle, and/or differential). For more information about where to go for oil changes, see the section on liquids and lubricants that follows.

It's usually wise to have your mechanic check the level and condition of the drivetrain oil when you have the motor oil changed. This is because accessing and checking can be difficult and the vehicle may need to be up on a lift. However, *you* must monitor the level of oil in your engine.

For accuracy, check your engine oil level with the vehicle on a flat surface. With the engine off and cold, have a look around the engine bay. While you may not know what everything is, become familiar with the general layout of your engine compartment. Since you are doing the job of a service station attendant, you must also assume his or her duties in looking for things amiss under the hood. The idea is to become acquainted with the way things are normally. Then if something frays, tears, breaks, or leaks, you will be able to spot it. If you don't check around and look for problems, who will?

Be sure to check the hoses connecting the motor to the rest of the car. Are they cracked or bulging? Are there any leaks? Using a flashlight, carefully examine the condition of the fan belt or belts.

If needed, consult your owner's manual for help in identifying the items under the hood. It is important to know the location of the following items: oil dipstick, transmission dipstick, coolant reservoir, brake-fluid reservoir, and windshield washer reservoir. Many modern cars have see-through liquid containers that allow you to check the fluid levels without touching anything. If your brake fluid, coolant, and windshield-washer reservoirs are made of translucent plastic, you should be able to see at a glance whether they are low.

Over time, the windshield washer fluid level should be the only level that goes down. If any other fluid level drops, there may be a leak; have your mechanic take a look. Leaking coolant or brake fluid can be a real disaster! Ideally, you will spot dropping fluid levels during your weekly under-the-hood inspections.

Tuning Up

In the old days, you could tell that your car needed a tune-up because the engine became hard to start. Modern cars don't act as if they need a tune-up, but if you miss your service interval, the ignition module may fail due to worn spark plugs, wires, cap, or rotor. Since the ignition module may cost $400, you don't want to let that happen.

Servicing Belts and Hoses

Careless installation of drive belts, timing belts, and hoses can cost you in other ways. While these jobs may seem simple, sloppy or incorrect installation causes the parts to fail prematurely and may even damage other parts (if a belt is tightened too much, the water pump or alternator will soon fail). Not all belts and hoses are the same quality, and cheaper ones don't last as long as good name-brand parts, such as Goodyear, Dayco, and Gates.

Because some cars require valve adjustments and special equipment to set the mixture and timing properly, tune-ups are best done by a mechanic who specializes in your car make or by your dealer. Using a cheap tune-up place can really cost you! In some cases, those mechanics are in too much of a hurry to get on to the next job and can carelessly create more problems.

Caring for Tires

You need to rotate your tires and check their alignment to get your money's worth from them. Find a local tire dealer willing to make a deal that includes periodic rotation, balancing, and alignment. Also, some shops give free alignment checks that involve driving your car over a metal plate. (See Chapter 3 for more information about tire rotation and alignment.)

Cleaning Injectors

Many late-model cars don't benefit from injector cleaning; new injector designs don't get dirty. The cleaning solvents can shorten the life of injectors. Don't fall for this ruse. Consult your owner's manual, contact your dealer, or call the manufacturer's customer service hot line and ask whether your engine's injectors should be cleaned and whether cleaning solvent will damage them.

Just because your local car dealership makes it a practice to clean injectors doesn't mean that doing so is a good idea. Some unscrupulous dealerships clean injectors even though the carmaker says not to. The dealer's service department is making extra money on a service that is not needed—and shortens the life of your injectors!

Replacing Shocks and Struts

Shock absorbers and MacPherson struts (depending on which kind your car has) are important in handling and preventing certain kinds of tire wear. Replacing them is a judgment call, and many times they are replaced needlessly. Get more than one opinion before having your shock absorbers and/or struts replaced. Also be aware that many different companies make shocks and struts. Some companies offer better handling, some offer a smoother ride, some offer lifetime guarantees, and some offer the cheapest price. Be sure to ask about these concerns because you may be buying a cheap shock or strut that will not perform in the manner you're used to: your car may not ride as well as it did before the shocks or struts were replaced.

Maintenance Intervals

In general, your owner's manual is the best source of maintenance interval information. But what if you don't have a manual? Also, you should know that the maintenance manual does not list all the items to be maintained. Some are left out so the manufacturer can get a better rating in car operating cost comparisons. In general, take the recommendations in your maintenance manual with a grain of salt. If you have any doubts, follow the advice in this chapter.

To keep your car running smoothly and to prolong its life, you need to keep it well lubricated and make sure that each type of filter is operating properly and not getting plugged up. Also, each part needs service after a certain number of miles or years. The following sections tell you when each service should be performed.

Liquids and Lubricants

Motor oil: Change every 3,000 miles or three months, whichever comes first. (**Exception:** Synthetic oil can easily last 7,500 miles or more.)

Automatic transmission: Modern front-wheel-drive cars, especially automatics, have *very* expensive transmissions. Because of today's low hood profiles, these units run hot and need more service. It's much cheaper to have the transmission serviced than to have it fixed, with repair costs ranging from $2,000 to $3,000.

Service the automatic transmission every 25,000 miles for most front-wheel-drive cars. Shorter intervals are recommended for city driving. Rear-wheel-drive vehicles can go 50,000 miles between changes. This service usually involves changing the fluid, pan gasket, and transmission filter. The transmission linkage and transmission bands (if your vehicle has them) should also be checked at this time. Some shops call this a *transmission tune-up*.

The most important service is an oil change. In general, oil in quart containers is better quality than bulk oil dispensed from storage tanks. When it's on sale, stock up on good oil (like Castrol, Valvoline, or Mobil). Bring your own oil to the service center and ask for a discount for supplying your own parts. Take advantage of advertised oil-change specials

Many automatic transmissions have transmission filters, which should be replaced when the transmission is serviced. However, some cars don't require transmission filter replacement; their filters are merely cleaned and reused. Find out which type your vehicle has by asking the dealer's parts department whether it cleans and reuses the transmission filters. Don't pay for a filter replacement if the filter is supposed to be reused, and don't let the mechanic reuse the old filter if it should be replaced.

The best place to go is a transmission specialist or dealership. Manual transmissions and differentials require much less maintenance and can withstand more abuse. Also, they don't have filters to replace. Both manual and automatic transmissions benefit from the installation of synthetic oil instead of the usual petroleum lubricant. Synthetic oil costs more but protects this very expensive part of your car better than petroleum oil.

Manual transmission, transaxle, differential: Change every 50,000 miles. Manual transmissions on front-wheel-drive cars also have an integral differential located in the front axle, which is called a *transaxle*. Rear-wheel-drive vehicles have a separate differential, located in the rear axle. Don't forget to have the differential or transaxle serviced, too.

Power steering fluid: Change every 30,000 miles (includes the power steering filter when applicable). Some carmakers don't call for power steering fluid changes, but dirty fluid can cause power steering failure. Power steering repairs are very expensive, but fluid changes are cheap insurance against major problems later on. Also, some cars (Volvo and Mercedes-Benz, for example) have power steering filters.

Brakes: Flush the fluid and inspect the brakes every 30,000 miles or two years, whichever comes first.

Brake fluid service is very important. You need your brakes! Having the fluid changed may prevent expensive brake repairs or catastrophic brake failure. Some antilock brake parts are easily ruined by old brake fluid and cost about $2,000 to replace. Save money by having your brakes inspected when they're being flushed.

Antifreeze Additives?

There are some cooling system additives on store shelves making claims that they do everything your cooling system needs and more. This may be true for a radiator that has old coolant in it, but for the money, forget it! If you service your radiator properly, these products are unnecessary and a big waste of money.

Regular coolant/antifreeze contains ethylene glycol, rust inhibitors, water pump lubricants, antifoaming agents, antiacids, and detergents. Actually, glycol is all that is needed to prevent freezing. The rest of the additives are part of the formula for maintaining the health of your cooling system. If the formula is for aluminum engines, it will also contain aluminum silicate or some other chemical to prevent corrosion. Most of today's cars have aluminum cylinder heads, and many have aluminum radiators as well. It's critical that the coolant be changed annually on these cars.

Antifreeze/coolant: Change every 25,000 miles or two years, whichever comes first. (Antifreeze and coolant are different names for the same thing.)

Modern engines use a great deal of aluminum, which requires a proper mixture of coolant and additives to prevent aluminum corrosion and acid buildup. If you skimp on periodic changes, you increase your chances of a blown head gasket and/or ruined cylinder head. Coolant turns acidic from combustion gases leaking into the cooling system. The more you drive, the more often you should have the coolant changed.

This service should be done by the dealer or someone experienced with your type of car. If it is done improperly, an air bubble can become trapped and cause a blown head gasket. Also, it is important to frequent a shop that recycles coolant rather than dumping it into the environment (it contains toxic heavy metals).

There is a new type of coolant on the market called *propylene glycol*. It differs from the traditional ethylene glycol coolant in several ways—mainly, it is much less toxic. It doesn't taste sweet like ethylene glycol and won't poison pets that wander by your car and drink some. If your vehicle leaks coolant and you are concerned that it might harm your pets, you may want to use propylene glycol. Be sure to check with your car's manufacturer about using it, as the use of some such substances voids the warranty.

Another new product is called DexCool™. This long-life coolant can be left in your system for up to five years or 100,000 miles. It also provides superior water-pump and corrosion protection. It's a little more expensive, but I think it's worth it.

How Long Can You Go?

Automotive engines depend on a steady diet of many things, and good, healthy antifreeze is one of them. Dirty, contaminated old antifreeze will shorten the life of the water pump, hoses, heater core, and radiator. These premature failures can add up to very big repair bills. The best way to prevent costly cooling-system repairs is to change your antifreeze regularly.

The Society of Automotive Engineers recommends that the antifreeze be changed every two to three years, depending on how much the car is driven. Actually, the main ingredient in antifreeze, ethylene glycol, never goes bad. It's all of the other ingredients that wear out or turn sour.

Just because the antifreeze passes the freeze-point test doesn't mean it's still OK. If it's over two years old, it may contain a harmful concentration of acids. Old antifreeze turns corrosive and attacks all of the internal aluminum and copper parts. The radiator, heater core, and water pump all take a beating. If your car has an aluminum/plastic radiator, you might want to change your antifreeze every 24,000 miles.

Always mix antifreeze with distilled water. Tap water contains too many minerals and chlorine, which will shorten the life of your radiator. Spend an extra dollar or two and mix with distilled water. If your car has an aluminum radiator or cylinder head, be sure that the antifreeze you buy is labeled "safe for aluminum."

Antifreeze Killers

Let's look at some of the things that can contribute to antifreeze going bad.

Water quality. One of the easiest ways to shorten the life of antifreeze is to use tap water when mixing. Distilled water should always be used.

Contamination. Oil seepage past the head gasket and other seals ruins antifreeze. Dirt contamination from foreign matter being drawn into the antifreeze reservoir also can ruin antifreeze. Exhaust leakage into antifreeze is impossible to prevent. Even the best head gasket cannot keep all of the combustion gases from seeping to the water jacket.

Aeration. If the cooling system is not pressurized properly, air bubbles can form in the antifreeze. In the presence of air, the coolant cannot resist oxidation.

Heavy metals. Breakdown of the inside of radiators, heater cores, and engine core soft plugs cause the antifreeze to become contaminated with heavy metals. Lead, tin, zinc, nickel, and copper attack the antifreeze and shorten its life. The more aluminum that comes into contact with the antifreeze, the faster it is depleted. Aluminum, when heated, turns into aluminum salts. These salts attack everything they touch, and build up in the radiator, eventually clogging it. Aluminum comes mainly from aluminum cylinder heads.

Cooling-system capacity. Modern cars have downsized cooling systems, meaning less antifreeze must do more work. Antifreeze becomes depleted more quickly on small cars than large cars.

Antifreeze temperature. Modern engines run hotter. The hotter the engine, the harder antifreeze must work. Antifreeze that comes into contact with extremely hot cylinder head parts breaks down quickly.

Galvanic coupling. Dissimilar metals inside the engine cause the antifreeze to become an electrolyte. Iron, brass, aluminum, nickel, and galvanized steel react with one another, causing a chemical reaction that turns the antifreeze acidic.

Engine dynamics. Ordinary operational factors like vibration, stress, load factors, and turbulence all cause antifreeze to break down. (So much for never needing to change your antifreeze.)

Filters

Oil filter: Replace at every oil change, or every six months if you're using synthetic oil.

Air filter: Replace every 30,000 miles (more often in dirty areas where there is a great deal of sand and dust on the road).

Fuel filter: Change at the tune-up. (There will be an extra charge for this service.)

Thermostats

Cooling systems are at the mercy of the engine thermostat. This little device can create a host of problems if it doesn't work as it is supposed to. It can cause the cooling system to be too cold or too hot. Either case can shorten the life of your car. Here's how the thermostat can damage things: If it opens too soon, the engine doesn't get a chance to warm up. The fuel burns improperly because of the cold cylinder walls inside the engine. The raw fuel condenses on the walls and mixes with the oil. This wrecks the oil's ability to lubricate the piston rings, and a terrible amount of wear occurs. Remember that 90 percent of an engine's wear takes place in the first three minutes of operation.

A cold running engine on a car with computer-controlled fuel can literally turn itself into a burning blaze of fire! How? Easy. The computer adjusts the fuel mixture according to the information it receives from its sensors. One of the most important is the coolant temperature sensor, which lets the computer do what the automatic choke used to do on carbureted cars. It makes the mixture rich when cold and lean when hot.

If the coolant sensor says the engine has never fully warmed up, the computer will *always* keep the mixture rich. The extra fuel causes the catalytic converter to overwork trying to burn up the extra gasoline coming out of the engine. But the catalytic converter can handle only so much of the extra fuel. It will get hotter and hotter until it becomes *red hot*. This can set the underside of the car on fire and burn the car to the ground. I've seen cars burned up this way.

If the thermostat stays open too far, coolant will move too fast in the system. Then the water pump and the radiator core will be destroyed by cavitation, which occurs when a liquid contains bubbles. Those bubbles then become a destructive force.

Always replace the thermostat with one that has the correct temperature range for your car. Use a name-brand part and change it every four or five years. It's a good idea to have the cooling system flushed out at the same time, because the thermostat must be removed to do a proper job of engine flushing anyway.

Killer Bubbles

When the water pump doesn't have the partially closed thermostat for a restriction to push against, it forms vacuum bubbles. When these killer bubbles pop, they do their damage. They attack the metal parts of the pump's impeller with the force of a 200-mph water jet. Little pieces of metal begin to flake off, eventually destroying the pump and/or its housing.

Cavitation can also cause the impeller blades of the water pump to form an air lock and lose their pumping force. The pump can't push coolant through the system, and overheating can result. If the thermostat doesn't open up enough, the car will overheat. Coolant can boil out or the engine can blow a head gasket or crack. A hot-running car can suffer from pinging, detonation, run-on, and a host of other drivability problems.

Cooling System

When was the last time you did something nice for your cooling system? If you have neglected changing the coolant, you face the possibility of major repairs in the future. One quick way to determine just how bad your coolant has become is to measure its electrical charge. As coolant ages, it becomes acidic. The more acidic it is, the more it acts like a battery. Eventually it will be so acidic that it will generate enough voltage to be read easily with a voltmeter.

To do the test, you will need a voltmeter that is capable of reading both AC and DC voltages. Ideally, the meter leads should be capable of reaching all the way from the radiator to the battery negative post. The meter should be able to read tenths of a volt; a digital voltmeter is best.

When doing these voltage tests, it is best to have the coolant at operating temperature. This means you must remove the radiator cap before you begin warming up the engine. Before you do this, remove some of the coolant from the radiator so it doesn't run out when it expands as it heats up.

Use a turkey baster to remove the coolant or siphon it off into a clean pail, bucket, or jug. You will want to save it to reinstall after you are finished with the test. An ideal container is an empty coolant jug or milk container. Be sure to continue to remove coolant as the engine warms and coolant expands in the radiator. Don't let it run out.

Once the coolant is hot to the touch, you are ready to begin testing. Here's the procedure:

1 Clip or probe the ground (black) lead of the voltmeter onto the battery ground terminal. Try to use the battery and not the engine block or vehicle frame. But if the battery is not available, you will have to use the engine block for a ground source.

2 Probe the positive lead (red) into the coolant. Be careful not to touch the sides of the radiator with it.

3 Take a reading of the DC voltage shown on the meter. If the reading is over ½ volt (0.5 volt), the coolant is contaminated and must be changed. If the reading is high, over 3 volts, the entire cooling system should be flushed. In addition, change the coolant. If the reading is less than ½ volt, go to the next step.

4 Turn on all the accessories: lights on high beam, air conditioner on high, rear-window defroster, radio, emergency flashers, wipers, and so on. If the coolant shows a DC electrical charge of more than ½ volt now, start turning off electrical accessories one at a time. When the voltage level drops, you have identified the accessory that has a grounding problem. Go to step 9.

5 Repeat the procedure outlined in step 4 with the voltmeter reading AC voltage. Again, identify the cause of high AC voltage readings by turning off each accessory until the voltage readings diminish. Any AC readings over 0.5 volt are caused by static electricity generated from that component. Go to step 9.

6 With the accessories still on, start the motor and observe both the AC and DC voltage readings. High DC readings indicate a ground problem between the engine, battery, alternator, and vehicle chassis. Go to step 8. High AC readings indicate the alternator is faulty and is putting AC voltage into the system. Replace the alternator.

7 If your vehicle has an electric cooling fan, run the engine until the cooling fan cycles on. Take another voltage reading while the fan is running. If you read more than ½ volt, the fan has a grounding problem. Go to step 9.

8 Move the positive meter probe to a good ground connection on the engine block. Try to find an unpainted shiny metal place. With the engine running but all accessories off, take a DC voltage reading. If it is more than ½ volt, the engine to battery ground cable is bad and should be inspected, cleaned, and/or replaced.

9 To cure other ground problems, attach a piece of 12-gauge insulated copper wire to the offending part and a nearby ground. Attach the wire to a good ground using an already existing screw or nearby bolt. Do not use any structural bolts or bolts that are torqued (like head bolts). If no fastener is handy, drill a hole in the body and install a sheet-metal screw to ground the wire. Here are some examples:

- Radiator cooling fan is grounded to the metal support brace.

- Radio gets grounded to an instrument panel support brace.

- Wiper motor gets grounded to the nearby body cowl.

- Electric blower motor for the heater gets grounded to a sheet-metal screw in the firewall.

Services

Tune-up: Follow your owner's manual. It's typically every 30,000 miles, though some newer cars can go 60,000 or even 100,000 miles between tune-ups. If you own one of these cars, be sure to take care of the other things (like fuel filters and transmission services) at the recommended intervals. If you wait until the tune-up to have these important services done, you may damage your vehicle.

Belts and hoses: Check the condition of the belts and hoses annually and replace every 60,000 miles or five years, whichever comes first. Replace the timing belt typically at 60,000 to 90,000 miles.

Tires: Rotate every 7,500 miles. Have them inspected for nails or cuts and check proper air pressure at every oil change. Check the alignment and balance when getting a tune-up. You have to pay extra, but this is a good time to have this service done.

M any modern engines have timing belts that **must** be replaced at 60,000 to 90,000 miles. On many cars, especially Asian imports, extensive engine damage can occur if you fail to change the timing belt and it breaks. Consult the dealer for the proper service interval for your engine and ask whether your engine will be damaged if the timing belt breaks. If not, the worst thing you risk by skimping on this service and driving until it breaks is needing a tow. Your choice!

General Intervals for Parts Replacement

If you don't have a service manual and wonder what to do when, here's a handy-dandy table for your reference. This table can also be used as a check to make sure a mechanic isn't selling you a bill of goods for replacement of some item that really doesn't need to be replaced. Remember, this is a generic chart. If the manufacturer calls for shorter intervals, follow that recommendation.

The type of driving you do has the biggest effect on how often you need to carry out the services listed below. If you drive less than 10 miles per trip, follow the shorter intervals. If you drive mostly long distances (50 miles or more per trip), follow the longer intervals.

General Service Intervals

Auto Part	Service or Replace
Shocks and struts	25,000–75,000 miles
Suspension, tie rods, and ball joints	50,000–150,000 miles
Tires	30,000–60,000 miles
Muffler and pipes	60,000–150,000 miles
Belts and hoses	60,000–150,000 miles
Front brakes	24,000–50,000 miles
Rear brakes	40,000–100,000 miles
Headlight bulbs	3–8 years or 50,000–150,000 miles
Windshield wiper blades	1–3 years

Radiator	100,000–200,000 miles or 10–12 years
Water pump	100,000–175,000 miles
Battery	2–6 years
Timing belt	60,000–90,000 miles
Timing chain	100,000–150,000 miles
Clutch (manual transmission)	80,000–150,000 miles
CV joints	80,000–150,000 miles
Universal joints	150,000–250,000 miles
Fuel injectors and fuel pump	100,000–200,000 miles

Getting More Bang for the Buck

Here are some mechanics' tips for making your car last longer and for getting the most from your car:

Buy the biggest and best battery that will fit in the battery tray. Long-life batteries hold a charge better, tax the alternator less, and power the starter better, making the alternator and starter last longer. Replace the battery six months before its warranty expires— an old battery causes the alternator to charge all the time, shortening its life.

Buy paint protection when you purchase a new car. Then apply a coating of silicone-type paint protection every six months (three months in polluted areas). Doing so makes your paint job last longer and helps to prevent acid-rain damage. If you want to do it yourself, you can buy the same paint protection from an automotive paint supply store and apply it at home—at a considerable savings.

Use synthetic oil in your engine and transmission. Longer engine life and better gas mileage more than compensate for the extra expense. While petroleum oil must be changed every 3,000 miles, synthetic oils last 7,500 miles or more. I like Redline synthetic oil best.

If there is room under the hood, install a bypass oil filter. Bypass filters really clean the oil and remove all contamination, making the engine last much longer.

Have your oil analyzed every year. Lube-oil analysis can detect potential problems long before they cause major engine damage.

Install a reusable lifetime air filter. These filters can be cleaned and reused indefinitely and do a better job of filtering the air.

Once a year, treat all the rubber weather-stripping on your car with a coating of silicone grease. Silicone prevents cracking from summer heat and splitting from freezing rain.

If you park outside, use a car cover. The sun's rays and environmental fallout really age a car. If you can't garage it, cover it.

Invest in an inexpensive, easy-to-use torque wrench. Mechanics use air-driven impact guns and overtorque the lug nuts, which can warp the brake rotors and permanently damage them. Retorque (retighten) your own lug nuts any time the wheels are off.

Don't forget your mechanic during the holidays. Spending a little on your mechanic now will pay off in the years to come.

Cleaning Your Car's Interior

Many people treasure their car's upholstery but don't know how to keep it clean and stain-free. Keeping it clean means reaping a higher resale value. The Car Care Council found that extra-clean cars can bring as much as 50 percent more when traded in or sold than not-so-clean cars with comparable mileage and equipment. Here are some general cleaning suggestions:

Nylon and polyester seats, interior, and carpeting: Use mild household cleaners made specifically for this purpose. Dip a soft cloth in the cleaner and wring it out. Don't use solvents, gasoline, acetone, naphtha, dry-cleaning solvent, paint reducer, or laundry detergent unless they are specifically called for.

Leather upholstery: Prevent leather from cracking by polishing it regularly with a cream made of one part vinegar and two parts linseed oil. Clean leather seasonally with a damp cloth and saddle soap. Rub a damp washcloth in the saddle soap until you create a lather. Shampoo the area one panel at a time. Finish with a cloth dipped in warm, clear water. Be sure to get all the pleats, folds, crevices, and seams.

Vinyl upholstery: Never oil vinyl; doing so makes it hard, and it's almost impossible to soften again. To clean, try sprinkling baking soda or vinegar on a rough, damp cloth. Then wash with a mild dishwashing detergent.

Fighting Stains

Work fast. Stains set with time and heat, making them harder to remove. Some items, like fruit juice and soft drinks, may turn yellow with heat and age. In a pinch, squirt the spot with shaving cream to help lift the spill. Rinse with cold water.

If possible, find a vacuum cleaner and vacuum up as much of the material as possible. Most car washes have vacuums that you don't need to clean (ugh!) after you're done. This alone can be worth the price. Don't push the material or liquid into the fabric with the vacuum nozzle. When making the first pass over the stain, don't touch the stain with the nozzle, but try to pass over it as closely as possible.

Let the vacuum do all the work, eliminating most of the offensive material. The second pass should lightly touch the surface of the stain area. Try to keep the attachment perpendicular to the stained surface to maximize its suction power. On your third pass, make contact with the surface and suck as much of the material out of the seat as possible.

To remove lingering odors, sponge the area with a solution of baking soda and water (1 teaspoon to 1 cup). Shaklee Basic-G works well.

If the dirty spot is only slightly dirty, you can clean it with cornmeal. Use a stiff brush to work the cornmeal into the rug or seat fabric. Then simply vacuum it out.

> **J**ohn F. Seets, Jr., drives a limo with a velour interior and frequently has to deal with stains. He says, "I know all about these stains and the vac is the way to go."

Rub soiled cotton fabric with an art-gum eraser (which you can purchase at a stationery store).

Quick and thorough drying is the key to ring prevention. Use a hair dryer, a heat lamp (don't scorch the upholstery!), or an air hose. If a ring forms anyway, redo the entire area. Use small amounts and avoid saturating the area. Try to wet only the cover, not the padding underneath.

Rub gently from the outside of the stain toward the center. Repeat until it is removed. Finish with a damp cloth dipped in warm water and wrung out.

Cleaning Specific Stains

Use the following tips to remove specific stains from your car. If one type of cleaner isn't available, use the other one(s) suggested.

Alcoholic beverages: Immediately sponge with cold water and then with cold water and glycerin (available at drugstores). Rinse with vinegar for a few seconds if the stain remains. These stains may brown with age. If a wine stain remains, rub it with concentrated detergent, wait 15 minutes, and rinse. Repeat if necessary. Rinse again with plenty of warm water.

Ballpoint pen ink: Apply slightly warmed glycerin (available from a drugstore). Blot frequently with paper towels, keeping the stain moist with more glycerin while working. Finish up with cleaning solvent. Other possible cleaners include denatured alcohol and petroleum jelly.

Blood: Rub off as much as you can first. Then take a cloth soaked in cold water and wet the spot. Immediately sponge it off with cold water, wiping as you go, to keep it from setting. In 2 quarts of warm water, mix 2 tablespoons of dish detergent with ¼ cup sudsy ammonia. Using a sponge, wet the stain, rub gently, and blot with paper towels. Repeat as needed. Rinse it right away with cold water. If the stain remains, work in detergent, using bleach that is safe for the fabric.

Candle wax: Use a dull knife to scrape off as much as possible. Try to blot as much as you can onto a piece of fabric or brown paper bag by pressing a warm iron over the blotting fabric or paper. Remove a colored stain with dry-cleaning solvent. Finish by washing with detergent and rinsing with cool water.

Chewing gum: Freeze the gum with an ice cube and carefully scrape the gum off using a dull knife. If needed, use some dry-cleaning solvent. Sponge the area with water to remove any sugar stain left behind.

Chocolate or cocoa: First, wipe it up with a napkin or paper towel. Then wipe with soapy water followed by cool water. Remove grease stains with dry-cleaning solvent. If color remains, sponge the area with hydrogen peroxide and wash again.

Crayon: Remove melted remains with the ice treatment for chewing gum. Finish the job with the lipstick-removal procedure that follows.

Deodorant: Sponge the area with vinegar. If the stain remains, soak it with denatured alcohol. Wash with detergent and hot water and rinse completely.

Egg: Scrape with a dull blade. Soak with cold water for at least 30 minutes. Remove the remaining grease with dry-cleaning solvent. Finish with detergent and warm water and rinse completely.

Fruits and fruit drinks: Soap may set the stain, so start by sponging with cool water until all traces are gone. Then use soapy water followed by a plain water rinse. If color remains, wash with detergent and bleach that is safe for fabric.

Glue: Try loosening it by saturating the spot with a cloth soaked with vinegar. Consult the glue container for solvent instructions. You can remove cement glue by rubbing it with cold cream, peanut butter, or salad oil.

Grease or oil: First, use kitty litter or cornmeal as an absorbent. Soak up as much as possible and vacuum the absorbent away. Pretreat with detergent or cleaning solvent. Brake-cleaning spray (available from auto parts stores) works well, too. Because cleaning solvents dissolve the stain and cause it to bleed into unaffected areas, use them sparingly. Start at the outside and work inward, using plenty of cleaner. Change the cloth often. Use dry-cleaning solvents (such as trichloroethylene) only in a well-ventilated area. In a pinch, pour salt, talcum, or baby powder onto the grease to soak it up.

Ketchup: First, wipe it up with a paper towel. If it's dry, use a dull knife to scrape off as much as possible. Soap may set the stain, so start with cool water until all traces are gone. Then use soapy water followed by a plain rinse. Ketchup is acidic, so use bar soap to neutralize it.

Lipstick and other cosmetics: Carefully wipe from the outside toward the center with dry-cleaning solvent to loosen the stain. Remove any remaining stain with a mild household cleaner, rubbing in the detergent until the outline of the stain is gone. Wash with warm water, detergent, and bleach that is safe for fabric until the area is clean.

Mildew: Pretreat as soon as possible with detergent. Wash thoroughly with hot water, detergent, and bleach that is safe for fabric. If any stain remains, sponge with lemon juice and salt. Allow the area to dry in the sun. Mildew is very hard to remove, so treat it promptly.

Milk, cream, or ice cream: Sponge or soak with cold water as soon as possible for 30 minutes. Wash with detergent. Remove cream grease stains with dry-cleaning solvent and wash again.

Mustard: Allow to dry and then scrape off as much as possible. Sponge with mild detergent.

Nail polish: Sponge with polish remover or banana oil. Wash. If stain remains, sponge with denatured alcohol to which a few drops of ammonia have been added. Wash again. Since some fabrics (acetates and triacetates) react with nail polish remover, first try the polish remover on an out-of-sight place to see how it reacts. You might also try carburetor cleaner and degreaser, acetone, paint remover, or dry-cleaning solvent.

Paint: *Oil based*—Sponge stains with turpentine, cleaning fluid, or paint remover. Follow with sponge and hot water. For older stains, sponge with banana oil and then with dry-cleaning solvent. Wash again. *Water based*—Scrape off paint with a dull blade. Wash with detergent and hot water. Rinse with cool water.

Perspiration: Sponge fresh stains with ammonia, old stains with vinegar. Soak with warm water and rinse. Wash in hot water. If fabric is yellowed, use bleach sparingly. If stain remains, dampen and sprinkle with meat tenderizer or pepsin. Let stand for one hour. Brush off and wash. For persistent odor, sponge with colorless mouthwash.

Road tar: Carefully scrape off as much as possible. Gently wipe toward the center of the stain with a cleaning solvent.

Rust: Soak in lemon juice and salt or oxalic acid solution (3 tablespoons oxalic acid to 1 pint warm water). Or use a commercial rust remover.

Soft drinks: Sponge off immediately with cold water and alcohol. Follow with soapy water and rinse with plain water. Note that heat or detergent may set the stain.

Handle poisonous rust removers carefully and keep them out of the reach of children. Never use oxalic acid or other rust removers around paint, as they can damage it.

Urine: Clean with soapy water after neutralizing with a little ammonia and water.

White water rings and spots: Dampen a soft cloth with water and put a dab of toothpaste on it or apply a paste of salad oil and salt. Let stand briefly. Rinse and blot with a dry cloth.

Vomit: Scrape up as much as possible. Follow with a solution of ½ cup of salt to 2 quarts of water. Rinse with plain water. Wash with soap and water and rinse again with plain water.

Daily Care for Your Car's Upholstery

Making these habits part of your daily routine can add to the life of your car's interior and increase its resale value:

- Park your car so that it faces a different direction every day. This prevents the sun from repeatedly bleaching the same area of upholstery.

- Keep the sunroof or windows cracked slightly open during hot days. This keeps the heat from loosening bonding adhesives and cracking vinyl in your car's interior.

- Use a dashboard cover or cardboard shield to protect the interior.

- Vacuum seats, carpets, and interior regularly to prevent dirt, dust, and food crumbs from being ground into the upholstery. Once a spill combines with food, it can be very hard to remove.

- Avoid using pointed vacuum cleaner attachments that can tear the upholstery.

- Spray fabric upholstery and carpets with a good fabric protector to repel stains.

Washing and Waxing Your Car

Caring for the outside of your car is just as important as caring for the inside. Salt and road ashes can destroy the finish and age your car prematurely. Dirt is an enemy because it attracts and holds moisture, which turns painted surfaces rusty.

Do-It-Yourself Washing

One of the simplest things you can do to preserve the value of your car is wash it regularly. Are you willing to put in a little effort and do it yourself? If you want to do a better job than a car wash can possibly do and want to preserve the factory finish of your car, read on.

What Not to Do

Beware of the pitfalls of doing it yourself. You can do more harm than good.

- *Don't* wash and/or wax it in the sun. *Do* park the car in a spot that will remain shady throughout the process.

- *Don't* wash a hot car. *Do* wait until the vehicle is cool to the touch. Let the engine and tires cool too.

- *Don't* apply cleaners to hot wheels, or their surface finish could crack. *Do* let the wheels cool first.

- *Don't* park under trees where birds perch. *Do* avoid having branches or leaves falling on the car.

- *Don't* begin by washing. *Do* rinse the car with cool water first to rinse away loose dirt and soften the stuck-on dirt.

- *Don't* use a high-pressure spray to loosen the dirt; this will push the dirt, road salt, and grime up into cracks and crevices, where it will remain. *Do* wash dirt off by hand.

- *Don't* wash with a dirty mitt or sponge. *Do* rinse them often. *Don't* use synthetic brushes, diapers, or T-shirts; they can hold dirt particles and scratch the finish.

- *Don't* use dish detergent or laundry soap; they are too harsh and can strip the wax and oils from the finish. *Do* spend a few dollars and purchase a car wash soap.

- *Don't* allow the car to dry while it is soapy. *Don't* allow it to air dry or you will get hard-to-remove water spots. *Do* rinse it often.

The Best Way to Wash

For the best protection for your car's finish, wash it weekly. If this is not possible, at least rinse it weekly to remove most of the road grime.

Here is my favorite strategy for washing your car:

First, rinse the car. After it is wet, wash the tires and wheels first. Use a spray-on cleaner made especially for wheels and tires with white sidewalls. To keep things simple, choose one product that will work fine for both wheels and tires—unless you need a separate cleaner designed for bleaching the tire sidewalls white. These products are very strong and will clean the brake dust, grease, and road tar off the wheels. Clean the tires while the car is still wet so that any overspray of the cleaner used on them will be diluted and not harm the delicate paint finish. Follow the directions on the product to avoid causing permanent damage to your fancy wheel covers or alloy wheels. Be sure to rinse off all traces of the cleaner when you're done.

Don't use the same bucket of soapy water for the entire car unless the car is not very dirty. Change the water at least a couple of times to avoid contaminating the sponge with abrasive dirt.

Rinse the wash mitt or sponge often and thoroughly, squeezing it and shaking it while it is immersed in the bucket of soapy water. This cannot be stressed enough! Small pieces of sand become embedded in the mitt and will scratch the finish. You won't discover the problem until after the job is done.

Work from the top down, front to back. Wash only one panel at a time. Use back-and-forth motions, not circular ones. Continually rinse the section you are working on to help carry away the dirt and abrasive sand.

Clean the windshield with the car wash soap to remove any abrasive sand stuck to it. Keep in mind that this is a preliminary step. You will be cleaning it again with window cleaner. For the final rinse, remove the spray nozzle and hose the car with a medium flow of water. The idea here is to make drying easier by allowing large sheets of water to form and roll off the vehicle.

Dry the vehicle with clean cotton towels or diapers. Change sides of the drying towel often in order to prevent streaking. Use several to finish the job, changing when one gets damp.

Wax On, Wax Off
For the best results in preserving the shine on your car and to provide maximum surface protection, wax it at least twice a year. Four times is even better. Do it in the late spring and in the fall.

If you don't have much time, use a product that is easy to apply and remove. There are many products on the market that clean, polish, and wax in one step. For the best shine, use a product that contains carnauba. This Brazilian wax is revered by perfectionists. It works well when combined with silicones and polymers.

Generally a paste works better than a liquid. Apply it with a very clean or new 100 percent terry cloth towel to avoid putting scratches in the finish. Change sides of the applicator often to avoid carrying abrasives from one spot to another. Don't do the entire car at once unless you are inside in a cool location. Instead, do one panel at a time. If you have an extra hour or two and want to achieve that "wet" look, use a cleaner, polish, and wax process.

First, apply the cleaner. It will use mild abrasives and chemicals to remove mild oxidation and chemical buildup in the paint finish without damaging the paint or clearcoat. Be sure to follow the instructions on the container.

Next, apply a pure-polish compound. It contains oils to feed the surface and clay to micropolish and fill as well as distillates to remove the old wax buildup. This will produce a shine with unequaled depth, clarity, and luster. Next, apply the wax. Paste waxes seem to produce slightly better results than liquid waxes, but they require a little more time to apply and remove.

Cleaning Up the Interior
If you plan on cleaning the interior of the car, you might want to do it first. That way you won't have to worry about getting smudges and grease prints on the exterior while doing the interior. Do this chore as needed. If the car is being operated in a dirty or muddy area, you may need to at least vacuum it every day. Otherwise, follow the same schedule as for washing and waxing.

Here is my favorite strategy for interior cleaning care:

Remove as many items from the interior as possible. Empty the glove box, console, and door pockets and remove any items from under the seats and floor. If the rear seat bottom can be removed, consider doing so. Ditto for any modular or removable seats. Slide the front seats as far back as possible to improve access.

If the floor mats are heavily soiled, put them in the washing machine. Set the load capacity on "max" and set on a gentle wash cycle, using carpet shampoo. Vacuum the entire interior, starting with the dash and door panels. Use a soft brush adapter to help ferret out dust and dirt from the nooks and crannies. Be sure to get the rear deck and down between the seats.

The instrument panel face (bezel) is usually coated with soft clear plastic and scratches easily. Be especially careful when cleaning it, as it will scratch if you dry wipe it. Use as little moisture as possible to keep from getting the dash electronics wet. Consider using a plastic or Plexiglas cleaner.

Using a straight-suction attachment, carefully go over the carpets, sucking out as much of the deep dirt as possible. If the carpets are heavily soiled, use a carpet shampoo. Be sure to allow plenty of time for drying. Once you put the floor mats back inside, any remaining moisture will be trapped. This will cause mildew and smells.

Wash all the vinyl surfaces with car wash shampoo or, better yet, a quality vinyl cleaner. Use a sponge or cloth to apply the cleaner, working it into the surface of the vinyl. Start with the dash and work your way around the inside of the car.

Rinse with plain warm water and dry with a fresh cloth or paper towel. Be sure to allow plenty of time for the vinyl to dry before using a vinyl conditioner. The conditioner is important because it will keep the vinyl from cracking and fading from the sun's ultraviolet (UV) rays. Choose a product that will give the type of look you prefer. Some produce a shiny luster; others have more of a matte finish.

Choosing the Right Car Wash

Although washing your car yourself is the best approach, it's far better to patronize a car wash than to neglect cleaning altogether. A little time and money spent on regular service will pay off in the long run. You will enjoy a clean car much more, and it will have a higher resale value when you decide to get rid of it. (And everyone knows that a clean car runs better.)

Deciphering Car Wash Buzzwords

Is there such a thing as a totally safe, nonhazardous, automatic car wash? It depends. If you own a new car, especially one that has a clearcoat finish, you want a frictionless or "touchless" car wash. If your car is older, the best bang for your buck may be one of the brushless types. If your car is a clunker and all you want is the bare minimum (probably free with a fill-up), you will probably be happy with a car wash that uses spinning brushes. I'll take a look at the advantages and disadvantages of each type.

Miters: These are the parts of the automatic washing machine that come into contact with your car. Miters can be made of plastic, nylon, cloth, or synthetic chamois.

Spinning brushes: This is the cheapest type of car wash, usually given away free with a fill-up. Those spinning cylinders covered with plastic bristle brushes do an excellent job of removing built-up and caked-on dirt. But the plastic bristles may be embedded with pieces of sand from the customers before you. That sand leaves millions of swirl marks on the finish, marks that usually cannot be removed. Spinning brushes are really terrible for cars with new or clearcoat finishes.

Brushless: These are nothing more than spinning strips of cloth called cloth miters. They are better than plastic bristles in that the cloth is less likely to get pieces of sand embedded in it. But this can still happen, especially if a number of dirty cars have come before you. The type of dirt found in your vicinity has much to do with how likely the miters are to be contaminated.

Dancing miter curtains: Overall, this is probably the best type of automatic car wash. Here, huge curtains of chamoislike material "dance" across the car. Because there are no fast-spinning parts and the miters move only a short distance, this type of car wash is the safest for delicate finishes. Dancing miters are not likely to snag antennas, rearview mirrors, or the trim.

Touch-free or frictionless: These systems use high-pressure water jets (up to 1,000 pounds of pressure) to remove dirt. This type of wash is the most modern and does the least damage—with a couple of exceptions. If there is salt on the car, the high-pressure spray can drive the salt crystals deep into cracks and crevices (like under weather-stripping) that wouldn't normally be contaminated. Also, if the car has peeling paint, watch out. The high-pressure spray will make it peel even more. Many frictionless car washes are actually hybrids; they use high-pressure sprayers along with miter curtains.

Finding a Good Car Wash
The hunt for a good car wash can be a chore. Here are some questions to steer you away from places that are likely to damage your car.

- **Is there a hand-drying crew?** Better car washes employ a staff to finish the drying job and clean the windows. Otherwise, bring along some paper towels and do it yourself as soon as you exit.

- **Do you see damaged junk in the pit?** Before surrendering your car, ask to inspect the inside. Walk along the track and look for pieces of trim and other objects that may have been torn from previous customers' cars. Do you see hubcaps, license plates, and sideview mirrors lying around? Bad sign!

- **Does the place have obviously old or worn-looking equipment?** Car wash equipment must be adjusted constantly. If not, it can damage your car.

- **Is the car wash clean?** A dirty car wash cannot produce clean cars. This also tells you how well the management maintains the place.

- **Are warning signs posted?** Look out for signs disclaiming responsibility for any damage caused to your car by the establishment. These can indicate a place that has terrible equipment that destroys antennas and rearview mirrors.

- **What does the Better Business Bureau say?** This agency maintains files of complaints about businesses. Ask how many complaints have been made. Watch out for places with more than one or two unresolved complaints.

Getting Good Results

To get the best wash possible from a car wash make sure that you do the following:

Spray your wheels with cleaner first. Before going through the machine, use a heavy-duty wheel cleaner and spray your wheels. This softens the buildup of brake dust and helps get the wheels cleaner.

Hold the carnauba wax. Don't purchase the wax job. It is dispensed via spray and gets all over everything, including your windows. The next time you drive at night, you'll think that you're in a dream with everything surrounded by halos and swirls of light. The fun really starts when you try to get the stuff off. (To clean carnauba wax off your windshield, see the section in Chapter 3 on cleaning the windshield.)

Get fresh water. Go early in the morning. Most car washes recycle their water, and as the day or week goes on, the water gets more minerals in it. In areas where there are water shortages, the water may not be changed very often. Ask the management when the water is changed and plan your visit around this time.

Check your car for damage before leaving. If you are missing a wheel cover or hubcap, you want to find out before you get very far. Ditto for any other damage caused by the machine. In particular, check the operation of your wipers and automatic antenna.

Winter Maintenance

With the chill of winter, many drivers will be faced with the usual seasonal concerns. Driving under treacherous icy conditions can be dangerous and frustrating, but there are steps you can take to ease driving problems and increase safety. According to the National Safety Council (NSC), maintenance and visibility are the most important aspects of safe winter driving.

Fluids: Be sure power steering, brake fluid, gear oil, and windshield washer fluids are at proper levels. Coolant should be strong enough to prevent freezing and fresh enough to prevent rust and corrosion.

Kitty litter: A cat may have nine lives, but you have only one. So before you go out driving this winter, use your safety sense—borrow something from kitty before you get behind the wheel. A heavy bag (10–25 pounds) of clay cat-box filler may be the best tip of all for emergency traction on slippery roads this winter. Keep it in your car's trunk and it will provide the extra weight needed when icy conditions prevail.

Cat litter can also help if you become stuck in snow or ice. The highly absorbent clay forms a rough, dry surface over packed snow and ice that will let a car go in snow. Simply clear the area around the rear tires (front tires for front-wheel drive), pour the cat box filler in front of the tires in the direction you want to go, and slowly drive away. A big plus is that clay won't contribute to corrosion the way salt does. With a few pounds of prevention, you may avoid the frustration of being stuck in snow, the expense of emergency road service, or even a life-threatening situation if you become stranded in a rural or isolated area during bitterly cold weather. (For more about driving in bad weather, see Chapter 7.)

Tire Chains

Now is the time to get out your tire chains and inspect them for damage. Remember, a chain is only as good as its weakest link. If they are old and badly worn, consider purchasing a new set. If you don't know a good chain from a bad one, have your local mechanic inspect them for you. Are the tensioning rubber bands and catch-hooks still functional?

To store tire chains, first rinse the salt and ashes off them as soon as possible to prolong their useful life. Then put them in the trunk in a container designed for wet conditions. A sturdy small cardboard box is ideal because it will absorb the moisture from the wet chains and keep them from rusting. Avoid placing them in an aluminum container, because electrolysis will set in and corrode them.

When driving with chains, do not go faster than about 30 mph. Faster speeds will quickly wear out the chains, and they may fling outward against the inside of the fender, damaging it. Chains wear an extra 10 percent for every 10 mph over 30 mph.

Winterizing Your Car

Rain, sleet, ice, snow, and salt all give cars a beating in the winter. Pounds of concern about winter driving can be addressed with an ounce of prevention now. Have your battery, brakes, snow tires, windshield wipers, defroster, and muffler thoroughly checked by a qualified mechanic.

Here are some other steps to take as you winterize:

A fresh *oil change* is a good start. Use a 5W-30 oil if the temperature drops below freezing at night and 10W-30 for cold operation from 32° to 50°F. The best advice is to use synthetic oil. Petroleum oil can be as thick as honey when it's freezing cold. This makes it very hard for all the moving parts in the engine to turn. Synthetic oils don't thicken on those cold mornings, allowing engine parts to turn and causing less drag on the battery. Of course, I recommend the best synthetic oil: Redline.

If your *battery* is at the end of its life, trade it in for a fresh one. Remember that it's the summer heat that kills batteries. The winter cold just signs the death certificate. Buy the biggest battery that will fit into your car. It will make your starter and alternator work less and will cost less in the long run. Clean the battery terminals and coat them with Coppercoat to seal out moisture.

Check the condition of your *tires.* You'll need all the traction you can get for those slippery roads covered with wet leaves or ice. Also, check the tire pressure as the thermometer falls. Every 10-degree drop in temperature translates to 1 psi loss of tire pressure.

The *wiper blades* should be changed if they are more than nine months old. You'll appreciate them when you are trying to see out windows streaked with mud, sleet, or snow. An alternative is to use 303 Wiper Treatment, which will rejuvenate the wipers and keep ice from sticking to them. Check to see if there are winter blades available for your car.

Check your *windshield solvent.* If there is just water in the solvent container, it should be removed or it will freeze and crack. **Note:** Some off-the-shelf washer solvents claim to be "freezeproof," but they are not. They will turn to slush and freeze in the spray nozzles. Always operate the windshield washer before shutting off the car when there is going to be snow, sleet, or freezing rain. This will help prevent the buildup of ice in the spray nozzles.

Check your *exhaust system.* Winter driving with the windows closed can mean carbon monoxide (CO) poisoning. Exhaust can leak into the rear hatch or trunk seal and poison you. Don't risk your life. Get a CO detector from Nutz & Boltz ($5 including shipping) (800) 888-0091.

If the time is right, get a *tune-up*. Ask to have the choke, thermostat, and thermostatic air preheating system checked.

Have all *belts and hoses* carefully inspected. If they are more than five years old or have more than 75,000 miles on them, get them replaced.

If your *engine thermostat* is more than five years old or has gone 50,000 miles, change it. A new thermostat will help the engine warm up more quickly (and you too).

Coat the *rubber weather-strip* around the doors and trunk with silicone. This will prevent the rubber from freezing to the door jamb, causing tearing when the door is opened. I recommend using 303 Silicone Treatment.

Give the body a good coating of *car wax*. Use a treatment for the chrome, too. This will help protect the car from the damaging effects of foul weather. I recommend Eagle-1 car care products.

Try out the *heater, defroster*, and rear-window *defogger*. These items must be in good working condition for safe winter operation. If you get a foul odor, disinfect the heater box.

Skid-test your *brakes*. In an empty parking lot, skid the car. Then get out and check for skid marks coming from each of the tires. With uneven braking, your car can be thrown into a spin and out of control when you try to stop on wet or icy roads. This is a good time to check the operation of your ABS (if you have it). If the brake fluid is more than two years old, change it. Old brake fluid contains moisture and can cause the brakes to freeze up.

Keep the *fuel tank* as full as possible. Try to maintain at least a half tank of gasoline at all times to avoid gas-line freeze-ups and ensure that you will have plenty of gas if you become stranded. I recommend Redline SI-1 to keep the tank free from water droplets, which can cause fuel-line freezing. Buy gas from the busiest station in your area to ensure that you are getting fresh, *winterized gas*.

If you don't have a garage, use a *car cover* to protect the windshield from snow, ice, and frost. Dick Tippie, transportation safety director for the NSC, says, "92 percent of the information that drivers need to perform the driving task comes visually. Seeing clearly what lies ahead is integral to the driving task and a clear windshield in the wintertime is of critical importance."

A product called the Frost-Blanket can end the wet, cold drudgery of scraping ice off your windshield. It is a specially formulated rubber cover shaped to wrap around and adhere to the windshield. Simply lift it off, shake it out, roll it up, and throw it in the trunk. You can also lie on the Frost-Blanket when working under your car or use it as a fender cover when working in the engine compartment. To get one of these time- and hand-savers ($19.95 plus shipping), call 800-FROSTED.

Put a bottle of Redline Water Wetter in the radiator to help the engine warm up more quickly. This will prolong engine life and will get the heater operating faster. There is now a special-formula Water Wetter made just for diesel engines; call (800) 624-7958.

Winter Fuel Robbers

Why does your vehicle seem to loose gas mileage when the temperature drops? Does Old Man Winter siphon gas from your tank while you aren't looking? Many things work against you and your vehicle in the winter to rob you of gas mileage and cost you more in operating expenses. Maybe if you had a better idea of what is actually going on, you might be able to avoid getting a bad case of the winter blues as you lose miles per gallon. Here are some of the biggest factors in loss of winter fuel mileage.

The winter wind is a big factor in loss of mileage. Buffeting wind can cut your mileage drastically, especially when you travel at highway speed. Cold air is also more dense and offers more resistance to your vehicle. Try to refrain from driving long distances when the wind is really whipping around.

Cranking times are always longer with a cold engine. Longer cranking costs fuel in two ways. First, the longer you crank an engine, the more fuel it uses. Second, longer cranking runs down the charge on the battery. This requires the alternator to work harder, which drains some power off the engine. This robs the engine of some of its efficiency, which costs in gas mileage.

When you use the heater in the passenger compartment, the engine takes much longer to warm itself up. The longer the engine takes to warm up, the longer it will run in a rich condition. Engines are designed to run at optimum efficiency when they are fully warmed up. A cold or even a cool engine is very inefficient and requires much more fuel in order to operate. Try not to use the heater until the engine temperature gauge starts to move from the cold position to slightly warm. If you don't have a gauge, wait three or four minutes before turning on the heater.

Using electrical accessories makes the alternator work harder. The alternator robs horsepower from the engine, which costs in gas mileage. The defroster, heater, wipers, and lights all cost in fuel mileage.

Rolling resistance of the tires is directly related to their ability to flex. Stiff tires don't flex and have higher rolling resistance than warm tires. On a frosty day, the tires may never warm up enough for the inner cords to become flexible.

Engine antifreeze thickens in the cold, which puts more strain on the engine to turn the water pump. Until the coolant warms up to full operating temperature, the water pump will drain extra energy from the engine. On a very cold day, the engine may never reach full operating temperature because the passenger compartment heater is draining so much heat away from the engine.

Winterized fuel has less energy than summer grades. It is blended for cold starts, not for performance. In many states, wintertime also means you are being sold oxygenated fuel, which is terrible for getting good fuel mileage. It is not unusual to see a drop of 15 percent fuel mileage just from reformulated or oxygenated gasoline.

Cold air tends to cause fuel to condense inside the combustion chamber. Fuel needs to be a vapor in order to burn efficiently. If the engine doesn't have a properly operating intake air preheating system (called EFE or Thermac), the engine will not run efficiently.

By far the biggest winter thieves of good fuel mileage are the lubricants inside the drivetrain. The oil thickens to the consistency of molasses and the grease becomes as hard as taffy. It takes a very long time for the gearbox and differential to warm up the gearlube, which is the consistency of toothpaste until it gets warm. To beat the cold in this department, change the entire drivetrain over to synthetic oil and grease.

Engine idling to warm up the car and keep it warm produces zero miles per gallon. Consider installing a block heater in the engine and add a bottle of Redline's Water Wetter to help the engine warm up faster.

Spring Cleaning

Spring is the time of the year we usually clean the house. It is also time to give a little extra attention to our car, truck, or van. If you live where the winter temperatures drop below freezing, springtime maintenance is even more important. Freezing weather makes rubber hard and brittle. Your engine's hoses, belts, and seals really take a beating when it freezes.

Salted roads are a major contributor to body rust. The salt finds its way into the door panels of your car by running off the windows and into the door. Salt collects on ledges inside the frame and engine compartment and does its dirty work. And rust never sleeps.

Here's an annual spring cleaning checklist to pamper your car after it has survived another winter:

General

Interior: Clean all traces of road salt from the carpets and mats. Coat the rubber weather-stripping around the doors and trunk with silicone.

Air conditioner: Does your A/C still work? Low Freon can cause undue stress on the compressor. There should be enough Freon to cool the car quickly.

Battery: Check the fluid level (if possible) and condition of the clamps and terminals. Corrosion can lead to electrical problems in other systems.

Fluids

Oil: Change it! Regardless of mileage, oil becomes contaminated by cold weather operation because the engine runs rich. The only exception is synthetic oil.

Coolant: Check the level in the radiator to make sure it is full. Check the operation of the electric cooling fan by letting the engine run until the fan cycles on.

Automatic transmission: Winter driving can toast the automatic transmission fluid. Smell it. It should smell sweet, not burned. If it smells bad, change it immediately. Don't wait, or it could cost you your transmission.

Power steering: The P/S fluid should be clean and smell like oil. If it smells burned, have it changed. Clean P/S fluid will prolong the life of the P/S pump and will help keep the seals from leaking.

Brake fluid: Inspect the fluid reservoir with a flashlight. The fluid should have a slight amber color. If it is too dark to see through easily, change it. Brake fluid darkens as it ages, when it is contaminated with water, or when it is overheated in the brake system.

Belts/hoses: Using a drop light or flashlight, carefully inspect the hoses for bulges or signs of seepage. Look for cracks or frayed edges on the belts. If your car has one long serpentine belt, look for hairline cracking on the smooth side of the belt.

Body

Wiper blades: Torn/worn blades mean poor visibility when driving in the rain. Freezing weather can cause the rubber to harden and lose resiliency.

Tires/spare: Check the tread for wear patterns or alignment-related wear. Spring is a good time to rotate the tires. Check the air pressure in all tires.

Lightbulbs: Walk around your car and inspect all lightbulbs for function. Operate the turn signals, high beams, and brakes. Have someone watch for burned-out bulbs.

Chassis wash: If you live with salted roads, the chassis of your car should be rinsed thoroughly. Drive the car up on ramps or a high curb and rinse the underbody with a garden hose. It's a messy, dirty job, so you may want to find a car wash that offers this service.

Body wash/wax: Thoroughly wash the outside of the car. Squirt water into the door cracks, trim, kick panels, trunk, and bumpers to remove all traces of road salt. Use a high-quality polish to preserve the paint. I like Eagle-1 wax.

Nicks/chips: Time to touch up the paint. A little dab will do a world of good in the long run. Untreated paint chips can turn to major rust.

Lubricants: Lube the door hinges with synthetic ATF spray. If there are grease fittings, grease the chassis with a high-quality, synthetic, heavy-duty grease. I recommend Redline CV-2 grease.

Road Trip Tips

Being on the road can be a happy or disastrous event. Seasoned travelers have long since learned the pitfalls of travel by car and know what to do to prepare themselves as well as how to handle bad situations. In this chapter, I will pass on a hundred years' worth of travelers' experiences.

Getting the Car Ready for a Long Trip

When getting ready to spend more than a day or two driving, there are some things you should do to reduce your odds of breaking down on the trip:

Don't have any work done on your car at the last minute. If something wasn't fixed correctly or completely, you'll find out in a few hundred miles—far enough away from home that you won't know a mechanic you can trust. If your car needs a tune-up, have it done at least 30 days before you leave.

Start your trip with fresh oil and a new oil filter. Use *high-quality* oil. Synthetic oil will keep your engine oil temperature lower and lengthen your change intervals. If the transmission and transaxle haven't had a fluid change in the last year or last 30,000 miles, change the fluid.

If the air filter and fuel filter are over 12 months or 10,000 miles old, have them changed.

Have all four wheels pulled so that the brakes, tires, and suspension can be inspected carefully. Check the spare, too. Now is a good time to seriously consider new tires.

If the brake fluid is more than a year old, have it flushed. When you're going down a mountain, old brake fluid can boil, resulting in dangerous brake fade. Has your brake pedal ever become mushy and gone to the floor? Pretty scary! Replacing the brake fluid in the master cylinder reservoir isn't enough. Flush the old fluid out of the entire brake system and replace it with new fluid.

If the wiper blades are over six months old, install a new set.

Have the headlights aimed with the car fully loaded with luggage and passengers. If your car doesn't have halogen bulbs, have a set installed. You will gain substantially better dusk-to-dawn visibility.

Have the coolant serviced if your last service date was more than one year or 12,000 miles ago. Be sure that the shop uses a 50/50 mix of coolant and distilled water.

Keep your own breakdown kit in the trunk. Stock it with six or more flares, a sturdy flashlight, spare fan belt, pliers, an adjustable wrench, a multipurpose screwdriver, some waterless hand cleaner, and a roll of paper towels. Also, take along a jug of water and an approved container full of fuel. (See Chapter 15 for a complete list of what to pack in your emergency road kit.)

CAUTION: Carry gasoline only in an approved container, intended for that purpose. **Do not** use any other type of container!

Keeping Yourself Awake, Alert, and Alive

Long road trips can be uncomfortable and boring. Boredom can lead to sleepiness, which can lead to sudden death. Here are some tips from experienced long-distance drivers that can help to make your trip more enjoyable:

Purchase a pair of clear-lens glasses. Very lightly tinted sunglasses will do in a pinch. Wearing them keeps your eyes from drying out in your car's ventilation draft. One of the biggest problems with night driving is sore eyes. Dry eyes become red, painful eyes. This tip came from a friend who used clear lenses so that he could continue wearing his contact lenses while driving at night. It works very well for anyone, whether or not you wear contacts.

Buy the best sunglasses you can afford. Defects and anomalies in cheap sunglasses can quickly tire your eyes. High-quality shades provide maximum UV protection for your eyes and keep them fresh longer. Better sunglasses cut haze and can reduce blindness from snow, fog, or dust. (See the section on choosing a pair of sunglasses for more information.)

Keep your car windows clean inside and out. Dirty windows cause excessive eyestrain.

Take Mom's advice: Don't slouch! Good posture can prevent back pain and improve alertness. Keep your head up and shoulders down.

Reclined seats are both sleep inducing and unsafe. A slight tilt may improve comfort, but overreclined seats defeat the purpose of seat belts. In an accident, you'll slide underneath.

A CB radio can help you stay alert and get the latest traffic reports. You might choose to leave it off when driving with children, however. Trucker language is often R-rated.

Books on tape are great, especially if you are driving by yourself. Listening to a story can keep you awake and make the long hours seem shorter. If you find yourself struggling to follow the plot, either it's time to stop and rest or you accidentally selected something by James Michener. (Just kidding.)

Chewing gum, preferably sugarless, can help keep you alert. Avoid sugared gum and candy because they will make you thirsty. Don't like gum? Chewing ginseng can give you a lift that's better than caffeine and doesn't make you irritable. Check local health food stores.

Stuff your ears with soft, self-forming earplugs. Prolonged exposure to road noise is tiring. These plugs, generally available at pharmacies, cut the decibels but still let you hear horns and sirens. Tired? Pull them out. The sudden rise in noise level increases alertness.

Keep the car's interior as cold as you can stand it. Heat encourages sleepiness. Every so often, lower the windows and circulate some fresh air. Put a damp washcloth in a plastic bag and keep it in your cooler for a wet wake-up.

Track a truck. If you have difficulty keeping a steady pace and your car doesn't have cruise control, find an 18-wheeler that is going at about the speed you want to travel. Get five to ten car lengths behind the truck and stay put. Drivers of the big trucks contact truckers going the other way and get reports about road hazards ahead. You can benefit by tagging along. In addition, tagging along gives you something to concentrate on and helps you stay alert.

Take breaks every two to three hours, before you feel the need. Have a light snack, do calisthenics, stretch your legs with a short walk, or even take a shower (many truck stops offer showers for a nominal fee). If nothing seems to wake you up, take a nap. Never mind the lost time: you may be preventing an accident. Pull over only in rest areas where there are other cars around or in a well-lit area where you feel safe. In a pinch, try the restaurant parking lot at a truck stop. Church parking lots are pretty safe bets, too.

For more information about driver fatigue, see Chapter 6.

Choosing a Pair of Sunglasses

Many people never buy a decent pair of sunglasses simply because they are afraid to lose them. But they are going cheap in a critical area where there should be no compromise. You cannot replace your eyes once they are damaged—and the sun can do permanent damage to your eyes if you don't protect them.

There are two kinds of damaging sunlight radiation, both in the form of ultraviolet rays. Long-wavelength ultraviolet ray A (UVA) is the aging ultraviolet ray. UVA is the main component in snow blindness and eye soreness from excessive outdoor activity. Symptoms include redness, excessive tearing, light sensitivity, and a feeling of grit in the eyes. The symptoms can take several hours to a couple of days to go away. Intermediate-wavelength ultraviolet ray B (UVB) can cause permanent damage to the retina, resulting in age-related cataracts, sunburn, skin wrinkles, and skin cancer.

The American National Standards Institute (ANSI) and Sunglasses Association of America call for 99 percent filtration of all UVB rays and 60 percent filtration of UVA rays. A quality pair of sunglasses should provide close to 100 percent filtration of both harmful types of UV radiation. Before buying a pair of sunglasses, find out how much protection they provide. Brands that say they provide UV protection but not how much are misleading and should be avoided. ANSI standard Z80.3 means that the sunglasses meet the minimum filtration requirements.

What about colored lenses? Drivers must be highly aware of the color of road signs and traffic signals. Sunglasses that incorporate spectral filters to filter out certain light wavelengths are designed for driving. They cause the primary colors to appear brighter, making red and yellow lights even more visible.

Some sunglasses offer enhanced blue-light filtration. Since blue light is more scattered than the rest of the spectrum, blue filtration limits the hazing effect that tends to partially obscure your vision. Some offer gradient lenses with more filtration on the top to reduce light from the sky in much the same way that the darkened strip across the top of the car windshield does. There are even double-gradient lenses with more filtration at both top and bottom—ideal for lifeguards and people who are around the water, since glare reflects off the water.

Becoming a Travel-Wise Traveler

Planning on doing some traveling this summer or winter vacation? Here are some timely tips to make things easier.

Getting the Cheapest and Best Gas

To find the best prices on gasoline when traveling, pay attention to roadside billboards advertising off-brand, cut-rate fuel. Take that exit even if you don't want to use that brand. Cut-rate gas stations are usually surrounded by name-brand stations also offering low prices on fuel. If you use high-test, one station will typically offer cheap high-test fuel as a loss leader.

If you use only one particular brand of gas, plan ahead. Write the company for a list of gas stations on the way that carry your brand. Name-brand stations are pretty much the same when it comes to open-highway engine performance. The differences in brands are usually apparent only in local stop-and-go driving.

Take a minute to drive around, checking out all the stations in the exit area until you find the cheapest fuel of the octane and brand you like.

Be sure to save the gas receipt from each purchase. If you buy a tank full of bad fuel and break down because of it, you will need proof of your purchase. It costs only a little extra time and may be the only thing that you have to prove that you got a load of "Robbie's rotgut watered-down gas."

Saving Gas While Using the Air Conditioner

Run the air conditioner at the warmest setting with the fan on high. This keeps the compressor cycling at a minimum. Also, choose the setting that has air coming out of the upper register vents. Because cool air normally falls, upper vents put cool air in the upper part of the car where it is needed most.

If You Miss Your Exit

Don't get flustered. As soon as you realize that you have passed your exit, start looking for the next exit with an on-ramp going in the opposite direction. Form a mental picture of where you want to go. Pay special attention to the place you want to exit when going in the opposite direction. Usually, you need to look behind you at the exit signs facing the other way.

Driving Defensively

Beware that many people run traffic lights in the bigger cities. As police departments downsize, there are fewer traffic cops to enforce these traffic laws. Be especially careful at intersections, even when the light is in your favor. Worst places: Washington, D.C., and New York City.

Preventing Back Pain

If you get back pain after driving for a long distance, vibrations from the car may be causing it. Chiropractors have found that these vibrations are close to the frequency at which the human spine vibrates, and lengthy exposure can hurt your spine. This is the most plausible explanation I have ever heard for back pain after long trips.

Sit with an inflatable pillow against your spine to help dampen the vibrations, and take short walking breaks every few hours.

Combating Dehydration

If you plan on traveling in a high-altitude region, beware of dehydration. Your lungs exhale more water in high, dry, oxygen-scarce air, and your thirst mechanism is suppressed. Symptoms of dehydration include dark yellow urine, headaches, and muscle soreness.

Drink at least 12 cups of water a day regardless of how thirsty you are.

Defensive Headgear

Bring along a baseball-type cap to wear when driving. You'll look like a local resident. Women should tuck their hair up inside the hat to give them a male profile when driving at night or in bad parts of town.

Parking to Avoid Crime

While in a roadside restaurant, always park your car in plain sight of the window. Ask for a table near the window so you can keep an eye on your car while you eat. At a motel, ask the clerk to assign you a room overlooking the parking lot where you can see your car easily.

At a rest stop, be wary of anyone hanging around the restroom or parking lot. Take a moment to scan the area for loiterers before you leave your car or enter the restroom. Stay with your travel companions if possible. Avoid parking next to vans; they are the perfect hiding place for thieves and muggers.

Avoiding Hotel Room Lockout

When leaving a hotel room without the key, remember that the door is spring-loaded. Prop it open securely using a chair or, in some cases, the door deadbolt.

Never leave your hotel room without your key or your pants, even for a quick trip to the candy or ice machine. Each time you leave your room, ask yourself: "Am I presentable to the people in the lobby as I am dressed?" If you're not careful, you may have to put that question to the test.

Heeding the Travel Guide Warning

Don't rely on a travel guide or tour guidebook, especially if it is an old one. Remember that restaurants, hotels, bed and breakfasts, and inns often change management, cooks, and menus. Your outdated guidebook may list a particular restaurant as being a nice, friendly place. Now, a couple of years later, Mr. Ripp U. Off works there.

Find a current travel guide, read the local newspaper's restaurant reviews, or ask local people for suggestions. Other good sources of advice: the hotel concierge, taxi driver, gas station attendant, or car rental agent.

Practicing Rental Car Safety

Don't rent a car that has a bumper sticker or other displays of the rental car company. Crooks know that you are from out of town and are probably a good mark. Always take your valuables with you in case someone steals the rental car while you are away from it. Avoid checking a map while sitting at an intersection—it's an invitation for a carjacking. In a strange place, stop during the day so that you are safely in your hotel by dark. You don't want to be driving on unfamiliar roads in the dark.

Rent a car from an agency near the hotel and use the hotel shuttle to travel to and from the airport. Off-airport rental agencies are usually cheaper. Also, most car rental companies usually have a free shuttle to and from the hotel. Ask the concierge or desk clerk for the name of a local, cheap rental company. Maybe one offers discounts for guests of that hotel.

Before leaving the rental car lot, do a bulb check on all the dash warning lights. Turn the key and don't start the car until you have familiarized yourself with all the indicator lights. If you don't know what a certain light means, ask the lot attendant. That way, if a warning light comes on while you are driving the car, you will know the cause. This also tells you whether the car is equipped with antilock brakes (ABS), air bags (SIR), and traction control (TRAC).

Avoiding Car Rental Insurance Traps

If you plan on using a credit card to pay for rental car insurance, be aware that it may not automatically include collision insurance.

Many credit cards and corporate cards, including American Express, lack collision insurance coverage for cardholders. If you rent cars often and your personal vehicle coverage won't cover a rental car (possibly because your car is still being used while you are away), consider getting a credit card that offers this service. The cost of collision damage waivers (CDWS) from rental companies can run as high as half of the daily rental rate.

Eating and Driving Do Mix

What do you like to eat when you drive along? Here are some suggestions.

Good Choices

Try unsalted or lightly salted popcorn, walnuts, cashews, peanuts, cheese, peanut butter on crackers, chocolate-covered raisins, yogurt-covered almonds, rice cakes, puffed corn cakes, granola bars, trail mix, yogurt, pudding, fresh fruits, or dried fruit/fruit leather. If you choose a variety of nuts, make sure that they are unsalted.

Generally, you want good, bite-size foods that are neat to eat, interesting in texture, and complex in flavor. Mix shredded wheat, unsalted pretzels, unsalted wheat crackers, and unsalted dry-roasted peanuts in a container, and the miles will roll away in a healthful and satisfying manner.

For drinks, try two-percent milk (chocolate or plain), individual juicepacks (freeze first), or lemonade. But water is best because it always quenches thirst.

Bad Choices

Try to avoid the following foods, which are messy and may make you more thirsty.

Sticky: Marshmallows and Gummi Bears

Greasy: French fries, potato chips, barbeque, pizza, and fried chicken

Crumbly: Cookies and pretzels

Sweet: Soda pop, punch, and candy (These contain too much sugar and increase thirst. The end result? Extra pit stops.)

Salty: Tomato juice and prepopped or prepackaged popcorn

Choosing a Motel

When traveling in a strange city, you often face the problem of choosing a motel. No one wants to spend too much, but a really cheap motel may not be worth the savings if you can't get a decent

night's sleep. This section gives you some tips for finding a motel when on the road or in a strange city.

Most motels are located on the way into or out of a city or at major interstate junctions. Don't stop at the ones on the way in or at the first one you see. Look them over and compare prices, which are usually posted outside. Typically, the closer you get to the center of town, the higher the prices are. Choose a motel on the way out of town that fits your budget and tastes. Don't be afraid to turn around and go back to one that you saw and liked.

Don't stay at the cheapest motels unless you like bad beds, noisy neighbors, all-night parties, faulty air conditioners, and rancid-smelling rooms. Also, beware of places that advertise weekly or monthly rates. These are usually so run-down and roach infested that only vagabonds and roadside rogues will stay there—keeping company with the cockroaches. The best "bargain" motels are those that were once luxury motels and are now under a different name. The original sign may still be there, but with new lettering covering up the old name.

Before you check in, always ask the price of the room. The price listed on the sign outside may be for only a few select rooms that are always taken. If one is available, it will most likely have a small bed and no bathtub and be inconveniently located. You may end up paying quite a bit more to get what you want, so ask first. Don't assume.

Always ask whether there are any special promotions, discounts, or freebies available when checking in. You may find that by signing up for a free club membership, you get free breakfasts. Ask whether you get a business discount for your company or your particular travel club or for being a senior citizen.

Selecting a Room

Ask to look at your room before checking in. Check the air conditioner or heater to see whether it works OK. Give the bed a try, too. You may find that it has no box spring or is a heated waterbed that is too hot. See if the TV works. If you are a light sleeper, always try to stay on the top floor so that heavy-footed occupants upstairs won't awaken you. Try to pick a room at the end of the hall so you won't have occupants on both sides of you. Doing so reduces your chance of having a noisy neighbor by 50 percent.

If you find something about the room objectionable, complain immediately. If you wait, there may not be another room available. Ask for compensation in some way for your inconvenience, especially when changing rooms. Ask for a room upgrade, a free meal voucher, or a discount on the rate.

Don't choose a room next to an elevator, staircase, ice machine, vending machine, or door leading to the outside. Elevators squeak, and doors to the stairs or the outside can become a noisy nuisance, opening and slamming all night long. Ditto for vending and ice machines.

Choose a room facing away from the highway. The sound of trucks, sirens, and traffic can spoil your sleep. The same is true for airport hotels, with runways and large parking lots where car alarms and jet engines can wail all night.

If you want a quiet room, ask for one. Alert the clerk to the fact that you need peace and quiet. If the room isn't quiet, ask for another room. If you don't get a good night's sleep because the room was not quiet, you can refuse to pay the bill.

Avoid a room that has an interconnecting door to an adjoining room. The lock on the door may be inferior and can easily be jimmied open from the other side.

Finally, always pay with a credit card. If a dispute about the bill arises, it is easier to file a complaint and get reimbursed if you charged the room cost.

Miscellaneous Items to Pack

Bring along the following handy items to make your road trip as trouble-free as possible:

- Moist towelettes and tissues or napkins for spills and quick cleanups

- Gloves to wear when pumping gas

- A cooler with a freezable, drinkable water pack in the lid, which saves on buying ice and provides drinking water

- An auto record book for keeping records of your car and travels (these are available at stationery stores)

- A funnel in a sealable plastic bag to use when adding oil to the engine

- A pillow from your own bed for better sleeping

- A hat with a sun visor to help when driving directly into the sun

- A pair of flip-flops for wearing in the shower and around the pool

- A small coffeemaker or immersion coil to make coffee or tea in your room

- Vitamins, antacids, Dramamine, aspirin, and other common medications

CB Radios

CB radios are a great deal for the money. For about $40 you can create your own talk radio, become your own broadcaster, or just have fun. What a wonderful way to meet interesting people and make new friends. There are plenty of people out there listening on their CB radios. just waiting for an opportunity to chat with you.

CBs are a great advantage in times of emergency. You can report emergencies or problems to other drivers, or hear about emergencies before you come across them yourself. Your CB can save you hours of delays and may even save your life. I heard about a snowstorm that was about to hit the Northeast while traveling north out of Florida. Instead of stopping, I drove straight through and was able to get home before the highways were closed by the storm.

If you do much long-distance driving, a CB is a great companion. You will be able to stay alert listening to the truckers' chatter and even contribute your own comments. If you make contact with a trucker ahead of you, he or she will know you are back there and will watch out for you. Truckers use CBs to while away the miles.

If you need local directions, your CB radio is better than a city map. If you want to know about a good place to have a meal, your CB will be better than a restaurant guide. How about a good motel? Truckers know all of the best places to stay and are usually happy to assist you.

Since many people have armed themselves with radar detectors, traffic police now use other methods to catch speeders. The problem is that once drivers see Smoky, they slam on their brakes. With your CB radio, you will be aware of police activity and be prepared when brake lights flash on ahead of you.

Emergencies

Planning ahead for a roadside emergency is a very important thing to do. What form of communication do you have to summon help? What if you are stranded, or go off the road into a ditch? What if your car is pinned between trees and you can't get out? What if you are stuck in a snowdrift during a blizzard? What if you are stuck in the sand on the beach and the tide is coming in? Who are you gonna call—Ghostbusters?

While a cellular phone is a great device to summon help, it has a few important drawbacks. It won't summon passing traffic. It must be close enough to a cellular antenna to work. It is expensive and a big target for thieves. On the other hand, a CB radio is cheap and requires no service hookup or monthly fees. While few cars carry CB radios, almost every truck does, and truckers are extremely helpful to stranded motorists. They keep their CB radios turned on and will quickly respond to a call for help.

In addition, the police and REACT monitor CB channel 9. CB REACT monitoring units are located all over the country, and these public-minded citizens spend thousands of hours listening to the emergency CB channel 9 for calls for help. Because of quirks in the atmosphere, radio waves can bounce off the ionosphere and travel hundreds or even thousands of miles. Your call for help in the rural bayous of Louisiana may be heard by a REACT member in Ohio. That person will contact the state police, who will relay the call for help to the police in your locale.

Police also have CB radios in their police cruisers and have channel 9 turned on in case a motorist needs to call for help. A trucker who sees someone driving in an unsafe condition or spots a stranded motorist will report it to the police on CB channel 9.

How to Call for Help

If you do become stranded and need to call for help on your CB radio, there are a few things you should know about operating the CB in an emergency.

Never use channel 9 unless it is an emergency. This channel has been nationally designated as the emergency channel. Turn down the squelch control until you hear white noise. This will allow you to hear distant broadcasts that normally would not "break the squelch."

Now turn up the volume until you can clearly hear distant broadcasts, but not so loud that a local broadcast will blast your ears. Give your location. This is called "giving your twenty." Look for a nearby intersection name, a mile marker, the nearest highway exit, or even the name of a building or mall.

Hold the microphone one to three inches from your mouth. Speak into the side of the microphone with louvers or vents cut into it. Generally, this is the opposite side of the hanger hook. Speak slowly and repeat all the information at least three times. Pause for a minute, listen for a reply, and then repeat your message.

Give the nature of the incident: fire, accident, or emergency. If possible, tell what type of assistance might be required. For example, "I ran out of gas. Help. I need a ride to get some gas." Tell if there are any injuries and what type of medical assistance might be required. For example, "There is a man who ran off the road and is unconscious. He appears to be alive and breathing but needs medical assistance"

Always give the name of the state you are calling from. For example, "My twenty is at mile marker 133 southbound in the ditch. I am south of the Idaho state line." Remember, REACT members can hear calls from clear across the country. You won't be able to hear them, but they may be listening to you.

CB Lingo

Here's a quick primer on talking on a CB radio. You might want to become familiar with these terms so you will understand what is being said:

- 10-4—I agree.
- 10-10—What time is it?
- Back door—I'm right behind you.
- Bear cage—Police station
- Bear in the air—Police in a helicopter or airplane
- Breaker 19—You want to talk on Channel 19
- Breaking up—Your signal is cutting on and off
- Bring it back—Answer me
- Chicken coop—Weigh station for trucks
- Copy—I heard that; I understand
- County mountie—County police
- Ears on—CB radio turned on
- Flip-flop—Return trip, change direction
- Front door—I'm in front of you

6

Highway Driving

When it comes to getting behind the wheel of a vehicle, just about everyone learns from the school of hard knocks. The longer you drive, the more you pick up about those unwritten rules of the road. Sometimes tragedies occur in the process of learning the ropes. Wouldn't it be wonderful if someone with a great deal of driving experience would pass on some of those valuable driving tips—especially to entry-level young drivers?

Sure, a good driving course teaches you a lot about safe driving. But there is so much more about being out there on the highway that no one ever tells you about. I have driven a truck coast to coast more than a dozen times and have driven in every type of driving condition there is. While on the road, I have collected a great deal of information about the pitfalls of highway driving.

Truck drivers log millions of miles and have to learn all the tricks of the road in order to survive. I learned much from talking with them on the CB and in person by observing their driving actions. In this chapter, I'll pass on some of the more important things I learned.

I highly recommend that parents make this chapter required reading for all young drivers in their family, especially the section on driving with big trucks. Big trucks are probably the most frightening things you encounter on the highway on a regular basis.

Foggy Driving

It comes in on cat's feet, sits quietly on its haunches, and then moves on. Fog is one of the most deadly adversaries drivers face. Driving in the fog is like playing Russian roulette with the road ahead—you never know what lies in your path.

The best way to deal with dense fog is to stay off the road. But that isn't always possible. The next time you find yourself having to go somewhere when it's foggy, remember these helpful driving tips:

- When entering into a patch of fog, don't wait to slow down until you are already into the fog.

- If you don't have fog lamps, use your low beams. High beams cause glare and impede visibility. Always put your lights on, even if you are driving in daytime fog—this will make it easier for other motorists to see you.

- Use the defroster to help keep the windshield clear. Turn it on high; crack the window if it gets too hot. Some of the fogginess may be on the inside, and a warmed windshield will stay much clearer. As needed, turn on the windshield wipers to keep the outside of the glass clear.

- Be especially wary of slow-moving vehicles ahead of you. Also beware of vehicles parked on the side of the road.

- Use the white stripe, fittingly called the "fogline," on the right side of the road as your guide. Stay away from the center line to avoid cars in the oncoming lane that may have strayed over into your lane.

- Keep lane changes to a minimum and try not to pass anyone unless your life depends on it.

- If you must leave the road, signal with plenty of time before-hand. Pull off slowly and carefully.

- When leaving the road, turn on your emergency flashers and leave them on while you are parked on the roadside. Don't use your flashers while under way. Other drivers may mistake your moving vehicle for a parked car.

- Try wearing sunglasses to help cut glare from your headlights. Some types of sunglasses actually improve visibility when driving in fog because they cut glare.

- Resist the temptation to drive at the speed limit. Instead, use the four-second rule: Pick an object as it comes into vision; it should take four seconds before you reach it ("one thousand one . . ."). If you reach it sooner, you're going too fast.

- Stay alert and concentrate on the fog ahead, moving your eyes from the white stripe on the roadside edge to the center line. Don't fall into a fixed gaze—this will slow your reaction time.

- Turn off the radio and listen. Fog muffles sounds. Hearing trouble ahead may allow you to stop in time.

Superhighway Driving

Have you ever wondered where on the road is safest to drive? Do you always drive in the right lane? Middle lane? Fast lane? How about when driving with other cars on the road? Do you follow behind, stay to the side, or lead the pack? Here are some tips for driving on freeways, turnpikes, and interstates:

Stay in your lane. Every time you change lanes, you risk hitting a vehicle that is in your blind spot.

When driving on a crowded highway with big trucks, watch which lane the trucks are in. If you see them changing lanes out of the traditional trucker's right-hand lane, a problem may lie in the road ahead. Truckers communicate with each other by CB radio and often know ahead of time that a problem is coming up. If all the trucks suddenly move to the passing lane, a lane closure may be ahead.

Watch out for "snake drivers," probably the most dangerous drivers on the road. They snake through the traffic, cutting back and forth between lanes to speed ahead. If you see snake drivers coming up in your rearview mirror, get over and out of the way. Don't let them sideswipe your car or cause you to make an emergency lane change to avoid hitting them as they fly by.

Be wary of driving alongside panel vans. Panel or delivery vans are especially dangerous because the lack of windows creates a huge blind spot and the driver may not see you. If you are driving beside a panel truck or van, make sure the driver can see you so that he or she doesn't decide to change lanes and suddenly pull right into you.

A modern travel tip: When you're traveling with a purse, briefcase, or laptop computer, it's wise to put it on the floor. If you leave it on the seat, a panic stop can throw it violently to the floor. If you must keep it on a seat, belt it in place with the seat belt. Securing it with a seat belt also makes it harder for a thief to pop open the door, reach inside, and grab your valuable item when you're stopped.

Pack Driving

Due to the increased congestion of today's roads, it is almost impossible to avoid being a pack driver. In general, driving in a group of cars is safer if you do it properly. Here are some pack driving tips:

Avoid driving in another driver's blind spot. If you can't see the other driver reflected in her rearview mirror, she probably doesn't know you are there. If the other driver wants to change lanes, you will be in a dangerous spot.

Avoid driving in another driver's escape path. This is the direction the driver is most likely to go if there is suddenly a road hazard ahead. He may not take the time to look to the left or right before making an emergency lane change—right into the side of your car.

Drive at the very front or very rear of the pack. Try to stay out of the middle. The middle is the most likely place to be trapped by the other cars if you need to make an emergency lane change.

Stay in the outside lane. If the pack is too big for you to maintain a position in the front or back, try to stay in the right-hand lane (or, if you must, in the left-hand lane). As long as you are in an outside lane, you have an escape path.

Always plan an escape path so you can make an emergency lane change. If something suddenly pops up in the road in front of you, you have a place to go.

Always give a gap. Be courteous to other drivers. If someone is trying to enter or exit the highway, either adjust your speed to open a place for the other driver or change lanes.

Is it better to go with the flow of traffic, even if that means breaking the speed limit with everyone else? This is a personal judgment call. Observing the speed limit only to have the whole world pass you by can be annoying. If you find this happening and don't want to go faster, get over to the right and let the other drivers spring all the speed traps.

Sleepiness Kills

Nearly one-third of the almost 50,000 people killed on U.S. highways every year die as a result of falling asleep at the wheel. This percentage is second only to that of people killed as a result of drunk driving accidents. Sleep-induced crashes can be exceptionally destructive because a sleepy driver may make no attempt to avert a collision.

It doesn't matter where you are going or how late you are; no one will give you an A for effort if you die in the process of getting there. Driving tired isn't heroic—it's suicidal *and* homicidal. Look at the following sidebar and see if you've experienced any of these symptoms on the road. Then commit the avoidance procedures to memory.

Five Signs of Driver Fatigue

1 **Focusing difficulties:** Reading the signs ahead becomes harder and harder. Your eyes burn and feel strained. Your blinking increases until the blinks turn into closed eyes. Your head nods or you can't stop yawning.

2 **Tracking difficulties:** You have trouble steering in a straight line and begin to weave from side to side like a drunk.

3 **Reduced reaction time:** You catch yourself about to nod off. You're driving erratically or at abnormal speeds, drifting, tailgating, or missing traffic signs. Your thought process, from perception of danger to avoidance, is dramatically impaired. For example, when a traffic light changes, drowsy drivers take far longer to react. This isn't a problem from red to green because someone will eventually honk. But if the change is from green to yellow to red, a sleepy driver may run the red light—with potentially fatal results.

4 **Tunnel vision:** Locking onto the road ahead without checking the mirrors or scanning the roadside indicates deteriorating alertness. Even worse, staring at something along the side of the road can lead to disaster.

5 **Time warp:** You have wandering, disconnected thoughts. You suddenly realize that you don't know how far you have been driving or what has been happening for some period of time. This may include going miles past exits and turnoffs, so now you're both sleepy and lost.

How to Avoid Sleeping Death

- Get a good night's sleep before driving. If you knew that staying up late was going to kill you the next day, how important would those "vital" last-minute details be?

- Share the driving with another person if possible. You may not like to, but the alternative could be death or permanent disability for you and your passenger(s).

- Eat smaller meals while on the road. A full stomach makes you drowsy. Snack if you need to, but avoid sugar-laden candy and sodas; they make your blood sugar go up and down like a roller coaster. Fruits and vegetables are better. Also try popcorn or beef jerky. (For a more complete list of foods to eat on the road, see "Eating and Driving Do Mix" in Chapter 5.)

- Drink coffee or tea sparingly. Caffeine increases alertness but can't replace sleep. Avoid over-the-counter stimulants, for both health and legal reasons. Some contain such powerful decongestants that some states require prescriptions for them. All provide a temporary lift, but the lift comes at the expense of worn-out nerves. A jumpy driver can be just as dangerous as a sleepy one.

- If you find yourself experiencing fatigue, find a safe place to pull over and rest. Good choices are rest stops and truck plazas. Look for places where you see big trucks resting. Staying alive takes precedence over staying on schedule. Remember, a brief rest period may keep you from killing both yourself and others on the road with you. Would you rather be "the late Mr. Jones" or "Mr. Jones, who arrived late"?

Encountering Big Trucks Up Close

Truck drivers are some of the hardest-working people in the world. Piloting huge tractor trailers (also called *18-wheelers*), they carry food and goods all over the country. The highway is their workplace, and their rig (truck) is their office. Big trucks require a driver's constant attention. A pleasant commute for you is a road full of little four-wheeled hazards (also called *four-wheelers*) for them. Maybe that's why truck drivers are pleasantly surprised when four-wheelers give them a little respect. The following sections give you some tips for driving safely around big rigs.

Stop Depending on Truckers' Vision

Don't depend on truckers to see you. Many trucks have convex mirrors, which distort distances. It's hard to tell how far back your car really is. Also, if the truck engine is causing the mirrors to vibrate, the driver may not have a clear view of anything.

The most dangerous place to drive is beside a truck, especially in the vicinity of the right front fender. If the driver changes lanes suddenly, you may end up in a ditch or beneath those tires. So if your cruise control has you lounging alongside an 18-wheeler, either complete the pass or drop back until you can. In the daytime, look for the truck driver's silhouette in his rearview mirror. If you can see him, he can probably see you. With practice, you will have a good idea of whether you can be seen when you're driving at night.

Get Out of the Way

Be extra careful while driving on the right-hand side of any truck. On the open road, truck drivers want to keep the right side clear, both for access to upcoming exits and in case they have to get off the road quickly. If they lose air pressure to their air brakes, which creates a serious brake pressure problem, they have only a few seconds to get off the road before the wheels lock up and the truck comes to a halt in the middle of the road.

In town, big trucks need to swing wide when making right-hand turns; otherwise, the trailer will run over the curb. Before you pull up on the right side of an 18-wheeler sitting in the left lane with his right turn signal on, think of how his right rear wheels will look planted in the middle of your trunk and back seat—or worse. When the truck's turn signals indicate that the driver wants to get into your lane, especially to the right, get out of the way! Truckers drive everywhere, often in areas that they don't know well. The driver may have just realized her exit is ahead and you're in the lane she needs. A desperate trucker may be tempted to run you off the road. Either fade back or finish passing, whichever is safer.

Subconsciously, truckers are always looking for a clear path to the right. The driver knows that the mechanical spring brakes will apply if the rig suddenly loses air pressure to the brakes. Unlike cars, which use hydraulic pressure to *apply* the brakes, trucks use air pressure to *release* their brakes. If the air pressure is low (say, if a hose breaks or a brake application device leaks air pressure), the brakes apply, causing the truck to stop dead in its tracks. The driver needs to get off the road immediately before the truck skids to a halt. If you follow too closely or linger to the right, you could end up underneath the truck.

Communicate on the Road

Truck drivers are acutely aware of each other's visual limitations. When they are passed by other trucks, they flash their headlights to tell the other drivers that the back end is clear of their cab. Wise four-wheelers do the same. In the daytime, flashing your high beams is the easiest. Do so when the trailer is far enough ahead of you to enter your lane safely. Do not flash your high beams at night. Instead, flick your headlights off and back on once. Did the trucker see you? If so, you'll see the truck's running lights flash to say thanks.

Avoid the Blind Spot

Don't drive directly behind a truck in the blind spot. Until rear-mounted video cameras become cost effective, 18-wheelers will always have blind spots. If the truck driver knows you're there, he or she may do some aggressive things to make you move. Oddly enough, truckers don't mind other trucks driving closely behind them. Almost all drivers have CB radios and communicate back and forth. But unless you are personally invited via CB radio to drop in among trucks in a group, don't do it.

Don't Be the Uninvited Guest

Truckers like to run in caravans to *slipstream*, or let the lead truck cut wind resistance for the others. They also drive together to intimidate speed-trap enforcement or just to chat on their radios. If you drop in, they will likely try to squeeze you out. Worse yet, if you are between two big trucks when the truck in front has brake-seizure problems, the truck in front of you and the truck behind you will do a "hammer and anvil" on your car—this is one way you *don't* want to lose weight!

Maintain Your Speed After You Pass

Want to make a trucker angry? Pass the truck, pull in front of it, and slow down. The trucker has to brake, check all the mirrors, look for the chance to downshift, and pass you again. Truckers hate passing because it involves a certain amount of risk. An unseen car may be in one of their blind spots. Truckers must build up great speed to pass, making them a perfect target for a speed trap. Passing also costs in fuel.

Be Aware of Trucks in Your Rearview Mirror

About that truck radiator in your rearview mirror: chances are it was your fault, at least from the truck driver's viewpoint. Passing a truck and pulling back into the lane too quickly can cause an accident. Only crazed truckers intentionally sit on the bumper of a four-wheeler; their insurance costs too much as it is. So when passing a truck, pull far ahead before reentering the truck's lane. It's best to wait until you can clearly see the truck's headlights in your rearview mirror.

Why do trucks pass on the right? Or, if you're in the right-hand lane, why do trucks sometimes loom up in your rearview mirror? Truck drivers must deal with one constant—the miles to cover—and two variables—time and fuel consumption.

Going uphill takes fuel and time. One of the ways truckers save fuel and precious minutes is to go fast on the downhill grade. If you're to the left and going slower, they'll pass on the right. If you're in their lane doing your "civic duty" by driving 55, you become an obstacle. It is not unusual to spend an hour or two in hilly country passing and being passed by the same truck, over and over. Flip on your CB radio and you will probably hear yourself described in unprintable terms.

If you see that big grille in your rearview mirror and the lane to your left is clear, move over and let the truck pass on the right. If you are already in the left lane, either speed up or move over to the right.

Keep glancing in the rearview mirror. If you see a truck bearing down on you *without* its turn signal on, get out of the way. If the turn signal is on, stay where you are but keep an eye on it. Remember, the driver is busy trying to keep a mammoth vehicle on the road. Your most important consideration is giving that truck *lots* of room.

Let Trucks Pass

Many people speed up when someone tries to pass them. Doing so while a trucker is passing on the right is called the *pushing effect*. Drivers accelerate as if to say, I was *not* driving slowly! If you speed up while being passed on the left, you demonstrate the *towing effect*. The higher speed of an adjacent vehicle encourages you to go faster as well. And some drivers out there just don't like to be passed.

If irritating the driver of a vehicle that outweighs yours by many thousands of pounds gives you a thrill, just don't let him pass you. Truckers hate it when a four-wheeler camps out in either the right or left lane, only to wake up and accelerate when the truck tries to pass. Do it often enough and the driver—or the driver's buddy in the next truck ahead—may just accidentally cut you off.

Stay Clear of Struggling Trucks

Stay away from a line of trucks struggling up a hill. The trucks following the lead rig are slipstreaming to make their job easier, and a small vehicle between them ruins the effect. It may have taken all the truck's effort to get up enough speed to make it up the next hill. The trucker may have planned this move way back, maybe miles back. In some cases, the entire caravan of trucks may be working in concert to save time and fuel on a particular hill. If

Truckers' Revenge

Truck drivers have some not-so-subtle ways of letting you know that they are displeased. You may be a little shocked by some of these methods, but put yourself in their shoes: After a few dozen sleepless hours behind the wheel of a big rig surrounded by little four-wheelers, you might become a little crazed, too.

CAUTION! I am not advocating that you attempt any of these tricks. They are listed only to alert you to them so you can avoid having them pulled on you. Here are truckers' favorite tricks:

Gravel bath: Here, the trucker pulls in front of you and eases onto the shoulder with his right tires. The trailer's wheels throw gravel and rocks, pelting your car. Say good-bye to your paint job and hello to a cracked windshield.

Brake hiss: The truck driver positions her truck so that the brake air-release valve is right next to you. Then the trucker taps the brakes, causing the valve to emit a loud hiss noise that may frighten you and cause you to lose control of your vehicle.

Killer trailer: This stunt is exceedingly dangerous! The trucker pulls ahead of you until the back wheels of the trailer are right next to you. He then cuts over into your lane, forcing you off the road.

Blockade: Several truckers get together and form a rolling roadblock that keeps you from driving by. They drive more and more slowly until you are really angry and try something stupid like passing on the shoulder.

Ramrodding: The trucker drives close to your rear bumper and tries to scare you off the road via an exit or the shoulder. Given the longer stopping distances for trucks, this is extremely dangerous.

Tattletale: The trucker uses her mobile phone to call 911 and gives a description of your car, saying that you are a drunk driver. Pretty soon, you're stopped by the county mountie.

you decide to slip into the middle of the trucks for no apparent reason, you may wind up experiencing truckers' revenge.

Avoid Trucks in the Rain

Stay away from big rigs in wet weather. Their wheel-splash will reduce your visibility to near zero, and the truckers may not see you for the same reason. Here's an interesting fact: Trucks can stop faster on wet roads than you can. Their front wheels squeeze out the water and their awesome weight improves traction. If they have to slam on the brakes and you are following too close, the result may well be fatal. The same applies on snow or ice.

In general, trucks have better traction in the snow, but they can suddenly *jackknife*, folding where the tractor and trailer connect. Just as deadly, you may lose traction and spin out while completing a pass, forcing the trucker to hit you or swerve off the road.

Watch Your Tail on Entrance and Exit Ramps

Where is the most likely place for a tractor trailer to crash? The answer is on an entrance or exit ramp leading to or from an interstate highway. Why? The truckers do not reduce their speed enough for the ramp. Many ramps are designed with curves that are poorly banked or too tight. A study conducted by the University of Virginia suggests that most accidents occur as the trucks leave the interstates because they don't slow down enough for the ramp.

In most of the accidents that occurred, a truck ran into the rear end of a smaller vehicle. The study posed the possibility that ramp speed limits are set for cars, not big trucks. So when you are leaving the interstate and a big truck is on your tail, watch out! That truck may not be able to slow down quickly enough to avoid you.

In summary, the two keys to driving safely around trucks are to give them plenty of room and to stay visible. By the way, don't expect all truckers to be courteous just because you show them respect. It may take them a while to recover from the shock.

Dealing with Deer Hazards

Each year, nearly 187,000 accidents involving vehicles and animals occur. An average of 1,700 people are injured or killed. Hitting a deer results in an average of $600 in property damage per accident—and the death of the deer. One year the Pennsylvania Game Commission recorded over 7,000 deer killings in January and February alone. In some states, more deer are killed by cars than by hunters with permits.

Deer are a greater problem to drivers during spring and fall, when they seek out new territory and cross the highways. Even though deer can accelerate from zero to 30 mph in 1.5 seconds, their size prevents them from changing direction easily. Once a deer begins to run into the path of your car, it won't be able to avoid a collision. It may even run right into the side of a stopped car in its path.

Deer like to forage in dense bushes alongside rural roads and appear oblivious to the sound of motor vehicles. They've been known to stand right in the middle of the road and watch a car run into them. Unless a deer has been hit by a car and lived to learn from the experience, it has no fear of vehicles.

For every five deaths involving deer accidents, one person will be killed by striking a deer; the other four will die trying to avoid hitting one. Deer kill more people than all other animals combined. Sometimes hitting the animal is a better choice than losing control of your vehicle. Slamming on your brakes can also lead to a rear-end collision.

Here are some tips for dealing with deer:

Use your high beams. When traveling at night where deer are prevalent, keep your high beams on as much as possible and scan the roadside ahead. The glow of the deer's eyes may be all the warning you'll get.

Avoid the road edge. Drive close to the center of the road as much as you can, assuming that there is no oncoming traffic.

Look out for deer crossing signs. Highway departments place these signs where accidents with deer have occurred. Slow down and be on full alert. Deer are creatures of habit, crossing at the same place year after year. Attempts to install "Press here to cross" buttons at these locations have met with limited success. (Just kidding.)

Be extra alert at dawn and dusk. Dawn and dusk are favorite times for deer to roam. These are also the times of least visibility for you.

Be wary of nice weather. Deer are more likely to be on the roam during a nice evening immediately following a period of cold weather.

If you actually see a deer, slow to a crawl. Deer are herd animals. Chances are good that more deer will soon follow the one you saw alongside the road or crossing the road ahead. Flick your lights from high to low beams and lightly tap the horn. Deer can become hypnotized by your lights, and flashing your lights can break the trance.

Plan an escape path. When driving in traffic, always try to have a lane that you can swerve into if a deer suddenly jumps in front of you. If you see no escape hatch, the best risk management may be to hit the animal.

7

Weather and the Elements

When you are the pilot of your car, you must fend for yourself in less-than-ideal driving conditions. What you do with the steering wheel, gas pedal, and brakes may make the difference between a safe trip and a nightmare. Many hidden dangers lurk along the way. This chapter will help you deal with skids, snow driving, and getting unstuck, as well as other weather-related villains.

Defogging Windows

Your visibility can directly affect the safety of your vehicle. Because most accidents occur within a few miles of home, the proper functioning of the defroster is important in those first few minutes of driving.

Here are some defogging tips that will help keep your windshield clear:

Always turn off the Recirculate option on the climate controls. Choose Fresh or Outside Air or turn the control to the setting that shows air coming in from outside the car. This step is critical for making the defroster function properly. While it may seem that recirculating warm air would work better, in fact, recirculating inside air makes it even harder for the defroster to remove moisture from the passenger compartment.

Always use the High setting for the fan. This fan speed produces the most dramatic results in defogging the windows. Try cracking open a window to speed things up. In some models, doing so facilitates the operation of the blower.

After the glass is clear, change to the proper mode selection for the air temperature that day. Turn off the defroster as soon as possible because it uses gasoline and forces the compressor to run all the time.

If the glass starts to fog again, avoid the temptation to run the defroster continuously, which costs you in gas mileage. Instead, increase blower speed, increase the amount of heat selected, crack open a window or two, and try to create a cross-breeze to carry moisture out of the car.

Most of the problem with window fogging comes from the moisture in your breath. If you can create enough of a draft to carry your moisture-laden breath out the window, you can easily solve the problem. Try keeping the windows on the left side of the vehicle open just a bit.

In a pinch, you can defrost the glass by cutting a potato in half and rubbing it on the glass. The potato makes the glass give up moisture and can really help when the defroster doesn't work. Don't forget to wipe the inside of the rear window glass to defrost it, too.

> **I**f you have chronic problems with foggy car windows, check the evaporator drains for clogging. If the evaporator can't drain the moisture out the bottom of the car, the system functions poorly.

Defrosting Icy Windshields

When faced with an ice- or snow-covered windshield, be extremely careful not to damage the glass. *Never* pour warm or hot water on the glass. In fact, just turning the windshield defroster on full blast can crack the glass if it is really cold or covered with ice and snow.

To prevent cracked glass, turn the heat on high with the blower speed on low. While it is gently warming the inside of the windshield, scrape the glass and clear the windows. If the glass has a heavy coating of ice, start by scratching a tic-tac-toe in one cor-

Your Car's HVAC System

The A/C compressor is the heart of the heating, ventilation, and air conditioning (HVAC) system. It is a small, round device about the size of a two-pound coffee can and is connected to the engine by a rubber drive belt—just like the other components, such as the water pump and alternator. The compressor compresses the refrigerant to very high pressures.

High-pressure refrigerant is very hot from being squished by the compressor. It is pumped to a special radiator, called the condenser, mounted in front of the cooling system radiator. The condenser looks just like the traditional radiator except that it's much thinner and is made from shiny aluminum. The high-pressure refrigerant gives up some of its heat to the outside air as the air passes through the condenser on its way into the engine compartment. This process makes the refrigerant ready to go inside and cool you.

The cooler refrigerant passes through another radiator located inside the passenger compartment, up under the dash. Inside this radiator, called the evaporator, the refrigerant is released from a very high state of pressure to a low state of pressure. When this happens, the refrigerant takes on heat from the air circulating in the passenger compartment and cools it. Now the low-pressure, warmed refrigerant is ready to be sucked back inside the compressor and be pressurized all over again.

Also located inside the passenger compartment, next to the evaporator, is a heater radiator. It warms the circulating air inside the passenger compartment and provides heat. When you choose Defrost mode, the air conditioner evaporator first cools the air. The evaporator gets cold and pulls heat out of the air to cool the vehicle. As it cools the air, moisture condenses on the fins of the evaporator unit and drips out of the car through the evaporator drain. The cooled air is then warmed by the heater core on its way into the passenger compartment.

If the air conditioner compressor doesn't engage for some reason (low refrigerant, faulty compressor, and so on) or the car doesn't have air conditioning, the heater core alone must defrost the car. This is especially difficult because the heater has no way to remove moisture from the air. Moisture removal is very important because moisture fogs the windows. Cars without defrosters have trouble defrosting windows.

ner to get through the ice. Now work your way to the center, clearing the rest of the glass.

Never scrape the ice off the windshield with any object that is harder than the glass, or you will scratch the surface. If you do not have an ice scraper handy, use a credit card or a plastic spatula (the kind designed for use in Teflon frying pans).

If the windshield washer solvent is frozen and won't squirt, pour hot water on the spray nozzle and the hoses that connect the nozzle to the washer bottle. (Be careful not to get the hot water on the cold windshield.) The solvent in the bottle usually doesn't freeze, but melted snow or ice can get into the nozzle or even the feed hoses and freeze there.

When you stop the vehicle for the night, turn on the windshield wipers and leave them up on the glass as you turn off the key. The wiper blades will be easy to free up and clean in the morning. (Some vehicles allow the wiper blades to be cocked and pulled away from the glass as well.)

Most people don't realize that their windshield wipers have an automatic "parking" mechanism that lowers the wipers when you turn off the wiper switch as you drive. If snow or ice builds up in the cowl area of your car (just in front of the windshield) and you turn off the wipers, the buildup prevents the wipers from returning to home position.

Because the wiper motor remains engaged as long as the ignition is on, it will continue to strain, trying to return the wipers to their home position. If snow and ice are in the way, the wiper motor can't finish its job and will die trying—all while you are driving along unaware of the trouble. If you notice this situation occurring, leave the wipers running at a slow speed until you can safely pull over and scrape away the buildup so they can return to their home position.

Snow Driving for Life

A friend of mine from Maine laughs at the thought of southern drivers panicking at the slightest hint of snow and schools and businesses closing at the drop of a hat. Drivers from up north know from experience how to handle snow. Sunbelt drivers do not. They wait for the forecast and venture forth only to buy emergency provisions. Or they ignore the conditions altogether and drive like maniacs. Instead, drivers should follow this game plan for best results.

Be Prepared

Before you venture out in the icy winter world, are you prepared to deal with the hazards of cold? If you get stranded, will you be able to survive for 12 to 24 hours without the vehicle's heater? Are you prepared to get out in blowing snow, blistering cold winds, freezing sleet, or rain and walk for several miles to get help? Don't underestimate how fast frostbite can get you. The effects of wind-chill can quickly rob your body of vital heat and turn you into a stiff long before the mortician ever sees you.

If you have a flat tire and have to change it, are you prepared? Are you carrying warm clothing? Do you have a heavy jacket with a windbreaker to protect your face? Do you have warm pants, gloves, boots, and head protection? Did you pack an emergency supply kit? (See Chapter 15.) Do you have a cellular phone or CB radio? Are they functional?

Staying Alive When Stranded

If you find yourself alone by the side of the road in a snowstorm, there are certain things you should do. Failure to do the right thing may cost your life.

It is usually better to stay in your vehicle and wait for help. If you are on a well-traveled highway, help will come soon enough. On the other hand, in a very remote area you may need to find help. Always try to remember any houses or farms you passed on your way and how far back they were in case you are forced to hike back to them.

If you can, wait out the force of the storm before trying to do anything outside the vehicle. The storm will usually abate within a few hours, and it will be much easier and less dangerous to venture out. Unless you are in immediate danger, stay inside during a blizzard. If you try to walk in heavy snowfall, it is easy to get lost and wander around until you die.

Run the engine just long enough to get the inside of the vehicle warm and then shut it off. When using the engine to warm the car, always crack open the window on the side opposite of the wind. Carbon monoxide (CO) gas is lighter than air and tends to gather at the top of the passenger compartment. When running the engine, slouch or lie down on the seat nearest the heater. If CO is leaking into the car, it will go out the window and be less likely to get you. Get out the blankets from your emergency kit to keep warm without running the engine too much.

Don't let yourself get dehydrated. Cold air will dry out your mucous membranes and make you thirsty. If necessary, eat snow to stay hydrated. Eat chocolate to give you energy and help elevate your mood. If you plan to venture outside your vehicle, take it along to eat for a quick energy burst.

Never Mind the Snow

The people in Finland don't use bad weather as a reason to stay home. Why? Because they are used to it. To them, there is no such thing as a snow day. The fact that it is dumping buckets of snow outside is no reason to stay home from work or to cancel school. Even ice storms have little effect on their lives. A Finnish National

Road Winter Traffic Project study found the Finns aren't scared of icy or slippery roads. More than half of those drivers don't consider winter roads slippery, and fewer than one in five calls very icy road conditions reasonably slippery. This may be why the Finns keep on driving during weather that would make you or me stay home.

Is winter driving really that bad? Well, anyone who has ever driven on icy roads knows how hazardous it can be. It is all too easy to lose control and wind up in a ditch—or even worse, slide into an embankment or an oncoming car! The key to driving in slippery conditions is traction. The more you have, the better off you are. Because the roads are icy so often in Scandinavia, drivers are allowed to use studded tires, which is forbidden on most U.S. highways.

But winter driving hazards aren't unique to any one country. Glare ice is just as horrible anywhere you encounter it and the result of losing traction is as universal as the laws of physics. The consequences of losing control are also universal. You either escape with your life or lose it. Between 1991 and 1993, only 4 percent of all fatal accidents were caused by drivers losing control while going in the same direction they were driving. More than 75 percent of fatalities occurred when cars slid sideways. This means that the amount of traction provided by your tires plays a bigger role than you might think.

Even if a snowy road is salted by the salt truck, it is still 11 times more dangerous than a dry road. A road covered by slush is 12 times more dangerous than a dry road. The most dangerous road is one that has glare ice on it. This road condition is 21 times more dangerous than a dry road.

Following in the Tracks

If you are traveling before the roads have been plowed, look for tire ruts made by other vehicles and drive in them. Maintain a constant speed. Avoid sudden acceleration or sudden braking; allow two to three times the normal driving distance between vehicles. This will let you travel at a reasonable speed while maintaining a safe stopping distance.

Think of driving in snow as slow motion. Every action requires calculation, anticipation, and added time to execute safely. Remember, when on slippery surfaces, traction is greatest just before the wheels spin. If your wheels start to spin, ease off the gas pedal until traction returns.

If the road is getting too heavily covered with snow, pull into a truck stop and wait for a truck to leave. Then follow in the ruts it makes. Don't follow too closely, however, since a heavy truck can stop much faster than you can in icy snow.

Braking and Steering

The rules are different for cars with antilock brake systems (ABS). But the most important rule remains the same for both ABS and non-ABS vehicles: Give yourself plenty of room to stop.

Non-ABS vehicles: If you feel the brakes start to lock up, pump them gently and lightly. Don't freeze and hold down the pedal. Release it and tap on it repeatedly. This pumping action gets the wheels rolling again. Remember, a rolling wheel has traction. A skidding one has very little.

ABS vehicles: Don't overrun your braking ability. Remember, the ABS system can't work miracles if you're driving too fast or following too close. Also be wary of the vehicle behind you, which may not have ABS and could skid out of control right into you.

If You Skid

Whether in a front- or rear-wheel-drive vehicle, first declutch or shift to Neutral, if possible, and steer into the skid. This will cause the vehicle to straighten out and stop skidding. Just before coming out of the skid, countersteer (turn the wheel the other way) until you are going in the right direction. Look where you want the vehicle to go.

Rear-wheel-drive vehicle: Be careful not to overcompensate in your countersteering, or the vehicle will continue to skid in the opposite direction. *Front-wheel-drive vehicle:* Control skids involving the wheels that steer the vehicle by steering in the direction your car is going. You must wait until the wheels begin to grip. Be prepared to use the brake to regain control once the drive wheels grip the road.

If You Spin Out

If you totally lose control and all four wheels are skidding, the best thing to do is lock up the brakes. Many people are injured when their spinning cars careen out of control into traffic, especially when the oncoming traffic is trying to dodge around them. If you lock up the brakes, your course will be predictable and you will be less likely to careen into others.

Getting Unstuck from Snow, Mud, or Sand

When it comes to going, all you have to do is push the gas pedal. But what happens if the wheels spin helplessly? You're stuck. If you make the wrong move, you may get stuck even further—or lose control and turn a sticky situation into a tragedy.

Have you ever skidded out of control, getting yourself so stuck in the mud or snow that you've been unable to get out? The following sections come from real-life situations and represent some of the more common maladies that you may encounter yourself.

In an emergency, quickly look them over and find the subject heading that best describes your plight. You can read the other sections at your leisure (before you get stuck in the first place).

Stuck in Snow

First, turn the defroster and fan on low to defrost the windshield and warm the car interior while you dig yourself out from whatever you have sunk down into. Keep a lightweight snow shovel in your trunk for digging out. Driving forward and backward in the parking space to pack down the snow with the tires may work as well. Be sure to accelerate gradually so that the tires don't spin. Spinning your wheels wears an ever-deepening rut, which is even harder to get out of. Point the front wheels straight ahead to minimize resistance to rolling.

Never leave occupants inside a closed vehicle while the engine is running unless a window is cracked and they are safely belted in place. Never leave a child loose inside a running car, as the child may put it in gear. Ditto for a dog.

Stuck in Mud

Mud is one of the hardest mediums to deal with because of its slippery nature. Mud also tends to "suck" the wheels down into it, deeper and deeper. Mud is an especially big problem for rear-wheel-drive vehicles. After you create enough traction for the drive wheels, the front wheels often sink down into the mud like a plow.

While front-wheel-drive vehicles are less likely to have the front end dig in, they are more likely to lose steering, and slide helplessly out of control into a nearby fence, guardrail, or building. Because the front wheels are used for both traction and steering, they also lose steering control when they break loose. Rear-wheel-drive vehicles don't have this problem.

But rear-wheel-drive vehicles suffer from the loss of power and just cannot climb a hill or sometimes even a small grade. Mud can contain a great deal of clay and is so slippery that even a four-wheel-drive vehicle will slip helplessly in the stuff. When the roads are slick with snow or ice, slipping in mud can be a very big problem. At that point, only front-wheel-drive vehicles can make it up hills.

Increase Your Traction

To get out of snow, mud, or sand, you need to increase the traction of your tires. You can use kitty litter, sand, ashes, fertilizer, or salt to increase traction. Salt is the worst for the environment, followed by ashes and fertilizer. Ashes are useless if the earth is the least bit wet and should be used only when the temperature is below freezing. Fertilizer and salt help create a small amount of traction, but their biggest advantage is that they turn snow into slush by speeding up the melting process.

In the winter, carry around an unopened bag of kitty litter in your trunk. It doesn't weigh much and will be handy if you get stuck.

Cardboard, carpet, or even the vehicle's floor mats can help give the wheels some additional traction. Cardboard boxes work well unless conditions are very wet or very muddy. Carry several large cardboard boxes broken down flat in the trunk of your car. You can also lie on the cardboard when working on the car in wet conditions (changing a tire, installing snow chains, or changing the oil, for example).

In a pinch, a wheel cover or hubcap makes a handy shovel. In sandy, snowy, or muddy conditions, sacrifice the wheel cover to help keep the jack from sinking. Just set the jack on top of the wheel cover to help give the jack firmer footing. Wheel covers are also a handy holding place for lug nuts, tire chains, or the drain plug.

You can use any type of wooden object to make runways for the wheels. If you can, jack up the vehicle and place the end of the piece of wood under the drive wheels. Then lower the vehicle onto one end of the piece of wood. Wooden objects you can use as runways include the following: planks, sheet paneling, several 1×1s placed alongside one another, two 2×4s or one 2×8 per wheel, a wooden lath, crates, wood chips, or sawdust.

Be sure to place enough wood under the tire so that the wood doesn't jack itself up into the undercarriage of the vehicle. If the wood does land in the undercarriage, it can damage the underbody or shatter as the wheel presses on the very edge.

If the ground is very soft and the wheels sink easily, jack up the vehicle and build a wooden bridge by filling the space below the wheel with wooden branches, small logs, firewood, or cut saplings. If the jack sinks when raising the vehicle, place cross-

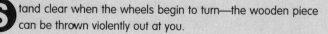

Stand clear when the wheels begin to turn—the wooden piece can be thrown violently out at you.

pieces of wood under it or use a jacking platform such as a large, flat piece of wood. Eight feet of a 2 × 12 works well with most jacks, though truck jacks require an even larger piece of wood.

In cases of dire need, use an ax or saw and cut saplings about three inches in diameter into three- or four-foot lengths. Lay them side by side and place the jack on top of them. If necessary, place another group of cut saplings across the first at a 90-degree angle. Keep building them up until the wheels are once again level with the road surface.

After you raise the vehicle, lay saplings down in its path to prevent it from sinking again until you can get it on drier, higher ground.

Using Tire Chains

Whether you're dealing with mud, snow, or ice, tire chains are your very best weapon in fighting the traction war. Unfortunately, you don't always have a set when you need one, and you may have to improvise. Any type of chain will do, as long as you have enough of it to place around both drive wheels. **Note:** Wrapping a chain around one wheel is practically useless with most drive systems except for true, full-time, four-wheel-drive systems.

Tire chains that are too large can still be of service. Shorten them by hooking onto a link further up on the wheel, trapping the extra chains under the adjoining side. Be very careful: If the extra chain is left to flop around on the outside of the wheel, it can hit against the underside of the fender and damage the car.

If the tire chain set is too short, you need only one extra chain set to lengthen the two short ones. With a hacksaw, cut apart the extra pieces needed and add them to the short set, making it fit. If the only chain sets available are too small for your wheels, creating a longer set can be a real lifesaver.

Here's an example of how this worked on my old Chrysler Cordoba: I was once stuck in the snow on my farm. I have a quarter-mile-long driveway that was covered with a three-inch layer of ice topped by several inches of snow. The only snow chains I had were too small. I hunted around the barn and found one old chain. In about an hour, I cut and fitted pieces of the extra chain onto the short ones. In a matter of minutes, I was able to drive the car out to the road—after a month of being stuck.

If no tire chains can be found, cut lengths of regular chain long enough to circle both rim and tire and then bolt them together. **Note:** This operation may scratch or ding the rim's finish! If there is time and enough chain, cut as many pieces as there are spokes in the wheel—the more the better. This method works even if you have only enough chain to circle each of the two main drive wheels once. If the vehicle is 4WD, always put the chains on the front for the best possible combination of traction and steering.

Here's another real-life example: When my truck was stuck in the mud alongside the Trinity River in Texas, I used a torch to cut my tow chain into two equal lengths. I wrapped each length around the truck's huge tandem rear wheels and tires and bolted the lengths tight, one on each side. The chains provided enough additional traction to get the truck moving up a slight grade to solid ground.

Using Rope
While not as durable as chain, rope has advantages: It usually doesn't damage the vehicle's rim or fenders, and it can be more easily fitted to the wheels. Its big disadvantage is lack of durability—rope works well only for short distances. Just wrap the rope around the wheel and back through the opening in the spokes as many times as you can. Tie a square knot after you're done.

One time I got my car stuck in the Florida sand and couldn't get enough traction to get out. All I had on hand was a towrope. I cut it into equal lengths and wove the two pieces around the car's rear drive wheels. This trick gave me just enough traction to get out of the sand trap.

Using Plants and Weeds
You can use local plants and weeds to add traction. Comb the area, looking for anything you can gather that will provide traction. Avoid using slippery objects like wet leaves or grass. Try to find things that are crunchy, like dry straw or hay, small dead shrubs, or weeds.

When my camper was stuck in the mud in the middle of the Painted Desert (it was the rainy season), I combed the empty desert and was able to gather dried weeds that looked like small sagebrush. Within a few hours, I had gathered enough small, dead plants to build a path and get the camper unstuck and onto firm, higher ground.

Using Other Assets
Cat litter, sand, or fireplace ashes can get you out in a pinch. Apply a layer about ¼- to ½-inch thick in the direction you want the tires to go. Bring it right up to the tire to get it moving. You need to put down only enough to cover the width of the tire. If continued application doesn't free the vehicle, try giving it a push from behind. Watch out for stones and gravel projected from spinning tires if you are standing behind them. Pushing forward and sideways on a rear quarter-panel may free the tire from a rut.

Dig a Runway

One of the most important things to get you unstuck is *momentum*. If you can't get the vehicle moving because of resistance in front of the wheels, you may have to dig out the area immediately in front and behind all four wheels. This added space may let you get the vehicle moving enough to get some momentum working for you. Dig a runway in the sand, mud, or snow long enough for the wheels to get moving. This allows the wheels to climb out more easily.

Dig Out the Underbody

Many times, the undercarriage of the vehicle comes to rest on the mud or snow as the wheels sink. Sometimes only a small bump or hill of mud, sand, or snow is interfering with the underbody and keeping the drive wheels from getting traction. You may have to crawl under the vehicle to dig out this material so that the drive wheels can get a foothold. Lie on carpet or cardboard to protect you from the wet or cold ground.

Practice Pushing

If more than one person is in the car, the weakest person should get behind the steering wheel and aim the car straight (the easy job). The other(s) help push it along. It may not seem like much, but even a small amount of pushing effort is sometimes enough to make the difference between go and no go. Usually, the most difficult part is finding a good foothold and something solid to push against. If necessary, dig footholds in the mud, ice, or snow. Let the vehicle rock backward and forward in the runway made by the wheels. Alternate pushing and pulling while the person behind the steering wheel gives it the gas when it is going forward (or backward, as the case may be). See the section called "Rock and Roll" for more information about this procedure.

The person behind the wheel can be the team leader, calling out "push" and "pull" when rocking the car. If the car has an automatic transmission, the transmission can be shifted from forward to reverse to help the car rock back and forth. If the car is a stick shift, choosing second gear instead of first may help keep the wheels from spinning as easily while still giving gentle power to get it going again. Use your legs to push; they are many times stronger than your arms. If possible, place your back against the vehicle and push your feet against the nearest object.

Make sure that you are completely clear of the vehicle so that you don't get crushed if it suddenly gains traction. The safest place to push is on the door frames. Roll down a window and push on the center or front door frame. Stay in the driver's line of sight so the vehicle can be brought to an immediate halt if you slip and fall.

Slide Sideways

If the surface you're stuck on is icy or too slippery and you have an assistant, push the vehicle sideways while the helper spins the wheels by pressing the gas pedal. The spinning wheels act like ball bearings, allowing you to re-angle the vehicle in a better line of traction.

A friend of mine got her Acura stuck going down an icy driveway. Her car suddenly slid sideways and jammed itself at an angle. I got her unstuck by pushing her car sideways on the front fender while she spun the front drive wheels. The spinning wheels allowed the car to be easily moved back into a straight position in the driveway.

Rock and Roll

The tried-and-true way to get unstuck involves rocking and rolling the vehicle until you have enough momentum to get free. While this is the best way, it can also be the most damaging to your transmission, transaxle, and/or differential. Attempt this maneuver with extreme care!

Sometimes you have to prime a pump with some water in order to get more water. Similarly, you sometimes must roll the vehicle backward in order to move forward. The alternating motion of going backward and immediately forward takes advantage of the reverse momentum generated when the vehicle has rolled as far in one direction as it will go and then starts moving the other way. The momentum is caused by the tires "ramping" up the end of the runway in one direction. Using this momentum can be like having another helper push you along.

For this method to work, you must change gears from forward to reverse in a hurry. This is easy in an automatic transmission vehicle but more difficult with a stick shift. On the other hand, it is *very* easy to damage the automatic transmission (especially on Hondas).

Other Tips

If your car is a rear-wheel drive and the wheels are spinning helplessly, try applying the parking brake. Because of the way differentials work, lightly applying the parking brake can limit the spin of the wheel that has the less traction, giving enough traction to the other wheel to get you unstuck.

If your car has a stick shift, try starting out in second gear to limit the amount of power going to the wheels and keep the wheels from spinning too fast.

Don't overspin your wheels! It may be a great way to vent frustration, but it does nothing to get you unstuck. It only buries the tire even farther and can cause major damage to the tire if you

When rocking an automatic transmission, be aware that the transmission fluid overheats in just a few minutes. If you don't let the fluid cool, it will literally cook the friction devices inside the automatic transmission. Let the liquid rest with the engine idling for 10 to 15 minutes after every minute or two of rocking effort. Doing so allows the fluid to circulate and cool down. **Never change gears while the wheels are still moving!**

spin it too fast. Because of the way your vehicle's differential works, one wheel is actually spinning at twice the speed the speedometer indicates when the other is stopped. If the speedometer says 70 mph, the tire is really going 140 mph. This speed can cause the tire to literally fly apart.

If the vehicle is a front-wheel drive, it may be to your advantage to back up a hill. Backing up puts the drive wheels at the rear of the vehicle and puts more of the vehicle's weight on the drive tires. To back up a hill, open your door and look behind you to see where you are going. Using the rearview mirror or even looking over your right shoulder does not gain you enough rear view to safely back up this way.

Always remember that momentum is your best helper. Many people forget this fact, slow down too much, lose their momentum, and can't get moving again. If possible, always keep moving. Go, go, go! Be aggressive and don't relent. Remember, once you slow down, you lose precious momentum and can't go over small bumps or hills.

Other Bad-Weather Driving Dilemmas

What do you do if someone is stopped or crawling along in front of you? Quickly and carefully judge the situation. You may need to pass that stuck or slow vehicle in order to keep moving yourself. If the road is clear, get over and stabilize your vehicle in the oncoming traffic lane before you try to pass. Don't try to do both at once. Once you're stable, ease on the throttle and pass gently.

Rolling wheels are *always* better than no rolling wheels. If you lock the wheels, you won't be able to steer and the rear end of the vehicle can easily slide out and spin sideways. Don't lock the brakes. Press gently on the pedal. If you start to feel the wheels skid, pump the brake pedal rapidly as fast as you can make your leg pump up and down. In many situations, merely slowing down and steering around an obstacle is better than trying to stop altogether and skidding into it.

C hanging lanes is very dangerous in bad road conditions, so be especially careful. You may lose control when passing, so try to be as clear of the other vehicle as possible before you attempt this maneuver. Pass only at great risk, knowing full well that you may wind up in a ditch.

Here's a life-threatening example of when ABS didn't help and I was almost in a terrible accident. I was coming down a steep, icy hill when I noticed that my antilock brakes were no longer slowing the car. Every time I pushed on them, all four wheels locked up and I started to slide. I tried to rub against the curb to brush off speed, but the curb was too ice-covered to do any good. The only choice was to aim down the hill and try to keep the car oriented straight ahead. Unfortunately, there were two vehicles in the roadway ahead, both coming my direction. At the bottom, a large van that slid against the curb was in my lane, and another car was slowly coming up the hill in the oncoming traffic lane.

There was just enough room to get behind the oncoming vehicle—if I could keep the car from spinning out of control on the way down. I kept pumping the brakes, even though they were doing nothing to slow the car. The pumping action kept the wheels rolling with just enough traction to keep the car under control. I wasn't able to slow down, but I did steer between the two vehicles—going about 50 mph as I passed the van!

Stuck in Deep Sand

If you're ever brave (or just plain dumb) enough to drive on a beach, you face the possibility of sinking into soft sand and getting stuck. Even worse, if the tide comes in before you get your vehicle out, you can lose everything! Be especially wary of the sand/shell mixtures next to the water. This "quicksand" surface is the most treacherous and should be avoided at all costs. If your Evel Kneivel days aren't quite over and you must drive on the beach, drive closer to the sand dunes when dealing with this kind of surface.

I f your vehicle has antilock brakes, **do not** pump the brakes. It reduces the effectiveness of the ABS and can even cause the brakes to fail. In order for antilock brake systems to function, you must apply firm, steady pressure on the brake pedal.

Here are some tips to help get you unstuck when you're up to your axles in the sand:

- Deflate the tires until they bulge a great deal, dropping the pressure just enough to provide some support without going totally flat. The added traction may help overcome the sinking sand.

- Keep the vehicle in a low gear, never in Drive. Avoid overheating the automatic transmission by excessive rocking. Rock for only a minute or two and then allow two or three minutes of rest so that the running engine can cool the transmission fluid. Excessive rocking can quickly fry the transmission. Also, avoid excessive tire spinning because the tire can fly into shreds and the differential can be destroyed.

- Use the foot brake or parking brake to limit wheel spinning without traction. Applying the parking brake gently while moving the vehicle can cause the wheel with less traction to slow down, giving the other wheel some added traction.

- If you find yourself sinking into a soft spot, floor the throttle and keep pouring it on until you get out (in low range or first gear). Don't worry about the tires spinning and sinking into the sand. If you let up for even a moment, you're stuck! The most important thing is to keep moving at all costs. Once you lose forward momentum, it will be very difficult to get going again.

- Keep the steering wheel straight. Turning the steering wheel in either direction will just cause the tires to dig deeper into the sand and make it even harder for your vehicle to get the momentum it needs to get moving.

- Use a wheel cover or similar implement to dig ramps both in front of and behind the tires. Digging ramps gives you a good starting point to rock the vehicle and gain some momentum to escape.

- Try to jack up the vehicle and put rocks, cardboard, boards, or other debris under the tires to give them added traction. Sometimes you can firm the sand by wetting it with ocean water. Look

Dig out the underside of the vehicle to reduce the drag of the sand on the undercarriage. **Do not place your body in a position where the vehicle can slip and crush you!** Use the spare tire as a safety device; keep it next to you at all times when you are under the vehicle. If the vehicle slips in the sand, that spare tire can save you from being pinned under a serious problem.

for dead brush, seaweed, or any plants that can be used to give the tires more traction. Install a set of tire chains or cables on the drive axle tires.

If you plan on venturing onto a beach, you may want to bring along some boards and tire chains just in case. Also, bring a cellular phone so that you can call for help in case you can't get unstuck.

Heater Odor Relief

The fall and winter months bring a variety of weather-related problems. Many drivers turn on their car heaters for the first time in months, only to be greeted with a weird locker-room odor of smelly socks.

Over the winter months, airborne microorganisms grow inside the car on the damp surfaces of the evaporator. During the warmer months, you can do several things to minimize the problem:

- Whenever possible, use the "Fresh" selection instead of using the "Max A/C" or "Recirculate" selection.

- Avoid parking under trees, where leaves or pine needles are likely to fall on the car.

- Avoid dirty or dusty roads. When you have to drive on them, use the "Recirculate" selection of the A/C unit.

- For short drives, avoid using the A/C at all.

- Make sure the evaporator drain is not plugged up. If the evaporator is not draining out all the water, it becomes a fertile place for microorganisms to grow.

- About half a mile from home, turn off the A/C, open the window, and turn on the heater with the blower on High. This helps to dry out the A/C evaporator before you turn it off, making it more difficult for microorganisms to grow inside the HVAC system.

If your nose is already faced with this smelly problem, you may find that the mold, bacteria, and fungi are aggravating your allergies. The professional solution is to disinfect the car with Airsept, a chemical available from your local dealer or auto parts store. This is a strong chemical disinfectant that will kill just about anything—including you if you don't use it correctly.

An attractive alternative to using dangerous toxic chemicals is to mix a teaspoon of Basic-G (sold by Shaklee dealers) and a pint of water in a spray bottle. With the car running, windows up, and defroster on high, spray the whole pint into the duct just in front of the windshield. Keep the windows closed, shut off the car, and let the solution soak in overnight (or for 12 hours). You're done. Repeat the treatment as often as needed, usually in the fall and again in the spring.

AC/Delco sells on "after-blow" module, which automatically turns on the HVAC blower fan for about ten minutes after you leave the car. This will help dry out the HVAC system, making the car less inviting for microorganisms. The module is sold by AC/Delco as part number 15-8632 or by GM dealers as part number 25533406.

Recognizing Carbon Monoxide Danger

One of the most deadly parts of winter driving is something that you can't see, smell, or touch. It is so insidious that it can snuff out your life before you ever know it exists. Even worse, as it starts to grab hold of you, your higher reasoning powers are lost and you won't realize that it has you. This treacherous villain is carbon monoxide (CO) poisoning.

CO poisoning takes the lives of more drivers than we will ever know because it is hard to tell when CO has done its dirty work. This type of gas is especially deadly because the first thing it attacks is your logical reasoning. You just can't figure out what is happening. Your mind becomes foggy and you can't think clearly. Without ever knowing it, you lose consciousness.

The biggest problem CO presents is that it dulls your thinking and you just can't react quickly enough to avoid a crash situation. With fuzzy thinking and slowed reflexes, you are unable to react in time to avoid the danger in the road ahead.

CO can get into your car from a leaking rubber seal in the trunk or exhaust gasket in the engine bay. In the earliest stages, CO makes you think you are getting the flu. Headaches, nausea, and dizziness that may be attributed to a virus can actually be caused by the vehicle you drive to work every day. People who suffer from 10:00 A.M. headaches at work often think it's the stress of their jobs, but they may be victims of CO poisoning.

I almost lost my life to CO poisoning and know firsthand how deadly it can be. In an effort to keep people from being killed by this silent assassin, I offer a life-saving carbon monoxide detector for $5 (including postage and handling). The detector is the size of a credit card and is designed for airplane pilots to stick on their instrument panel. A pink patch of chemically treated material is mounted in it. If the patch turns dark, you are in the presence of deadly CO gas. The detector is good for one year and can be used at home or anywhere you suspect CO gas poisoning. Call Nutz & Boltz at 800-888-0091 for more information or write Nutz & Boltz, PO Box 123, Butler, MD 21023.

Avoiding and Coping with Accidents

The moment an accident happens, the whole thing seems to be in slow motion. Or it's over so fast that you don't know what happened. When you're in shock after an accident, it's hard to know what to do. This chapter gives you strategies for keeping your cool so that you can avoid accidents, and it also leads you through post-accident trauma with advice that may save you a great deal of trouble—and expense—later on.

Deadly Ejections

Surprisingly, a significant number of people still believe it is safer to drive without wearing seat belts. If you question them, they will invariably say that they know of someone whose life was spared because he or she was thrown free from a vehicle. Trying to argue with these people is fruitless; their minds are made up and they will even risk breaking the law by not wearing their belts. All this despite the proof that safety belts provide better protection than any other safety device.

What about ejection? Are you better off being thrown free, as those who shun belts would have you believe? A study conducted by the Centers for Disease Control and Prevention focused on this issue. The study found that seat belts are great. It also uncovered other very interesting findings:

- Occupant ejections occur in only 1.5 percent of vehicle crashes but are responsible for a disproportionate number of injuries and fatalities. Rollovers occur in only 8 percent of all crashes but cause more than 50 percent of all ejections.

- Side-impact crashes increase the likelihood of passenger ejections. Ejections are also more likely to occur in sport utility vehicles, vans, and pickup trucks.

- As expected, ejected occupants were found to sustain much greater injuries than those who were not ejected. The study surmises that those ejected would have been much better off if they had remained in their seats.

- While safety belts are highly effective in preventing occupants from being ejected from their vehicle, they do little to prevent partial ejections. This is when the occupant's arm or head gets thrust out a window or open door.

- While the numbers of people using their seat belts have grown rapidly during the past decade, the numbers of people being ejected have remained the same. The study concludes that people who are involved in crashes generally refuse to wear safety belts. Could there be a connection between unsafe driving and refusal to buckle up?

- For those who were ejected, almost all of their injuries were a direct result of the ejection from the vehicle—not from the impact with another vehicle or other object.

- When similar crash conditions were compared with belted versus nonbelted occupants, the nonbelted occupants had much higher odds of dying than those who wore their belts.

- Open windows are not necessarily more dangerous and closed windows do not necessarily contain the occupants. In half of the occupant ejections, the person was thrown through a closed window on the front, side, rear, or roof of the vehicle. The most likely path of ejection was through a closed side window. Ejection through the door, rear hatch, or windshield was less frequent.

- When a person is ejected through a window, the window is usually shattered by the force of the vehicle impact, not the force of the person's body. The exception is the windshield, where the occupant usually creates a hole when being ejected.

Dealing with Panic Driving Situations

For this chapter, I interviewed an expert driving instructor, Myriam Shotland, who is an instructor for the Porsche Club and for the BSI Advanced Driver Training School. She also teaches high-performance driving and counterterrorism and knows a great deal about handling panic driving situations.

What to Do If You Skid

If you try to make a turn and your vehicle begins to skid and keeps going straight, what do you do? Actually, your wheels are turning; it's the mass of the car that's going straight. You go into a skid because you've asked your car to do more than it can do at one time. Obviously, you're going too fast.

When your car is going straight even though the wheels are turned, your tires aren't grabbing the road. You have zero steering control. The more you turn the wheel, the worse the skid gets. Instinctively, most people turn the wheel even more because the car stops responding. Then panic sets in, and you hit the brakes.

Do not hit the brakes! By doing so, you're just adding another item to your car's list of things to do. Ease off the gas and straighten the steering wheel. Do everything gently! Just straighten the wheel and be patient.

Rear-End Skids

What if you start to turn and the rear end of the car starts to break loose and skid? First of all, you have to determine which way the rear end is skidding. In correcting a rear-end skid, the most important thing is to *look in the direction you want the car to go*. Next, you must figure out how much to turn the steering wheel. If you look where you want the car to go, you will automatically make the correct adjustments to the steering wheel to regain control of the car. You don't even have to think about it.

Two Wheels off the Road While Turning

Suppose you're making a left-hand turn and the car starts sliding to the right. Your instinctive reaction is to try to keep the car on the road, but the wheels have gone off the road onto the soft shoulder. Those right-side wheels have no traction, and you've got the wheel turned in the opposite direction. Most likely, the two wheels off the road are going to give way. You're going to spin—generally into oncoming traffic!

In this situation, you've asked the car to do too much at once. Deal with it by asking the car to do less. By jerking the car back on the road, you lose traction on one side of the car, which almost always throws you into a spin.

Fight your instincts. Take your feet off the gas and brakes: no brakes, no gas, no nothing. Straighten the wheel. Now, most important, look in the direction you want the car to go. After the car has slowed down, you can ease it back onto the road. But no matter what, don't deny that you're going off the road. Fighting to stay on the road is where people lose control.

Collisions at Intersections

Suppose you're coming into an intersection and a car runs a red light and heads right across your path. You don't want to broadside the car, which would transfer all the momentum from your vehicle to the car you hit.

Aim for the back end of the car. You'll spin the other car out of the way, because you hit its lightest end. Don't hit the brakes.

Coast into it—or even better, stay on the gas. Just like jumping out a window, it's not the fall that hurts you. It's the sudden stop! The same principle operates here.

Why would you want to stay on the gas? It helps you transfer all the kinetic energy from your car to the rear of the other car so that no one gets hurt. You may think that pressing the accelerator would cause you to hit with more force than slowing down. But hitting the brakes, or even letting off the gas, actually increases your chance of suffering more bodily harm.

When you stop, you are actually thrown forward. What can hurt you is the transfer of your body weight. Not only the mass of your car but also your body continues to go forward. When you stay on the gas, all the weight transfer goes to the rear of the other car, meaning that your body is not slammed forward very hard, if at all.

Both your car and your body are already moving in a forward direction. If you slam on the brakes, your body has even less distance to go before coming to a stop when you hit the other car. Your body has a greater deceleration rate and you are more likely to be hurt. As the laws of physics say, "A body at rest tends to stay at rest, and a body in motion tends to stay in motion."

T-Bone Side Crashes

If someone is about to run into the left side of your car at, say, 30 mph, what do you do? Your car is going to be pushed to the right. You, a loose object in the car, are going to be smashed back to the left at 30 mph (especially if you're not wearing a seat belt). The laws of physics say that for every action there is an equal and opposite reaction. Your hitting the door at 30 mph is the equal and opposite reaction.

That you are going to be hurt is almost a certainty. It's not the impact of the other vehicle hitting your car that's going to hurt you, but the impact of your body being thrown over to the left side of your car. Your instincts tell you to lean over toward the passenger seat to try to escape the crash—but that's the worst thing you can do. If you're being hit from the left, the car is going to move to the right.

The best way to deal with this situation is to lean against the door being hit, which absorbs the energy of the car hitting you. Most certainly, you're going to feel a bump. But you will not be hurt as much as if you leaned over to the passenger seat and got thrown back against the driver's door at 30 mph.

Unintended Acceleration

It was a hot, overcast Sunday morning. The scene began innocently as a woman left church with her two grandchildren. They got into her car. The girl got in beside Grandma, and the boy hopped into the back seat. Suddenly, as Grandma started to pull out of the parking lot, unintended acceleration (UA) struck like lightning.

The car jumped into the street at full throttle. Terror froze Grandma at the wheel. She didn't understand what was happening; all she could do was hold the steering wheel as the car bolted into the street. Desperately, she yelled, "Whoa! Whoa!" She was panic-stricken.

The car hit the median strip in the center of the road first and then roared past the median, catapulting over the curb on the far side and flattening a street sign. It continued across the lawn on the opposite side of the street. By the time the car struck a brick building head-on, it was going about 45 mph. Eyewitnesses said that they never saw the brake lights come on. Apparently, it all happened too fast for the driver to react.

Understanding UA

Typically, the authorities blame such an incident on "a problem with pedal misapplication"—where you mean to press the brake pedal and instead press the gas pedal. Did a seasoned driver like Grandma misapply the pedal, or was this truly a case of UA?

Close scrutiny of the vehicle didn't turn up a single clue. If the woman had pushed the gas pedal instead of the brake, her foot would have driven the pedal into the floor, leaving "witness marks." There would have been a lasting imprint where her foot drove the gas pedal into the carpet and sheet metal when the car hit the brick wall. But there were no marks. Very suspicious!

Examination of the car's throttle mechanism revealed nothing that might have caused it to jam. The throttle was found to be closed, not stuck in the open position. What, then, could have been responsible?

Could a supersonic transport plane (sst) taking off nearby turn on the car's cruise control, causing it to go haywire and opening the idle speed controller? This would cause an engine to rev up. The sst has a very powerful radio transmitter, which often causes electromagnetic interference (emi) in areas where it takes off and lands. The sst might be responsible, but no one could prove it.

Shortly after Grandma's accident, the vehicle manufacturer changed the design of the idle speed controller. Coincidence?

This isn't the only case of radio emi causing electrical problems with vehicles. When computers were married to cars, they gave birth to electronic poltergeists. In the 1970s, auto companies became aware of *electronic smog* in the airwaves. Specially equipped trucks were sent to check the electronic environment. The amount of radio noise they discovered, even in remote places, was amazing. This radio and microwave smog can cause the automotive fuel, ignition, speedometer, cruise control, and other on-board computer systems to "lose their minds."

Here's a classic example: A Chicago tour bus used to screech to a halt whenever it tried to cross a certain bridge. The culprit turned out to be a radio tower atop a nearby skyscraper. The steel bridge picked up the radio signal and reflected it into the bus's antilock brake control computer.

During certain times of the day, some microwave transmission towers can shut down any passing computer-controlled car. Local tow trucks just tow the car in and jump-start it. Police cars experienced problems when two-way radios were installed in computerized cars. As soon as the officer pressed the talk button, the car died.

Truckers who have beefed up their CBs with illegal linear amplifiers can electronically interfere with the cars next to them. And I'll bet you didn't know that traffic-sensing wires embedded in the road, used to activate traffic signals, can cause cars to stall. Improperly installed car phones, car alarms, CB radios, cruise controls, and sound systems can interfere with the normal operation of electronic fuel-management systems.

Reacting to UA

If your car suddenly accelerates, turn the key off and press the brake hard. **Do not pump the brakes.** Often, braking alone is not enough to prevent a crash. Practice the following maneuver on a large, unoccupied parking lot or back street: Take a friend and a broomstick or yardstick with you. Have your friend suddenly press the gas pedal with the stick when you aren't expecting it. *Quick*, turn off the key and hit the brakes! Do so several times until you can do it well.

Avoiding UA

You can decrease your car's chances of undergoing unintended acceleration by observing the following guidelines:

- Don't drive with the cruise control on unless you're using it.

- Press the brake hard when moving the gear selector into Drive or Reverse (in cars with automatic transmissions).

- Don't idle in Park for long periods of time. Instead, shut off the engine until you are ready to move. Then restart the car and put it in gear.

- Don't drive with two feet, using your left foot for the brake. This can totally confuse the computer.

- Have a professional install your car phone, sound system, or CB radio. Improperly installed speakers and power wires can affect computer sensors, screws can interrupt chassis wiring, and improperly shielded antennas can irradiate computer circuits and induce resonance, confusing your car's computer.

- Have high-quality original equipment spark plug wires installed. Make sure the wires are factory length and are secured in their holders. Spark plug wires lying near a sensor wire can induce current in the sensor wire.

Most Vulnerable Situations and Types of Cars

Unintended acceleration is more likely to occur:

- in cars with automatic transmissions
- in cars with computer-controlled idle speed
- when you engage the transmission immediately after starting the car
- when you shift the transmission into Drive or Reverse
- after you idle for long periods in Park and then shift into Drive
- while you're traveling in very cold weather
- when you apply the brake and gas pedals simultaneously

What to Do After an Accident

One out of every five people reading this book will have an automobile accident of some consequence in the next 12 months. The question that everyone should be able to answer is: "What do I do after being involved in an accident?" Here's a handy checklist of what to do—and what not to do:

1 Activate your four-way flashers.

2 Calm yourself by taking five to seven deep breaths.

3 Call an ambulance for the injured; call a fire truck if gas is spilled; and call the police.

4 *Do not* leave the scene of the accident.

5 If you're not hurt, get out and start moving around. Doing so helps to clear your head so that you can more rationally appraise the situation. Try not to yawn; it might appear suspicious, as if you were driving under the influence or were asleep at the wheel.

6 If the vehicles are blocking the flow of traffic, quickly mark
their locations on the ground and move them out of the roadway.

7 Get out your safety kit and set up reflectors, flares, or triangles.

Take Pictures

After you take these preliminary steps, prepare for the next step:
dealing with the insurance company. If you have a camera handy,
get it out and take pictures of the accident. Tell your story with
pictures. Shoot positions of everything before anything is moved.
Photograph the following:

- Other vehicles as they are going down the road

- The other parties, especially if they are moving about in apparently uninjured fashion

- Any passengers and their positions in the vehicle(s)

- Traffic control devices; skid marks; shiny, wet, or icy pavement;
obstructions

- Rust or dirty damage to the other vehicle from previous accidents. Be shrewd. Does the damage correspond to where your
vehicle hit the car? What looks fresh and what doesn't? Look
for rust and dirt buildup on old damage. If you don't get this on
film now, you may be held responsible for damage that you didn't
cause.

Gather Information

Next, get this important information about the other driver and his
or her vehicle:

1 Name, address, home phone number, and work phone number

2 Place of employment and name of someone to contact (perhaps
a co-worker) in case the driver is absent

3 Insurance company, policy number, and coverage period

4 Make, model, and year of the vehicle, as well as its condition,
color, and license number

In addition, get names and phone numbers from witnesses. Make
sure the names are spelled correctly, and double-check all numbers. Ask for names of others who can speak for the witness if he
or she is not available.

From the police officer, get this important police information:
rank, badge number, precinct, phone number, and an address to
write to get a copy of the police report. Get the facts regarding all

injured parties, including passengers. Take down names, addresses, dates of birth, sex, and the extent of injury.

Safety Kit Items

I suggest placing the contents of this kit in a sturdy plastic shoe box, tackle box, or toolbox and keeping it in your trunk. You may wish to add other items or to combine this kit with the emergency roadside kit described in Chapter 15.

- Roadside flares, fuses, a blinking flasher light, or emergency reflector triangles

- "Send Help/Send Police" cardboard sunscreen dash cover

- Disposable camera

- Notepad

- Crayons, colored pens, or markers

- First aid kit

- Bright-orange safety vest

- Poncho or lightweight raincoat (a jumbo plastic garbage bag will do)

- Nutz & Boltz personal reflector (call 800-888-0091 for information)

- Fire extinguisher

- Flashlight with alkaline batteries (keep the batteries in a separate plastic bag to preserve them)

- Portable CB radio

Look for Suspicious Signs

If you wind up taking the accident to court, you should be especially alert. A little sleuthing now can pay off in big rewards in court. Here are some things to watch out for:

- Watch for things that the other driver(s) may be tossing away or tucking out of sight. Do you see alcoholic beverages being hidden? Is a marijuana cigarette being tossed out the window?

- Do you smell drugs or alcohol?

- Do you smell gasoline? Leaking gas may have affected the driver's judgment.

- Listen to what the other parties are saying to each other. Are they blaming one another for the accident?

- What are the other parties saying to the police? Are they making up a story about how you were at fault?

- Is anyone acting in a way that seems strange or out of place?

- Is the other driver sleepy? Yawning? Lethargic?

Get out your notebook and write down everything at the scene. Draw a diagram, making sure to note road names, numbers, accesses, mile markers, lanes, and the direction each vehicle was heading. Try to make your view as wide as you can. Don't trust your memory; your emotions may erase big parts of the scene.

Parking Lot Perils

Parking lots can be hazardous to your health and the well-being of your vehicle, too. Low-speed parking lot fender benders are not easy to track because most incidents are never reported. Why? They don't usually involve personal injury and are considered nonreportable incidents by the police. The police responding to the incident typically just instruct those involved to exchange drivers' license numbers and insurance information.

In an effort to learn more about urban low-speed crashes, the Insurance Institute for Highway Safety surveyed passenger cars at 16 insurance company drive-in claim centers in four big cities. The survey found that about 20 percent of all claims were from parking lot accidents. Many of the claims occurred while the vehicle was not in motion, but was parked or standing. Damage from bumper underride was common.

Bumper underride occurs when one vehicle bumper goes underneath the bumper of another vehicle, usually resulting in extensive damage to the fascia, lighting, and grille. Here's a list of reminders to help you avoid problems with parking lot fender benders:

- Park next to four-door cars. Their doors are shorter than those on two-door models, so your car is less likely to be whacked.

- Park next to a new car. New car owners are normally careful with their cars.

- Avoid parking next to hulks, beaters, or bombs. Such owners often give their cars little thought and could leave a lasting impression on your car.

- Look out for station wagons or vehicles with toys in the back window. These are signs of children, who are likely to slam their door open into your nice, new paint finish.

- Don't park behind a van, truck, or RV. They have poor rear views and big strong bumpers.

- Avoid the end of a row. This is an unprotected area and a likely spot for an accident.

- Park in the middle of your space. This distances you from cars on both sides.

- Stay away from guardrails, curbs, and poles. It's easy to back into them if they are in your blind spot.

- If your car has an air dam (spoiler), back into the space. The dam you save may be your own.

- If there are two spaces facing one another, drive through the first into the second so that you will be able to leave without backing out.

With the colored markers or crayons from your safety kit, color the events with colored pens to identify their relation to each other. This will help fix them sharply in your mind. Consider the following examples:

- White cars against snow or sand

- Gray day, overcast, fog, rain, sleet, smoke, and so on

- Red cars at dawn or dusk

- A driver wearing a parka that could restrict head movement or obstruct vision

- Rear of the car full of junk or other objects that prevent proper rearview vision

- Driver wearing sunglasses at night

- Car windows covered with sunblocking tint so dark that you can't see in or out

Keep Your Cool

Watch your own behavior, too. Don't be arrogant. Here's the ideal attitude:

- Remain a little on the positive side of neutral.

- Choose your language carefully. Use small words and talk politely.

- Don't admit fault or distraction.

- Avoid further discussion with the other parties. They may be fishing for information to use against you.

- Don't volunteer information about the extent of your insurance coverage.

> **I**f you have any type of injury, even if the soreness doesn't appear until a day or two later, see a doctor. You must establish that you were injured by creating a medical history. Even a visit to the emergency room for a once-over examination is important if you expect to seek damages for pain and suffering later on. If you wait too long to see a doctor, it will be very difficult to establish that you were injured by the accident and not from something else. Don't tough it out.

See a Doctor

If you are injured, don't try to tough it out. Never state, in conversation or in writing, that you were not hurt. You may regret it later. Until you are examined by a medical professional, you really don't know.

9

Blowouts and Bad Brakes

Do you know what to do if a tire blows as you're driving down the highway? How about knowing the right way to change a tire? A mistake here could cost you your life. How do you know when your brakes are about to fail? If you don't know, you might not be able to stop, which is certainly a life-threatening situation. What to do if you have to make a panic stop? What do you need to know about ABS brakes? What does that angry dash warning light mean? Read on for answers to all these questions and more.

Taming a Blowout

Tires almost always go flat when you're on your way somewhere, especially when you're late. There you are, cruising along, brain occupied with the details of life, and—pow! A blowout.

Let's say your right front tire just went flat. Quick, do you:

Ⓐ Slam on the brakes?

Ⓑ Keep pressing the gas pedal?

Ⓒ Steer into the flat?

Ⓓ Steer away from the flat?

Ⓔ All of the above while babbling hysterically?

Your first reaction to a blowout is probably to hit the brakes. Maybe you think stopping the car will save the tire. It won't. That tire is already destroyed.

Hitting the brakes is the *last thing* you want to do. The vehicle is stabilized by its forward momentum. A collapsed tire doesn't cause serious instability until the vehicle slows below 50 mph. Vibration and noise are worst between 50 and 40 mph, the range at which some people lose control of their vehicles. As the car slows, the sideways pull of the flattened tire has a greater effect.

Against all instinct, you need to keep your foot on the gas pedal when a blowout occurs. Choice B is the correct answer. The vehicle's forward momentum is your ally because continuous engine power helps you steer the vehicle. Maintain it and steer as you would in a sudden strong crosswind.

Don't let those strange noises generated by the flat tire worry you. Grip the wheel firmly at the 10 and 2 or 9 and 3 o'clock positions, and make steering corrections only as needed—no wild wrenching on the wheel. Begin decelerating gently, all the while looking for a good place to pull off the road. Soon enough, the side with the blowout will begin to drop lower to the road.

Forget the tire and wheel. Avoiding an accident is far more important than some silly pieces of rubber and metal. Besides, stopping in a traffic lane will almost guarantee an accident. Keep going slowly until you find a safe place to get off the road. If you are on a traffic-filled freeway, it may be better to continue to the next exit. A flat is good for up to $\frac{1}{3}$ mile before you are riding on the rim, and the rim can go for up to two miles before it becomes scrap metal. Remember, your life is more important than the tire.

Flat-Tire Blues

No matter how much you try to avoid it, tires occasionally go flat. Knowing how to deal with it can help you avert a disaster.

First, calm yourself. You can't inflate a tire with steam, so blow off your steam later. Take heart in the fact that practically anyone can change a flat with a few instructions.

Remember, it's most important to get off the road safely and avoid an accident. If you save the tire but die in the process, no one will be impressed.

If your flat is on the driver's side and you must stop on the shoulder, park way off the road. Changing a driver's side tire close to traffic could get you killed.

Put on the emergency flashers and place flares or reflectors 75 to 100 feet behind your car. Flares and/or roadway reflectors are must-have items for your emergency road kit. (See Chapter 15 for a complete list of items to keep in your kit.)

Changing Your Flat Tire

Changing a flat tire is a dangerous job. The car could slip off the jack and roll onto you. Always work on a level place. Never lie under the vehicle. Be sure that any passengers are out of and away from the vehicle.

To change the tire, you need the following items:

- A working jack

- A lug-nut wrench or tire spanner

- Firm ground below the car to support the jack

- A spare tire that is inflated and ready to use

Ten Tire-Changing Commandments

I. Immobilize the vehicle. Put the shift lever in Park or leave the manual transmission in first gear (engine off). Set the parking brake. Look around for a rock or other object to chock the wheels.

II. Mount the jack in its place on the body or bumper of the vehicle. There are many types of jacks and jack mounting points for various makes and models. Don't assume that the car is the same as your last one—read the manual. Operate the jack until the vehicle just begins to rise up and then stop.

III. Remove the wheel cover (hubcap) and set it nearby to hold the lug nuts after you remove them. To remove some wheel covers, you need a special tool. The tool should be in the glove box and looks like a lug nut with the adapter part built right into one end of it. Be careful; wheel covers have sharp edges and can cut you.

IV. Loosen the lug nuts about halfway, but don't remove them. Getting them to move may take muscle work. Don't hurt your back! Push with one arm and pull with the other simultaneously. Use your legs to help muscle the lug wrench.

V. Play it safe. Put the spare tire on the ground next to the jack. Slide the spare tire under the vehicle as soon as there is enough clearance so that it will serve as a catch if the vehicle falls from the jack.

VI. Raise the vehicle with the jack until it is high enough that you can put the spare tire on the vehicle.

VII. Remove the lug nuts and place them in the wheel cover. Then install the spare. Remove the flat tire and put it under the car for added safety.

VIII. Tighten the lug nuts, but not too tight yet. Make sure the metal wheel is snug against the hub or brake drum and not cocked at an angle. A cocked wheel can give the false impression of being correctly mounted but later break loose and cause an accident. When you're certain that the wheel is not cocked, tighten the lug nuts snugly with the lug wrench until the wheel begins to move.

IX. Lower the car carefully. Move the old tire out of the way. Now tighten the lug nuts with the wrench some more. Use a star-shaped pattern, skipping over each second nut until all are very tight.

X. Pack up. Put the flat tire and wheel cover in the car. Go to the next service station or garage and have the wheel lug nuts torqued to the correct foot-pound tightness for the vehicle. Consult your owner's manual for the exact torque value.

Lug-Nut Lessons

Your car's lowly lug nuts are more important than you might think. These simple fasteners can make the difference between a safe car and a death trap. If the lug nuts suddenly fail to hold, the wheel can come off, and you'll completely lose control.

Tightening the lug nuts to the proper torque value is generally overlooked by mechanics, but the importance of this simple task cannot be stressed enough. I heard about one woman who will never walk again because the lug nuts on her wheels were not tightened properly. They came loose, the wheel came off, and the car rolled over. The accident broke her back and she instantly became a quadriplegic.

The initial tightening should be done in whatever manner is easiest. Most mechanics prefer to use an air impact wrench for this step. Next, tighten the lug nuts in a star pattern, using a torque wrench to achieve the proper torque.

If the repair shop has removed your wheels for any reason, check the lug-nut torque before driving away. Use a beam-type torque wrench to determine whether your wheels were torqued properly. If the lug nuts were improperly torqued (the usual situation), you can prevent the brake rotors from warping by retorquing the lug nuts before the brake rotors become hot.

Failure to torque the lug nuts properly often results in a danger-ous condition. If the lug bolts are torqued too tightly, the brake rotor usually warps, causing brake pedal pulsation and poor braking. If the lugs are not tightened enough, the wheel can come off.

Improper lug-nut torque is the most common cause of warped brake rotors, which cause the brake pedal to pulsate when you brake. A man with an expensive car came to me complaining that his brakes kept on pulsating no matter what the dealer did. He had returned to the dealer several times and was charged for a brake job and machining of the rotors each time.

I explained that the car's lug nuts were probably installed with an impact gun rather than a torque wrench. He had asked the dealer, who said the lug nuts had been properly torqued with a torque wrench. I said, "Let's see," and tried to loosen the lug nuts using a beam-type torque wrench. The lug-nut torque ranged from 40 to 150 pounds of torque on the same wheel! The dealer had lied to him and was, in fact, the cause of his brake problems. The problem was the same from the beginning—the mechanic was lazy and installed the wheel with an impact gun.

If you are a mechanic and have a hard time remembering to torque the wheels properly when you are finished, lay the torque wrench on the driver's seat. That way, you have to pick it up to move the car out of your service bay. This technique will remind you every time.

Application of antiseize compound or lithium grease to the lug-nut threads and contact areas helps to maintain proper torque val-ues consistently, especially with aluminum or mag wheels (because lug nuts are always steel). Steel and aluminum create an electrolytic action against one another and become stuck to each other. Every time the wheel is removed, metal is galled from the rim. Over time, the rim is ruined by this process.

Antiseize is preferable to lithium and can be bought from any hardware or parts store. Just wipe some antiseize on the threads and mating surface of the lug nut, wheel stud, and rim mounting hole. While you're at it, put a dab on the mounting/centering hole where the wheel meets up with the hub so that you can get the wheel off the hub more easily next time.

If a lug nut or bolt is frozen in place, try smacking the head of the bolt with a large hammer. This can free a stuck lug, espe-cially when the rim is aluminum or alloy.

No Brakes!

It's a motorist's worst nightmare. You're zooming along the open road, you step on the brakes, and—nothing. The pedal is mushy and won't slow the car. Or it goes all the way to the floor with no effect. What do you do? Here are some ways to slow down in a panic situation:

Pump the brake pedal: Pumping may repressurize a leaking circuit temporarily. After the pedal comes back and gets firm, stop pumping and hold it.

Use the parking brake: They don't call it the emergency brake anymore because it does a poor job of stopping the car. The faster you are going, the longer it will take to slow down.

Scrape the rails: Race-car drivers call grazing the nearest guardrail, wall, or curb "scrubbing off speed." Let the friction of car against object slow you down. It means body work later, but it's better than a fatal crash.

Don't shut off the motor: Shutting off the motor won't stop the car. Besides, you need to keep the engine running in order for the power steering to work.

Downshift (manual transmission only): Be careful. This can slow the car dramatically. If you are not traveling in a straight line, downshifting can make the car spin out. You may also damage the transmission. If your car has an automatic transmission, downshifting will probably have no effect.

Put the car into reverse: The only way to use an automatic transmission to stop a car is to throw it into reverse, which may ruin the transmission. Brace for a shock when doing this—the wheels will quickly lock up. This procedure is more complex on some cars and trucks, so here are some extra tips on this emergency maneuver:

- Never put the transmission in reverse while going forward unless absolutely necessary. This is not a trick to play around with. Each time you do it, you risk causing significant damage to the transmission, transaxle, or driveshaft(s).

- Always be concerned about the wheels breaking loose and causing the vehicle to spin out or become impossible to steer, especially if one wheel is on a slick surface and the other wheel has more traction. The wheel with more traction will grab the pavement, sending the vehicle into a spin.

- The amount of throttle is critical to making this maneuver work. If you take your foot off the gas pedal when you slam it into reverse, the engine will most likely stall, and the transmission will lock up the wheels. To get the transmission to engage in reverse on some vehicles, the engine speed must be raised slightly. This will cause the drivetrain to engage in the opposite direction instead of just freewheeling without any engagement of the wheels.

- Too much gas, and the wheels will smoke and spin out of control. Too little gas, and the engine will stall. In this procedure, the throttle pedal becomes a pseudo-braking system; its application causes the braking action of the wheels.

- This doesn't work with computer-controlled transmissions, which are found on many newer cars. If you don't know whether your car has one, ask your local dealer. In general, a computer-controlled automatic transmission will not let the transmission engage reverse while rolling forward.

Ten Brake Failure Warnings

Have you ever had the brake pedal fall to the floor—a complete loss of brakes? It has to be the worst experience a driver can have. Your brake warning light is only one indication of impending brake failure. Check your vehicle for these 10 brake failure warnings and their possible causes:

Low brake fluid: Random checking of brake-fluid levels by the Car Care Council found that one out of three was low on brake fluid. Some cars have warning indicators for low fluid level; some do not. Modern cars have clear brake reservoirs that allow you to see the level without removing the cap. Low fluid means one of two things:

- The brake pads are worn thin, making the caliper pistons extend, which causes a drop in the fluid level. This condition is normal and indicates a need for new brake pads.

- The car has a leak somewhere in the hydraulic system.

In either case, the brakes need immediate attention. If you don't know how to check your brake-fluid level, consult your owner's manual or have a local mechanic show you.

Low brake pedal: With the engine on and brake pedal pressed, you should be able to get your foot between the pedal and the floor. A low pedal can mean something as simple as maladjusted brakes. Or it can indicate much more serious problems, such as bent/distorted brake shoes, improper shoe/drum fit, or a loose wheel bearing that's causing caliper piston kickback.

Pedal sinks to the floor: In this condition, your vehicle is an accident waiting to happen. Typically, the master cylinder is about to fail or there is a leak in the system. If the fluid level isn't dropping, the master cylinder is probably at fault.

Hard brake pedal: If you have to put strong leg pressure on the brake pedal to stop the car, the booster or pump may be malfunctioning. Other causes of a firm pedal include grease-soaked, glazed, or hard brake linings, vacuum supply problems, or frozen wheel cylinders. All of these possible causes are pretty complicated and technical and will require a visit to the shop for further diagnosis if you are not very technically minded.

Spongy pedal: The usual cause of a soft or spongy pedal is air trapped in the system. Other causes include vapor locking from old brake fluid, brake hose(s) ballooning (and about to burst), warped brake shoes, new shoes or pads that don't fit properly, or brake drums worn too thin, causing *bellmouthing* of the drums. (When the brake drums are too thin and expand outward as the brake shoes put pressure on them from inside, the drums assume a bell shape.)

Sensitive pedal: Brake grab (when your brakes apply almost as soon as you touch the pedal) can cause loss of directional control, particularly on slick roads. Oil/grease/brake-fluid contamination on the friction material is the usual culprit. Other possible causes include a faulty metering valve, system failure for the rear half of split brake systems, a slipped power booster reaction disc (located between the master cylinder and the booster), organic pads installed where asbestos is required, or a loose caliper.

Pedal pulsation: When the brake pedal bounces or pulsates against your foot, a rotor or drum is out of true. Like a washing machine with all the clothes on one side, the pedal pulsates when the drum or rotor has more metal on one side than the other. If the wheels have been removed recently, the rotors were probably warped by improper tightening of the wheel lug nuts. Other causes include loose wheel bearings, a bent drive axle, or warped rotors from using metallic pads on rotors designed for organic brake pads. If your brakes were relined recently, the wrong type of brake pad material could have been installed or the wheels could have been put on with an impact gun. The root cause is difficult to discover after the fact. See "Slaying 'Dragon Brakes,'" in Chapter 2 for more information about brake pad material. **Note:** Some ABS-equipped vehicles have a normal pedal vibration when you apply the brakes with force.

Dragging brakes: Dragging brakes are usually accompanied by a loss of fuel mileage and a burning smell from the affected wheel(s). This condition causes brake fade (spongy pedal) and will probably lead to complete brake failure. Typical causes are a restricted flexible brake hose or driving with both feet and resting your left foot on the brake pedal. Other causes include improper brake adjustment, sticking parking-brake cable, frozen hydraulic piston(s), brake pedal linkage binding, loose/worn front-wheel bearings, weak brake spring(s), overfilling the master cylinder, debris in the master cylinder compensating port, or a defective quick-take-up valve in the master cylinder. See "Slaying 'Dragon Brakes,'" in Chapter 2 for more information.

Brake pull: If the car pulls to the left or right when you apply the brakes, you can lose control and have an accident. The brakes always pull toward the side on which the brakes function properly. The most common cause is a restricted brake line or hose. Other causes include contamination of the friction elements; frozen or tight wheel cylinder/caliper pistons; incorrect, unmatched, or unevenly worn linings; nonparallelism or excessive runout of the rotor; a drum that is out of round, threaded, cracked, glazed, bell-mouthed, or damaged; brakes out of adjustment; a broken shoe return spring or a grooved backing plate; a faulty combination valve in a cross-type system; or an eccentric radius arm bushing worn on one side of the car and new on the other.

W hew! This is a lot of technical stuff to digest and may not mean much to you. All these possible causes are pretty complicated and necessitate a visit to the shop for further diagnosis if you are not very technically minded. But if you are a do-it-yourselfer and want a list of possible causes, here it is. Also, if your mechanic is stumped and needs suggestions, show him or her this book.

Noise: The brakes make a loud noise when you apply them. Many cars today have built-in brake pad wear detectors that make a high-pitched chirping noise when you begin to apply the brakes. This noise tells you that the brake pads have become thin and need to be replaced. The other most common brake noise comes from the brake pads vibrating against the rotor. This awful squeal is usually caused by worn or weak antirattle clips or springs, glazed pads, or corrosion buildup between pad and caliper.

Another dangerous brake noise is a scraping sound, possibly accompanied by a squeal. This noise can be caused by caliper mounting bolts that are too long, a loose rotor rubbing against a caliper, or brake pads or shoes that are worn down to the metal. A rattle at low speeds on rough roads with the brakes not applied usually means that there is excessive clearance between the pad and caliper; the anti-rattle clips or springs are worn, missing, or improperly positioned; or the rotors were turned at too slow a feed speed. A chatter noise accompanied by pulsating pedal during brake application means excessive lateral runout or parallelism of the rotor, a loose wheel bearing, a bent drive axle, or improper lug-bolt torque.

Panic Stop!

Do you know what to do and what not to do when making a panic stop? Quick thinking and lightning-fast reactions can eliminate or at least minimize your injuries and losses in a panic situation. It's a good idea to rehearse these items in your mind beforehand so that you are mentally prepared for the day when you have to make a panic stop. Here are some tips:

Are you clear to the left or right? If so, a quick turn into an empty traffic lane may allow you to avoid a collision. Truckers make a habit of checking to both sides for this very reason.

Look in the rearview mirror. Someone may be so close behind you that he or she can't avoid hitting you and causing a rear-end accident. If you have time, pump the brake pedal to catch the attention of the driver who's on your tail. No way to avoid being rear-ended? Then let that driver hit you first and force you into the car in front of you. Otherwise, your car will be against the vehicle in front and the collision will have a more violent hammer-and-anvil effect. Also, for insurance reasons, it's better to be forced into the vehicle ahead.

The best defense against panic stop problems is to follow the Coast Guard motto: "Semper paratus," or "Always prepared." The time to think of the following items is *before* you have to slam on the brakes:

- Seat belts are a must! Make sure that they are snug against your body.

- Don't forget that lap belt if your shoulder belt is automatic.

- All loose baggage, including packages, groceries, and personal belongings, should be secure inside the car. You can use the seat belt to secure briefcases and purses as well.

- Don't keep items on the rear deck of the car. Even a small thing like a library book can cause a nasty blow to your head in a panic stop.

- Secure pets with an auto pet harness. Otherwise, a panic stop may throw your pet against the door frame or windshield. Never allow the pet to ride in your lap; you could crush it against the steering wheel, even in a minor accident.

- If you are transporting a load of cargo in the back seat or behind you in a station wagon, make sure the cargo is secure. If the cargo is high enough to hit you in the back of the head, you are asking for trouble. In a panic stop, the cargo will slide forward and can snap your neck or slam into the back of your seat with tremendous force.

- Install the best tires you can afford. Your tires might make the difference between a near-miss and a disaster.

- If someone suddenly pulls out directly in your path and you think you're going to hit his car, aim for the rear fender. By the time your vehicle gets to that point, with luck the other vehicle will have already passed and you will miss it.

- Make sure that your brakes are working properly. Practice a few panic stops in an empty parking lot or deserted road to check your brake system. If your vehicle pulls to the left or right or stops poorly, get the brakes repaired before they cost a life— that of a small child darting out from between parked cars . . . or your own!

Antilock Brake Systems Explained

Is ABS best? Since the advent of air bags, many people have become complacent about driving safety. Some think that an air bag is all they really need. But air bags deploy in only about 1 percent of all emergency situations. According to Pontiac general manager John Middlebrook, "The average individual will use an air bag once every 175 years but will use antilock brakes in an emergency once a year." It's better to avoid a dangerous situation, and that is where antilock brake systems come into the picture.

The advantage of ABS is twofold: In most cases the vehicle can be stopped faster with better directional stability, even under adverse conditions. Think of the last time you slammed on the brakes and skidded. Were you able to steer while your vehicle was skidding? If you tried to turn when the wheels were locked, you found that the vehicle didn't respond. Why? Because they didn't have any traction.

A vehicle with ABS acts differently. The wheels don't skid; instead, they continue to have traction, which allows the driver to steer through a panic stop. The vehicle can still be controlled and, in many cases, steered out of harm's way.

ABS Flaws

ABS isn't always best. Sometimes it can actually work against you, so some carmakers offer an ABS off switch to allow the driver to turn off the antilock function. Consider the following situations:

- When the entire road surface is slick, ABS may not function properly and can keep the driver from having full control of the car. For example, when you are driving on gravel or dirt roads or driving on sheet ice, the antilock computer cannot tell what is happening because the computer uses input from each wheel to compare with the other wheels. In this situation, the computer releases the braking effect on the first wheel that starts to slip, causing the other wheel(s) to lose traction more quickly. After the second wheel loses traction, the computer releases both wheels, which can cause instant directional instability.

- When the driver is not familiar with ABS brake operation, he or she may try to pump the pedal when making a panic stop.

- When the driver is not familiar with ABS, he or she may panic when the ABS makes the brake pedal pulsate. A frightened driver may release the pulsating brake pedal.

Before blaming the ABS computer for turning on the yellow ABS light, check the basics. Some of these items are easy to fix without the need for a repair manual and high-tech tools.

> **I**f you don't use it, you'll lose it! Use your ABS at least once a month, or the ABS controller can fail prematurely from lack of use. Find a deserted parking lot and make a full-on panic stop, causing the ABS to operate. Also, periodically testing the ABS gives you practice in it, so you will not be inclined to let up on the brake pedal in a panic braking situation when the ABS starts cycling and the pedal vibrates against your foot.

The heart of the ABS's logic is the rotational speed of the tires. If one or more tires are worn or are of a slightly different size, the ABS is affected. The system has built-in tables that look up the tires' handling characteristics. Logic for tire height, profile, traction, and slip ratio is part of the ABS computer program. If tires with lower stability are installed, for example, the ABS computer can become confused. The system may still work, but hard braking can cause the car to shimmy and possibly slide sideways. Even a badly underinflated tire can throw the system off and trigger the ABS light.

The wheel sensors cause most of the havoc in ABS because these parts work in a grueling environment. Moisture, salt, dirt, slush, small rocks, and metal particles can all cause problems. There is usually a critical gap between the sensor and the tone wheel. If dirt or a small rock gets into the gap and moves the sensor, the ABS failure light is triggered.

Cleaning the engine compartment contaminates the sensors' connectors. When the ABS does its self-test procedure and the sensor doesn't respond as it should, the ABS light is triggered. You can cure this condition easily by cleaning the weatherpack connector. Road salt can do the same thing and can also be cleaned off. Use electric contact or electric motor cleaner to service the connector. Coat the terminals with silicone grease to prevent further problems.

Metal particles are the biggest headache of ABS. The roadside environment is full of iron particles from brake drums. The ABS wheel rotation sensor contains a permanent magnet, and the magnet starts to collect metal filings. Pretty soon it looks like a porcupine with metal particles sticking all over it. The presence of the extra metal eventually prevents the wheel sensor from responding correctly to the tone wheel as it turns, triggering the ABS light. You can easily clean the sensor to fix the problem.

ABS speed sensors installed in the differential housing are also a problem. During the differential break-in period, the ring and pinion gears seat against each other. Small metal particles are worn off these gears and become attached to the ABS sensor magnet. Just clean the magnet—or better yet, change the gear lube after 5,000 to 10,000 miles and eliminate the source of the problem.

The heart of any computer system is the power source. Battery voltage is critical for the system to function properly. ABS requires a constant supply of voltage; if the supply is too high or low, the ABS fails and turns the light on. If the charging system fails to keep the battery charge up at least 9.5 volts, even for a fraction of a second, the ABS shuts down. If the alternator produces nonrectified alternating current (AC voltage) levels in excess of a few volts, the ABS computer can be damaged. One of the first things to check when troubleshooting the ABS is the battery voltage, both DC and AC. If there is more than about ½ volt AC in the electrical system, the alternator is shot because it has a bad rectifier (diode).

Dash Warning-Light Dilemmas

For the past decade or so, carmakers have been producing dash warning lights in two colors: amber and red. When an amber (or yellow) light is on, a problem exists. When a red light is on, the problem is much more serious and usually requires immediate action. One of the more serious things a warning light can indicate is a charging system failure.

What do you do when the alternator or battery symbol comes to life on the dash? Must you stop immediately, or can you drive until the next opportunity to stop? How long can you go without hurting anything?

The answer really depends on the drive-belt configuration of your engine. If your water pump is driven by the same belt as the alternator, stop immediately. Don't turn off the motor until you check whether the belt has broken or is not turning the water pump and alternator. If the belt is still there, the alternator has failed, and you can probably drive for a little while—at least to the repair shop. If you don't know whether the water pump is also driven by the alternator fan belt, ask your mechanic to look and let you know. This is an important fact you should know about your vehicle.

If the alternator belt has broken and the water pump isn't turning, shut off the engine immediately. If you drive any farther, you may blow a head gasket and maybe even crack the engine block. If your vehicle has an engine temperature gauge, you can use it to determine whether the problem is the belt. **If the engine temperature goes up, stop your car immediately!**

If you are satisfied that just the alternator is out of service, try to find a place to stop where you won't have to start the car again.

Before you just go out and have the alternator replaced, consider having the entire charging system checked. In fact, have it checked both before and after the alternator replacement. It's a good idea to get a printout showing how much amperage your old alternator was producing and how much the new one is making. Some replacement alternators can be as defective as the one they replaced. Having this test done both before and after gives you some insurance that the new alternator was installed correctly and is putting out a good amount of charging amperage.

After you shut off the engine, it is quite likely that you *won't be able* to start the car again because the battery will be too weak. Look for a garage or service station that may be able to fix the problem, or at least find someplace where you can safely leave the vehicle until you can have it fixed.

If you plan to tough it out and want to drive as far as you can go on battery power, don't use any accessories. Turn off the radio, heater, and air conditioner. Don't use the turn signals and try to stay off the brakes as much as possible. Try to maintain a minimum speed of 45 mph, the most efficient speed.

If your vehicle is carbureted and the battery still has a good charge, you may have four to five hours of driving left. Fuel-injected vehicles use much more energy and will go for only about one hour on the battery. Pay attention to the engine. As the battery weakens, the engine will begin to misfire, especially at higher rpms. When that happens, cut your speed. You have only a few minutes of battery life left at this point, so look for a safe place to come to a final stop.

If you are driving at night, the driving time will be cut considerably. Watch for the lights to begin dimming. When they do, start looking for a place to get off the road. I once had my charging system go out while leaving Tallahassee, Florida, on my way to Tampa. I had already driven for over an hour and knew that my battery wouldn't make it. It was a Sunday night and everything was closed except for a gas station. I was able to purchase a new battery there and complete the trip.

What do you do if you have no lights, if there isn't a gas station nearby, and you must move your vehicle? Have two vehicles escort you—one in front and one behind, acting as your headlights and taillights.

Stalled Cars and Other Nightmares

Just when you least expect it, the engine won't start. It just cranks and cranks. In this chapter, you'll find out all the mechanics' tricks for starting an unwilling engine. What if it's running hot? How do you deal with an overheated engine in the breakdown lane, and what steps do you take to remedy that hot condition? What if the car catches fire? You'll learn the three things the fire department would like you to do before you leave a burning vehicle.

You may have to give up altogether and have your car towed. In that case, you should know that all tow trucks are not equal. Some types can damage your car and should be avoided. Read on for all this information and more.

Starting a Stalled or Unwilling Engine

Have you ever wondered whether you can do anything to get your car to start after it stalls? The engine cranks over but doesn't catch—it cranks and cranks and never fires up. This section gives you some mechanics' magic tips for getting it to start. Some of these hints are simple, and some are a bit technical. If you don't understand them, have your mechanic review them with you so that you will be able to carry them out if you get stranded and your car just won't start.

A no-start condition is when the engine turns over (cranks) but fails to catch. This condition is different from a no-crank condition. If nothing happens when you twist the key—the starter motor doesn't turn the engine at all—read on to find out how to troubleshoot an engine that won't crank.

Also remember that excessive cranking ruins the starter motor. Crank for 30 seconds at the most, followed by a one-minute rest to let the starter motor cool down. Be sure to turn the ignition key all the way off between cranking attempts.

Some of the following procedures can cause a fire if you are not careful. **Always have a fire extinguisher handy**, wear safety goggles, and dress appropriately (short sleeves, no jewelry, hair tied back). Please be careful!

Here's the procedure for getting that engine to start:

1 Lift the hood and let the engine cool down. You can overcome heat-induced ignition module problems by letting the module cool down. Ditto for vapor-lock problems. You'd be surprised at how many unwilling engines are happy to cooperate after they cool down. That's why the darn thing starts when the tow-truck driver arrives.

2 Remove the air filter. If the engine is flooded or the air filter is dirty, removing the air filter helps to clear out the unburned gas. This trick works great if the engine has been cranked and cranked and may be flooded.

3 Pop the gas cap and let the fuel tank breathe. Sometimes the fuel-tank vapor vent valve fails, preventing fuel from being drawn from the tank. This vent valve is located under the car, above the gas tank, and is very difficult to get at. Sometimes it clogs up and makes the tank build pressure—or the opposite: the tank won't vent properly and the gas can't come out. You can circumvent this problem simply by removing the gas cap.

Turn the key all the way off before you crank the engine so that you reset the computer. After you do so, the engine control computer can recognize a failure of some sensor. If turning the key off doesn't help, try disconnecting and reconnecting the battery cable. Make sure that the car and all accessories are turned off before you mess with the battery cable, or you can fry the computer. Disconnecting the battery may cause the engine to idle funny for a short while, and you may lose the memory in your radio. Also, if your radio has a security alarm, this trick may shut it down until someone reenters the code.

If you own a GM car, take note: You can easily put the engine in limp-home mode by connecting two of the leads in the ALDL connector. If your engine is equipped with a mass airflow (MAF) sensor (which is a fairly common component that causes problems), disconnect it when the engine is off, forcing the computer into limp-home mode. Ask your mechanic to show you where the ALDL and MAF connectors are.

Create a Spark

If you get no spark at the spark plug or from the coil in an engine *with* a distributor, stress the module. Remove the coil wire from the distributor, holding it one inch from a good ground. As the engine cranks, slowly move the wire closer to the ground until it begins to spark. Repeat this procedure as necessary. After it starts to produce spark, plug it back into the distributor and start the engine.

If you get no spark at the spark plug or from the coil in an engine *without* a distributor, check the connections to the electronic ignition module, the coils, and the crankshaft sensor. Wiggle them to check for a tight fit and unplug them to look for corrosion and terminal ends that may have backed out of the holder.

Dry Wet Plug Wires

Use any type of lubricating spray (or ideally a silicone spray) to dry off the plug wires and coil wire. If none is available, use a dry rag or towel. Don't forget to remove the distributor cap (if your car is so equipped) and dry it inside. If neither a spray nor a dry rag or towel is available, just open the hood and let the sunshine and air dry things out. It may take a little longer, but eventually the moisture will evaporate.

Give It a Shot of Fuel

If your vehicle is carbureted or throttle-body fuel-injected, put a little fuel (half a shot glass full) in the throttle inlet to get the engine to fire up. This should cause it to start up and run, at least for a moment. Sometimes the extra rpm surge that occurs when it fires up causes the stuck float, fuel injector, or weak fuel pump to come back to life. After the car is running, you can get it into a shop and have a mechanic fix the problem. If you don't know whether you have a carburetor, throttle body, or what, have your mechanic go over the engine compartment and show you what you have and how it works.

While this procedure won't work on multiport fuel-injected engines, you can use ether or starting fluid to achieve the same result with a fuel-injected car. Follow the instructions on the can to give it a shot of gas and get it to fire up for a moment with the same results described for carbureted cars.

C **aution!** Exercise extreme care when working with gasoline or starting fluid, especially around a hot engine. Use of too much can cause an engine fire or explosion. If you are inexperienced or wary, do not attempt this procedure!

Jump It

What if no fuel is going into the engine, and the engine just starts and dies when you give it a shot of fuel or ether? Listen at the gas filler hole while someone else turns the ignition key. Do you hear the fuel pump run for a few seconds? If not, the electric fuel pump may be the cause of your no-start. Just about every car made since 1980 has an electric fuel pump. When the pump fails to run, you can sometimes coax it to life with a jump-start (see the procedure in Chapter 2). After you connect to another vehicle, start the other vehicle and run it for 15 minutes at a fast idle (give it some extra gas to make it idle fast) to put an additional charge on your battery. Leave the jumpers connected and try starting your vehicle. The extra voltage sometimes makes the fuel pump motor come to life.

Thaw It Out

Is freezing weather causing your no-start? Is the engine cranking over v-e-r-y s-l-o-w-l-y? If so, try a different battery or a jump-start. If you already did so, the motor oil may be too viscous. Try draining the oil and installing 5W-30 oil in the engine. Does the electric fuel pump run? (See the preceding procedure for instructions on checking the fuel pump.) You can revive a frozen fuel pump by using a drop light to heat it and thaw the frozen fuel/water inside it. You can revive frozen crankshaft position sensors the same way. If using a drop light isn't possible, try pushing the vehicle into a heated garage. (No, it's not a good idea to build a fire under the car to warm it up.)

Air It Out

You suspect the engine is flooded because you smell gas after several attempts at cranking it. First, make sure that you don't have a gas leak. If you *see* any signs of a gas leak, *stop!* You could start an engine fire. If you *smell* gas, the engine is probably flooded. Simply remove the air filter and let the engine air out for 15 minutes. Now crank it over. Hold the gas pedal on the floor to clear out the extra gas and let the engine draw in fresh air. If you don't know how to remove the air filter, consult your owner's manual or ask your friendly mechanic.

Dry the Ignition Wires

Stalled because of rain or going over a big puddle? The ignition wires may be wet. It's best to remove the plug wires and dry them out one by one (so you don't get them mixed up, silly). Ditto for the distributor cap. Spray the wires, cap, and rotor with WD-40, 5-56, LPS, or silicone spray. In a pinch, you can displace the moisture by using any spray solvent (such as brake cleaner or carb cleaner).

Be careful not to start a fire! Let the solvent dry thoroughly before you attempt to start the car. If an appropriate spray isn't available, just open the hood and let the air and warm sun dry out the under-hood area. It may take longer, but it works.

Unplug the Exhaust System

What if the engine cranks OK and seems to be trying to start, but it just can't seem to catch? It almost starts but then pops or sputters, and you see no exhaust fumes coming out of the tailpipe. This is a good indication that the exhaust system is plugged. An easy way to get the engine to start is simply to remove one spark plug. More difficult ways are to remove the oxygen sensor or loosen the exhaust pipe somewhere in front of the muffler (or catalytic converter) to let the exhaust leak out. Removing a spark plug lets the car start, but you can't drive it to the shop this way. Loosen the exhaust flange or remove the oxygen sensor to make the car drivable.

Overheating? Don't Blow Your Cool

What do you do if your engine is drastically overheating, steam has started to spurt from the hood area, and the temperature warning light is on? Follow these steps:

1 **Pull over as soon as possible.** Another mile or two can turn a minor repair into a blown head gasket or, even worse, a cracked block. In some cases, the cost of repairing the damage can exceed the value of the car.

2 **Turn the heater to its High setting and open the windows.** This draws heat away from the engine and helps to cool off the radiator.

3 **Unless the engine is steaming, smoking, or on fire, don't turn off the ignition.** If allowed to idle, the engine can throw off more heat because the engine's coolant is circulating. Shutting off an overheated engine can turn the oil to varnish, which can cause engine bearings to seize up, ruining the engine.

4 **If you have access to a hose, spray water into the grille of the car in the area of the radiator.** Make sure that you cool down the hood area to avoid getting burned when you lift it. The engine should still be running.

5 **After the water has cooled off the radiator until it is cool to the touch, carefully open the radiator cap and pour water into the radiator until it is full. Then replace the cap tightly. CAUTION: Take extra care opening the radiator cap. It can still be hot!** If water isn't available, leave the engine on but use gloves or towels to open the hood.

6 **Remove the oil filler cap carefully—it's hot—and add a quart or two of oil.** You should add oil even if the dipstick indicates that the engine is full. For a short period, the engine can handle the excess, and the oil will help cool the internal engine parts.

Be careful not to spill oil on the hot engine. It could cause a fire!

Wait until the engine/radiator is cool (about an hour) before driving again. Just be sure to have the oil drained as soon as possible—which is a good idea anyway if the engine overheated and burned the oil beyond its useful life.

Important: If you do not have water or oil and turning on the heater doesn't help, turn off the engine as a last resort. Wait an hour or so until it is cool before trying to start it again.

Beating the Heat

How important is heat reduction in an engine? The cooling system of a diesel engine, running under load, has a great deal of heat to remove. So much, in fact, that if it weren't properly cooled, the heat generated could reduce the engine to a molten blob within an hour. About 9,000 gallons of coolant pump through the cooling system each hour. In one day's operation, that's enough coolant to fill a large swimming pool. Consider this: The cooling system accounts for less than 60 percent of the engine's cooling capability. The rest of the heat is left for the oil to dissipate.

Here's a compilation of tricks and tips for preventing overheating in the first place. Look over the list and pick one or more that will work best for your situation. Some are simple, and some are very technical. If you don't understand a particular suggestion, consult your mechanic.

- Use a 50/50 mix of coolant and water. Too much coolant can cause overheating. People think, "If a little is good, more must be better." Then they drain out all the coolant/water mix and refill with straight coolant. Bad idea! Coolant doesn't cool. They should have just called it antifreeze. I told them, but no one would listen.

- Have your thermostat and radiator cap changed every four years or 60,000 miles. A faulty thermostat is the most common reason for cars to run hot and/or overheat. Be sure to buy only name-brand parts, such as Stant or Robertshaw. Cheap imitations will fail and cause a major breakdown. Is it worth it to save a few dollars?

- Use synthetic oil in your engine and drivetrain. Synthetic oil can reduce engine oil temperature by 50 degrees and is much better at getting rid of engine heat. It is also much more slippery, which lets the engine run with less internal friction—further reducing engine heat.

- Put the gear selector in Neutral if your transmission is an automatic. If you are stuck in a traffic jam and not moving, let the engine and transmission idle freely in Neutral. This speeds up circulation through the transmission cooler, which helps to cool both the engine and the transmission.

- Be sure that the radiator is clean inside and outside. Have the inside checked when the coolant is flushed every two years. With the nozzle on your garden hose or a self-serve car wash spray wand, spray high-pressure water from the inside of the engine compartment toward the outside to remove bugs, dirt, leaves, and so on.

- With the engine cool, squeeze the lower radiator hose. You should feel a spring inside. If the spring isn't there or has corroded away, the water pump's suction can cause the hose to collapse. This condition usually indicates that all the hoses are old and need to be replaced. Ditto for the coolant. If it was acidic enough to dissolve that spring, think what it must be doing to the rest of the cooling system.

- As a general rule of thumb, change the cooling system hoses every four to five years or 40,000 to 60,000 miles. This helps to prevent a hose from rupturing and leaving you on the side of the road. Pay a little now or a lot later.

To help avoid overheating, try using Redline Water Wetter, a cheap and easy method for reducing cylinder head temperatures. A small amount of the product added to the radiator can decrease cylinder head temperatures by as much as 50 degrees.

Overheating First Aid

If your car does overheat, **do not under any circumstances open the radiator cap until it's cool**. A safe procedure is to spray water into the grille with the engine running. Direct the water into the radiator and keep spraying until the engine is cool. Turn off the engine and continue to spray the radiator until it's cool to the touch. Now you can safely open the radiator cap.

Causes of Overheating

Some causes of stubborn, hard-to-find overheating problems are simple, and you can easily fix them yourself. Others are a bit technical and require the assistance of a mechanic or radiator repair specialist. Rest assured that if your car is running hot, you'll find the reason in this section.

Leaks in hoses, water pumps, timing covers, radiators, and heaters/hoses often leave green puddles on the ground under the car. (See "Identifying Trouble Puddles" in Chapter 11.) If the source of the leak is not evident, use a cooling system tester to pressurize the system. Do this on a hot engine using 15–20 psi and let it cool down. Repressurize as needed to maintain this amount of pressure. Some components leak only when hot; others leak when cold. If you don't have a pressure tester, have a radiator shop test your car for you.

Don't drive your vehicle with a low coolant level and overheat the engine, or you may turn a leak into a blown head gasket! If you do need to drive, loosen the radiator cap and keep adding water (bring along a few jugs full) as needed until you reach your destination.

Both the radiator cap and the cooling system should be able to hold the tester's pressure for at least five minutes. Loss of pressure means that the coolant is leaking out somewhere. Also, the radiator cap must hold the correct rated pressure printed on the top of the cap.

Do you see coolant being forced out the overflow of the radiator or out the top of the overflow bottle? If so, you may be seeing the effects of a blown head gasket and you are in for a pretty big repair. It's not a good idea to drive the vehicle with this problem because the leaking head gasket can cause further engine damage. Get it checked out right away.

A low coolant level can cause all kinds of mischief. It can make the coolant temperature sensor read incorrectly and make air bubbles form in the hot parts of the engine. The heater may not work properly and, most important, the engine may overheat.

If the coolant solution is mixed with too little or too much coolant, the system may overheat. Too much coolant (more than 75 percent) causes the engine to run too hot because it cannot transfer heat into the strong mixture of coolant. Too much water can cause the system to boil over because coolant is supposed to raise the boiling point 20 degrees above that of water.

If the engine oil level is too high, it causes oil to foam at high speeds. Foamy oil doesn't lubricate the inside of the engine, so the engine runs hotter. A low oil level causes overheating from friction of the poorly lubricated engine parts.

Rear-wheel-drive vehicles only: If the radiator fan clutch fails to keep the fan engaged, the fan clutch is the wrong type or is made to turn in the opposite direction. The engine will overheat only when you drive at slow speeds. On the highway, it will be fine. With the engine hot and not running, give the radiator fan a good spin. Does the fan spin more than five revolutions? If so, the fan clutch is definitely bad.

Front-wheel-drive and some rear-wheel-drive vehicles with electric cooling fans: If the electric fan comes on too slowly or not at all, the engine will overheat only when you drive at slow speeds. On the highway, it will be fine. The fan should operate when the temp sensor is grounded (except for Mazdas and some Toyota models).

Radiator blockage causes internal restrictions and reduced flow rate. A quick check for internal radiator blockage is to feel the outside of the radiator (with the engine turned off). The radiator should feel hot at one end and then cooler as you move your hand across it. A blocked radiator will feel cool in the center and hot around the edges. Another test is to remove the cap and look inside the radiator with a penlight. First, open the petcock, drain out some of the coolant, and check whether fluid is left standing in the tubes. Standing coolant indicates that the tubes are blocked. Next, run the engine with the coolant level still low and check for good flow. It should have plenty of circulation, kind of like a waterfall.

New cars have air dams and use airflow channeled through the bottom of the grille opening. This is the "bottom feeder" airflow design. If airflow through the radiator is blocked by missing or damaged air dams, or leaves and debris are blocking the air scoop, overheating will occur.

Internal engine cooling system restrictions in the engine water jacket caused by scale or blockage are the hardest cooling system problems to deal with. Usually, you have to remove the engine block core plug (also known as a *freeze plug*) to look inside the engine cooling jacket for blockage. The only way to clean out this type of blockage is to pressure-flush fluids from the engine block. In extreme cases, the freeze plugs will have to be removed and the junk physically cleaned through the plug openings.

If the hood's felt insulation liner falls down in front of the radiator, it will restrict the airflow. This problem is plainly visible. A similar but less visible problem occurs when the sealing rubber around the radiator and air intake area is damaged, falls off, or is not reinstalled after the car is repaired. This sealing rubber channels the air and forces it through the radiator. Without it, the air can simply bypass the radiator and not do its job of cooling.

The cooling system thermostat may be sticking closed, be the wrong type, or be installed upside down. To pinpoint this problem, remove the radiator cap and run the engine at high rpm (2,000 or so) for a few minutes to get it hot. Turn the engine off and let it heat-soak for a minute so that the heat travels throughout the engine and cooling system. This procedure should cause the thermostat to open fully. Next, have someone start and rev the engine while you watch for the fluid level. If the thermostat is working and has opened as it should, the liquid level in the radiator will drop and you will see lots of coolant flow. It will really churn the coolant. Now, continue to idle the engine. As the engine cools down to normal temperature, the coolant flow should slow down, indicating that the thermostat is working properly and has begun to close.

The water pump impeller blades may be broken or eroded, or the impeller itself may have come loose. If you see a great deal of red rust accumulation inside the cooling system (like the Rio Grande), this condition may be caused by the engine block or water pump impeller blades rusting. The pump must be removed and examined for further diagnosis of this very tough-to-find problem.

The air conditioning may have been overcharged during a recent A/C service, which can cause the engine to labor and run hot. Does running the A/C make it overheat? Does the engine seem to have much less power (than usual) when the A/C is running? This condition is very easy to correct. Have some of the refrigerant removed from the A/C system. Go back to the shop that serviced the A/C and have them check the A/C system pressures to see whether the pressure is too high—an indication of an overcharge.

The brakes may be dragging. If so, the wheels will be hot to the touch and the car will not coast very well when put in Neutral. (See "Slaying 'Dragon Brakes'" in Chapter 2.)

The exhaust may be restricted, causing the engine to run hot. This is another difficult one to pinpoint. The best way to find out if there is an exhaust restriction is to have the exhaust system back pressure tested. It should not have more than about 2 pounds of back pressure with the engine running at 2,000 rpm (no load on the engine).

The engine may be getting hot air all the time, meaning that the EFE (heat riser) is stuck closed or the Thermac is stuck on hot (depending on the type of vehicle you have). You can easily pinpoint this problem by removing the air filter and filter cover, thus letting cool air into the engine all the time. If this makes the problem go away, the "heated air" system must be checked out by a mechanic.

Timing for the ignition system may be retarded. Many things on many different engines can retard the timing. Finding the cause will require the help of a tune-up or engine drivability specialist.

A worn camshaft causes poor engine efficiency. This condition is usually reflected in a lowered engine vacuum. A simple engine vacuum test should nail this cause down. The vacuum should be 18 to 21 inches at idle, without any fluctuations. Ditto for a timing belt that has jumped off just one tooth.

The lower radiator hose may be collapsed, restricting coolant flow at highway speeds. A missing spring inside this hose usually causes this problem. Give it a squeeze to feel for the spring.

Air locked in the system may be preventing coolant flow. Any time the cooling system is opened up for service, there is a danger of getting air locks in the system. If the air is not removed (burped) from the cooling system, the engine can overheat. In extreme cases, this can damage the head gasket.

Prop the thermostat open with two aspirins when replacing it. This will bleed the air out, especially if the thermostat is mounted on the water pump. This simple procedure can prevent air locks and make the cooling system purge itself of bubbles more easily.

Any source of air leaking into the suction side of the water pump (between the pump and the lower radiator hose) will allow air into the cooling system and cause air locks. Loose hose clamps are the usual cause for air sneaking into the system.

If the radiator is too small or the wrong radiator is installed, your engine will never run cool—especially on the highway under heavy loads or when going up hills. Heavy-duty core radiators are available at your local radiator shop.

The engine belts may be tight, worn, smooth, or frayed or may not fit on the pulley properly. A slipping fan belt can prevent the water pump from turning at the proper speed and coolant from circulating as it should. It can also run the water pump in the wrong direction.

If the pump has a smooth pulley, it is made to rotate counterclockwise. If the pulley has a groove or V, it rotates clockwise or the same direction as the crankshaft.

A lean air–fuel mixture makes combustion temperatures too high. Have the exhaust gas analyzed to pinpoint excessively lean mixtures. This condition is usually accompanied by the presence of engine ping, knock, or detonation.

Chariots Afire!

You smell smoke. It's coming from under your hood. Your engine is on fire! What do you do?

First and foremost, get safely off the road. Be sure to turn off the ignition when you stop—this simple act may stop the fire from spreading and help the fire to go out on its own. (Remember that when you shut off the engine, the power steering and power brakes will stop operating, so be sure you're off the road before you turn off the ignition.) If the fire is coming from underneath the car or from the rear, get a safe distance away from the car as fast as possible because the gas tank may explode.

If you are squeamish or don't care if the car burns up, just pull over and get at least 100 feet away from the vehicle. If you have children on board, get them out first—as fast as possible!

Stand away from the car. If possible, wave down a passing truck; truckers carry fire extinguishers. (Don't forget to offer to pay for the fire extinguisher afterward.) Someone with a car phone can also summon more help.

Warning: Attempt these procedures only if you have been trained in working with car fires, if the fire is small, and if you are in dire need. Otherwise, leave the job to the fire department. Vehicle fires burn toxic materials whose fumes can kill you. They can also blow up: the gas-filled struts and shock absorbers can explode when heated, not to mention the gas tank. A car can be replaced. Your life cannot!

If you do want to attempt to put out the fire or do some things that may assist the firefighters when they arrive, read on.

- First, try to shut off the ignition as soon as safely possible. This shuts off the fuel pump, which stops the flow of fuel.

- Get to the side of the road as quickly as possible. While you're rolling, air flowing through the grille fans the fire. Make sure the doors are unlocked because the battery may soon lose electrical power.

- Once stopped and after you are certain the doors are unlocked, close the car windows and sunroof, making the inside as airtight as possible. (**Note:** You may need to turn the ignition back on again for a moment to get the windows to go up. However, the fire department says that doing so before exiting the car is smart because it keeps the fire from spreading into the passenger compartment.)

- Before you get out of the car, pop the hood and gas cover levers. The fire department will need to get into the engine compartment and will have a harder time if you haven't released the hood latch.

- After you are out of the car (if you have time and the fire isn't spreading too fast), loosen the gas cap to prevent fuel tank pressure from forcing more gas into the engine.

- If you plan on fighting the fire yourself, open the trunk and get out the trunk mat, blanket, floor mats, or anything else that you can use to smother flames. Take the jack handle or tire iron as well.

The hood will probably be too hot to touch. If so, use the tire iron to work the safety catch. **Important:** Leave this job to firefighters if the heat is too intense.

- If you open the hood and are greeted with flames, do not try to smother the fire. Shutting the hood may slow the fire until help comes. Don't close the hood completely. The firefighters will need to open it again when they arrive.

- If the fire is small, smother it with the trunk mat. You may be able to find sand nearby that you can use to smother the fire. In some cases, you can pop off a hubcap to shovel sand onto the fire.

Fire Extinguishers

A fire extinguisher is an invaluable piece of equipment. Purchase one and keep it in your car. Be sure the fire extinguisher is FM- or UL-approved and is specified for class A, B, and C fires. The best ones have gauges that let you know they are still full.

Water-Charged

This type of extinguisher is practically useless unless you are trying to put out an upholstery or carpet fire. Water is likely to cause burning gasoline to spatter and spread the fire to other parts of the engine compartment.

CO_2 or Halon

This type of extinguisher is good for all types of fires except electrical and magnesium–alloy metal fires. CO_2 is discharged at a temperature of less than $-210°F$ and is not very effective in open areas, where the wind can dissipate the discharge stream. Use CO_2 for fires in confined spaces under the dash and in the engine compartment, where wind isn't a factor. CO_2 does not leave a chemical residue behind and will not damage expensive electrical equipment.

Dry Chemical

This type of extinguisher is good for most automotive fires, but it has one serious drawback—it leaves behind a caustic powder that is highly corrosive. The chemical must be washed out of the area as soon as possible before it attacks wiring and paint. Also, this type of extinguisher must be recharged once triggered, regardless of how little is used. After the seal is broken, all the propellant leaks out.

Metal-X or Purple K

This type of extinguisher uses a potassium-based chemical that stops magnesium fires. Fires in engine blocks, transmission cases, and magnesium wheels are impossible to stop without this type of extinguisher.

- If the fire is caused by an electrical short and appears to be in the electric wires, try to disconnect the battery. If you can't get at the battery, or the clamps are too tight to wrestle free, you may need to cut the battery cable. Always try to disconnect the ground cable because it won't make sparks if you accidentally ground it to the frame. If no tools are handy, you can try using the jack handle and pry or knock the post off the battery to disconnect it. Be careful and forewarned: Sparks can cause the battery to explode!

- **Note:** Electrical fires are not affected by CO_2 fire extinguishers unless you can spray the CO_2 directly onto the short, cooling it down and depriving it of oxygen. In general, electrical fires continue to create heat until the battery is disconnected. Also, if the engine block or wheels are made of magnesium–aluminum alloy and catch fire, they can be extinguished only with a special purple foam (Class D) fire extinguisher.

Locked Out?

When was the last time you locked your keys in your car? Have you ever lost your keys? Sooner or later everyone has the awful experience of being locked out. There are some things you can do ahead of time to avoid the situation and there are some things you should know in case you do need to break into your own car.

Using a Slim Jim or Coat Hanger

First, check with the local police. Some carry slim jims around with them. Also check with parking lot attendants and nearby garages and gas stations. If you have no luck, you may find a slim jim at an auto parts store. Usually you will have to bend the slim jim to accommodate the curvature of the door.

If a slim jim is not available, use a coat hanger. Try to find one that is made from thick wire. Bend it straight and put a slight J-hook on one end. Be careful not to damage the car's rubber weather-stripping or paint. You might protect the car with duct tape. Move slowly—if necessary, use saliva to lubricate the coat hanger.

Try gaining access where the rubber molding surrounds the window, especially where it seals the rearmost edge of the passenger door window. You can always get in here in convertibles. Try entering with the coat hanger and snaring the door latch.

Always work on the passenger side door; this lock is usually easier to access. The driver's door may have additional electronic locking and window control units that make it harder to gain access to the lock mechanism.

Use a wooden wedge to pry a space between the window and the door. Put your face against the window and watch the door lock button or lever. A flashlight will help you see where you're going. When you are right on the lock mechanism, the button/latch should wiggle. If necessary, have an assistant watch the latch and report to you when you are making the latching mechanism wiggle. Now work the slim jim or coat hanger up and down as well as sideways until it opens.

After you successfully make contact with the latch mechanism, gently bang on the door with your fist or knee while jimmying the lock. Doing so helps the latch slip into the unlocked position in much the same manner that banging on the side of a pinball machine helps the ball go into the hole.

Sometimes the lock will open when you pull up on the latch, sometimes when you press down, and sometimes when you move it to the side. Experiment with different ways. Watch the latch to see which way makes it move a little and continue until it unlocks.

If the car has electric locking buttons, use a strong, stiff wire and press the unlock button.

Getting into an Asian Import
On some Asian import models, you can simply bend the top of the door frame away from the body to access the latch. Bending back the frame when you're done is easy.

Last-Resort Techniques
If you must break a window, pick the vent window or a small side rear window. These are the cheapest to replace.

Sometimes breaking a window is not an option. As a last resort, destroy the lock mechanism. If the door lock is separate from the latch assembly (especially in Asian imports), use a big screwdriver to turn the whole lock, tumbler and all. Insert the screwdriver just like a key and force the whole mechanism to turn. You can repair the hole in the door later with epoxy.

Other Ways to Get In

Dealer duplicates: Most newer cars have key codes listed at the dealership. All you have to do is contact the dealer who sold you the car and order another set. Sometimes the key code is listed in the paperwork that comes with the car.

Lock barrel dupes: In some cases, the door-lock key barrel can be removed and another key created using the tumbler setup for the doors. A locksmith will copy the pattern used for the door locks and create a master key that will operate the ignition. Of course, this won't work if the door key doesn't fit the ignition lock.

Hide-a-key: It is a good idea to buy a hide-a-key box and hide it somewhere secret under your car. The box has a magnet attached so you can hide it somewhere out of sight. Some car thieves are wise to this trick and will crawl under your car and try to find the hide-a-key. To foil them, put only a door or trunk key in the hide-a-key box, not an ignition key. Put the ignition key in a secret place inside the car or trunk. The thief will only be able to unlock the door, not start the car.

Call police: Calling the police, fire department, or other public servants is a last resort. These people don't always have the tools or knowledge needed to open your car without damage.

Home spares: It is wise to keep a spare set of keys at home in case you need them. You could call home and have someone bring them to you. Or it might be cheaper to take a cab to retrieve your spare keys than to hire a locksmith to break into the car.

Locksmith: You can get into your car faster and protect it better by seeking the advice and service of a specialist. Look for a member of a trade association for locksmiths. Members are trained in automotive-lock opening, tested regularly, and kept up to date on current materials and technology. Look for one or more of the following credentials: Associated Locksmiths of America (ALOA), Certified Registered Locksmith (CRL), Certified Professional Locksmith (CPL), or Certified Master Locksmith (CML).

Lost Key Risks

If a crook has found your keys and you have a name tag attached to the key ring, you face the possibility of having your car stolen right from your driveway. All the thief has to do is show up at your place late at night, unlock the car, and drive it away. If this possibility exists for you, it might be a good idea to have the lock cylinders changed. (See Chapter 14 for more information on avoiding car theft.)

Laser-Cut Keys

More expensive cars have keys that are cut using lasers. The key has double rows of notches on both sides of the key. These keys are very expensive to duplicate. On the plus side, the lock is impossible to pick; no thief can pick that many tumblers at once.

To Tow or Not to Tow

Your car has a problem, so you call a tow truck. What are the chances that towing your car from your driveway to the garage will do additional damage?

Towing isn't what it used to be. With the advent of computerized transmissions, front-wheel drive, four-wheel drive, unibody construction, and plastic air dams or fascias, towing modern cars is a big problem. If the vehicle is towed on its drive wheels, the damage to a transaxle can run as high as $5,000. The following sections describe the three commonly used tow methods and list their pros and cons.

Sling Towing

Sling towing is the traditional tow method—and is the one most likely to damage your car. When the sling is attached to the car's front end, it is likely to damage the front bumper. The sling also attaches to the frame under the car and, if the operator is careless when placing the hooks, front-end parts of your car can be damaged. A sling should never be used if there is an air dam or if the car has plastic front bumpers. Automatic transmissions in rear-wheel-drive cars will be damaged if the car is towed more than 25 miles.

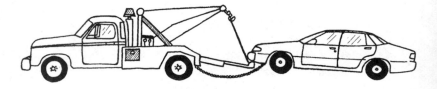

Wheel-Lift Towing

Wheel-lift tow rigs are the accepted norm of the towing industry today. They don't require attachment to the undercarriage and don't use the bumper to stop the car as the sling does. However, because this type of towing lifts by the front wheels, cars with air dams can still be damaged. And automatic transmissions in rear-wheel-drive cars will still be damaged if the car is towed more than 25 miles.

Flatbed Towing

Flatbed towing is the most expensive type, but it is also the best. The drawback of flatbeds is that they are unwieldy and require more room to maneuver into place. Also, it takes longer to load the car. After it is on the truck, the car is essentially out of harm's way. If not properly secured, however, the vehicle can still be damaged by the securing hooks or by shifting and hitting the front of the tow truck's headboard.

A good towing operation will have both wheel-lift and flatbed tow trucks. Although sling-style tow trucks are relics of the past in big cities, rural towing services still use them. If you have a late-model car and a sling tow truck shows up to tow you, refuse it! A reputable towing operation will ask you the year, make, and model of your car when you call. Consider asking the towing service what kind of truck it intends to dispatch.

Ten Breakdown Commandments

I. **Be calm.** Clear thinking is very important. If you get excited, you lose your ability to think clearly and react effectively. Stay calm. Stay alert.

II. **Move over.** You want to exit the road immediately. So as soon as you discover that your car has a problem, begin moving to the right-hand lane. Use your vehicle's momentum to get off the road. It is better to tough it out trying to cross traffic to the shoulder while you are moving than to break down in the middle of the road. Hesitation here may be deadly.

III. **Flash on.** As you're pulling over, put on your right-hand turn signal, not your four-way emergency flashers. If you put on your emergency flashers, traffic behind you won't know which way you are going. After you're off the road, turn on your emergency flashers.

IV. **Go right.** The right-hand shoulder of the road is the best place to stop. Truckers call this the breakdown lane. Pull as far off the road as possible, within reason. If the road has a hard shoulder and soft dirt beyond the shoulder, stay off the dirt. You don't want to be broken down and stuck, too.

V. **Avoid curves.** Get as far away from curves in the road as you can. Your car will be very hard to see on a curve. Keep going until you are a safe distance from the curve.

VI. **Exit right.** If you want to get out of your car, slide over to the passenger side and exit from that door. Watch for oncoming cars before you exit.

VII. **Seek safety.** If possible, climb up an embankment safely away from the car. If you can't get a safe distance from your broken-down car, it is better to stay inside with your seat belt on. The passenger seat is the safest place, away from the steering wheel. If there is only a guardrail and no room to get a safe distance from the car, don't leave your car.

VIII. **Stand alone.** Never stand directly in front of or behind your car or between two vehicles, such as the tow truck and your car. Stand near the front, as far away from the road as possible. If someone runs into your car, you don't want to be crushed!

IX. **Make yourself more visible.** Open the hood, even if you have only a flat tire. An open hood is the universal signal of a vehicle in distress. Light flares (if you have them) and put them 25 to 50 feet behind your car. Even a lantern or flashlight is helpful in making your car more visible at night. Put the "Send Help!" sign in the rear window. Tie a light-colored cloth to the antenna.

X. **Beware of strangers when you call for help.** If a stranger stops and offers you a ride, don't accept it. It's safer to ask the stranger to help you by contacting the police. Give the person some money and ask him or her to call for some help. If you do leave your vehicle behind, leave a note with your name, the date and time you left, the direction you're going, what you are wearing, a description and license number of any vehicle you get into, and the name of the driver.

Trouble Symptoms and Bad Vibes

Your car will usually give you telltale signs if it is having a problem or is about to leave you stranded. This chapter shows you how to recognize what your car is trying to tell you so that you won't wind up stranded on the side of the road—or even worse, broken down in the middle of the road. Your car can't talk, but it may still be trying to communicate with you. Here's how to listen.

Identifying Trouble Puddles

The puddle under your car can mean a lot of trouble if the puddle is not water. You can tell a great deal by checking out the color of the puddle.

Match the color to the problem, making careful note of the puddle's location:

- **Green puddles** mean leaking cooling system parts. If the leak is from the front engine area (where the drive belts are), the water pump is suspect. Leaks from the grille area are probably related to the radiator. Leaks from the dashboard area could be from a hose or heater core. Fix the leak before you ruin the engine.

- **Red puddles** are made up of automatic transmission fluid if the leak is in the area of the transmission. If the leak is from the radiator area, the cooler hoses from the transmission to the radiator are leaking. Fix the leak before it ruins the transmission.

- **Clear or light red puddles** indicate power steering leaks. This fluid is usually clear, although some cars use red automatic transmission fluid in their power steering units, which may fool you. It is important to pay attention to the exact location of the puddle.

- **Clear, thick, oily puddles** point to manual transmission or differential leaks. Gear lube has a strong, heavy-machinery smell. Finding the source of the leak will tip you off to what is leaking.

- **Blue puddles** indicate a leaking windshield washer bottle.

- **Dirty, dark, or black puddles** mean that you have motor oil leaks. Keep track of your oil consumption. If the engine is using more than a quart every 800 miles, the engine oil leak can be dangerous. If the oil is leaking on the exhaust system, it can cause a fire. *Tip-off*: Does the engine show signs of smoke after you shut it off?

Oil Leaks

A leak of one drop of oil every 20 feet approximates a loss of one quart of oil every 100 miles. A typical quart contains 36,000 drops of oil. Another common loss of oil is through the combustion chamber. For example, let's take a six-cylinder engine. One drop of oil passing by the rings on each piston every 1,100 firing strokes will consume one quart per 1,000 miles. Two drops will burn a quart every 500 miles. Putting it another way, if one-thousandth of a drop of oil passes by the rings on each firing stroke, the engine will consume a quart every 1,000 miles.

Checking for Leaks

Oil leaking out of the engine can be detected using a black-light leak detection system. A special fluorescent dye is added to the oil and the engine is operated until it leaks. When subjected to a black light, the fluorescent dye will leave a visible trace leading right to the leak.

The lazy way to find a leak is by placing a piece of cardboard under the car overnight. Make sure the cardboard doesn't touch the hot exhaust system. If there is oil on the cardboard in the morning, you have an external leak. Locate the place the leak is coming from by checking for the telltale spot on the cardboard.

To check for leaks that happen only when the engine is at road speed, tie a piece of light-colored cloth under the engine (be careful of hot exhaust parts). Oil on the cloth will indicate that the source of the leak is external.

An inexpensive way to find leaks is by using common foot-spray powder. First, clean and degrease the engine. Next, run it until it is dry. Finally, spray white foot powder on the suspect area and watch for the oil to start seeping out of the engine. It will leave a dark stain on the white foot powder.

Here are 19 reasons for oil loss or consumption, divided up into internal, external, and operational causes:

External Reasons for Oil Leaks

External gasket leaks: Valve cover gasket, drain plug gasket, fuel pump gasket, oil pressure sensor. These gaskets leak most when the engine is hot or under load.

External seal leaks: Front and rear main crankshaft seals and cam seals. These seals leak most when the engine is running at high rpms.

Fuel pump seal: A worn mechanical fuel pump can leak oil out its weep hole. Oil pressure sensing unit: Leaks most when the engine is hot at high rpms.

Internal Reasons for Oil Leaks

Worn or damaged bearings: Crank, rod, and cam bearings with excessive clearance throw off too much oil. The crankshaft tosses the oil up into the cylinders, which are flooded with more oil than the rings can handle. This extra oil goes into the combustion chamber and is burned.

Cylinder problems: Worn cylinders, improperly torqued head bolts, accessory mounting bolts distorting cylinders. Tapered or out-of-round cylinders permit oil to get past the rings into the combustion chamber.

Positive crankcase ventilation: Pcv valve not functioning. Crankcase ventilation is extremely important for controlling crankcase blowby gases that come from combustion slipping by the rings. A clogged pcv valve or hose or a dirty vent filter or valve cover baffle can stop pcv. Modern valve covers have a problem with the baffle coming loose, which allows oil to be drawn directly into the pcv system.

Piston ring problems: Worn or broken ring grooves, cracked or stuck rings, or rings installed improperly will permit oil to escape into the combustion chamber.

Valve problems: Worn valve guides, valve stems, or valve stem seals. Intake manifold vacuum will draw oil into the combustion chamber, especially during high-speed deceleration.

Connecting rod: A bent or misaligned rod will not allow the piston to ride straight in the cylinders, so oil leaks past.

Clogged oil passages: Oil drainback passages can prevent oil from returning to the oil pan. Accumulation of oil in the cylinder head will force oil past valve stem seals into the combustion chamber.

Cooling system: Poor engine cooling from rust, scale, or sediment can cause localized hot spots in some parts of the cylinders.

This distorts the cylinder bore, causing cylinder scuffing, scoring, and piston ring damage.

Operational Reasons for Oil Leaks

Fuel mixture: Too lean a mixture will overheat the pistons and rings, causing the rings to stick and break. Too rich a mixture will wash oil off the cylinder walls and wear the rings, too. Both lead to oil consumption.

Dipstick: Too much oil in the engine due to inaccurate dipstick readings will cause oil to be consumed. The crankshaft will churn the excess oil, making it splash.

Late valve timing: A stretched timing chain can cause the intake valve to stay closed too long after the intake stroke has started. This increases cylinder vacuum, sucking oil past the rings into the combustion chamber.

Oil pressure: A faulty pressure relief valve can let pressure get too high. The rods will squirt too much oil into the piston skirt, flooding the cylinders with oil.

Oil type: If the oil has too little viscosity, it will be drawn past the rings in excessive amounts. Switch to a heavier grade.

Driving habits: High-speed driving, pulling heavy loads, and jackrabbit starts cause high engine vacuum and crankcase pressure. These will push oil past the rings.

Short-trip driving: Causes the oil to be diluted with moisture and unburned gasoline. This keeps the oil level from dropping. Then, on a long trip, the oil level drops drastically because all of the gasoline is boiled out of the oil. Short trips do not warm the engine enough to boil out contamination.

Oil volatility: A large amount of oil is lost to boiling. Hot oil evaporates and is drawn into the combustion chamber through the crankcase ventilation system. One easy way to reduce oil consumption is to switch to synthetic. Petroleum oils are more than twice as volatile as Redline 100 percent synthetic oil.

Identifying Trouble Smells

Your nose can be a great diagnostic tool. Notice when a smell comes from your car. Is it when you start up, after you drive a while, at night, or when it is raining or damp out?

Match the smell to the problem:

- **Acrid chemical smells** that arise soon after the engine heats up mean that coolant is leaking onto hot exhaust parts, causing a strong odor similar to that of the inside of a new plastic bag.

The odor may be stronger if you are standing in front of your car because it is coming from under the hood. You also may smell it coming out the tailpipe if the coolant is leaking into your combustion chamber. Carefully check the coolant level and watch for a loss.

Get plastic smells checked out right away! They can cause a fire because coolant may catch fire and burn.

- **Chemical smells** inside the car after you've been driving it indicate that coolant is leaking from the heater core inside the car. This is sometimes accompanied by oily film deposits on the inside windows, especially the windshield. Sometimes it smells like an old refrigerator or new Styrofoam.

- **Rotten egg smells** can occur when you first start the car and at other odd times. This is a normal condition of an overly rich fuel mixture. The catalytic converter is too cold to properly burn off the rich mixture coming out of the engine. If this smell persists, something is causing the engine to run rich all the time.

- **Burned plastic smells** are most commonly caused by overheating wiring. Turn off all electrical accessories to see if the smell goes away. Carefully feel the fuse box to determine whether it is the source of the smell. Unplug the fuses one at a time, feeling each for telltale evidence of the heat problem. Also smell each wheel for dragging brakes. (See "Slaying 'Dragon Brakes'" in Chapter 2 for more information about this problem.)

- **Burning leaves smells** may arise if you park under a tree. Sometimes leaves get into the heater duct and fall against the blower motor resistor. This resistor gets red-hot and burns any debris lodged against it. Try removing the resistor to determine whether burned leaves are stuck to it.

Identifying Trouble Sounds

Does your car make a clunk when hitting a bump? Do you hear a squeak throughout the week? Tracking down persistent automobile noises is a real chore, but you can narrow the search by familiarizing yourself with some common causes.

Noises that change with *vehicle* speed include the following:

- Brake pad wear indicators rubbing on the rotors make a scraping noise. A stone caught in the rotor housing also makes this sound. Does pressing the brake make the noise go away?

- Loose, glazed, or slipping fan belts cause chirps, squeaks, clicks, and rattles. These noises are more common when you first start the car or when you're using an accessory such as the air conditioner or rear-window defroster. Does the noise happen when you're turning the wheel, when the A/C compressor cycles, or when you call the alternator into action by using the accessories?

- Clutch chatter or clunking when accelerating or stopping can be caused by a broken engine mount or engine strut. Pinpoint the problem: Does the noise become worse when the engine is in gear and the brake is applied (automatic transmissions) or when the clutch is released with the brake applied (manual transmissions)? Try Reverse as well. Also check for driveshaft noises by putting the car on a lift and listening to the driveshaft while someone inside the car shifts between Reverse and Drive with the brake applied.

- Exhaust noises come and go when the engine rocks back and forth. The exhaust doughnut sometimes leaks exhaust gas when the engine flexes the pipe. Do you feel exhaust residue at the pipe junction? With your fingers (when the engine is cold), rub the area around the exhaust joint. Do your fingers come up black from the leaking exhaust soot?

- U-joints (in rear-wheel-drive vehicles) make a clunk when they are too loose. U-joints can also become tight and cause a hard-to-find vibration at speeds greater than 45 mph. Remove the driveshaft and physically check the U-joints. Are they too loose? Do they bind?

- CV joints (front-wheel-drive vehicles) may knock, click, or cause steering wheel vibrations. Inner CVs clunk like U-joints when worn and loose. They also cause vibration at speeds over 50 mph.

- Wheel bearings make noises similar to U-joints and CV joints but usually at lower road speeds, especially on curves and turns.

- Driveshaft center bearings (RWD and 4WD vehicles) make noises similar to bad wheel bearings but are not affected by turns.

- A driveshaft imbalance (RWD and 4WD vehicles) is apparent at speeds above 45 mph, causing a high-speed vibration.

- Radial tire runout (egg-shaped tire) is most noticeable at low speeds. Lateral tire runout (bent rim) is most noticeable at higher speeds.

- Unbalanced tires (weights missing) are noticeable at speeds above 50 mph.

- Transmission tailshaft bushing (RWD and 4WD vehicles) causes a scraping or squealing noise that is detectable when you're accelerating or decelerating.

Noises that change with *engine* speed include the following:

- Misaligned pulleys and broken brackets for the alternator, A/C compressor, or power steering pump cause underhood engine noises. Do you see a broken brace?

- Timing belts make noise when loose. If the belt strikes the belt housing, it rattles or knocks. Loose timing belts cause backlash snapping inside the distributor (a knock or rattle), similar to a worn distributor bushing. Take a long hose and listen for the source of the sound. Where do you hear it coming from?

- Exhaust leaks make noise when cold and are quiet when hot. This is especially common in exhaust manifold leaks. The cast-iron manifold expands as it gets hot, partially sealing off the leak. Use a long piece of hose, such as a stethoscope, and listen for the source of the noise. You will hear the sound of escaping exhaust gases.

- Poorly installed exhaust systems clunk, rattle, buzz, or make droning noises. Sometimes the noises happen when you're accelerating, stopping, going over bumps, or idling.

- Air pump silencer mufflers lose the dampening material in the muffler and make noise when the air pump is vented to the outside. This sound is normal.

- Air conditioner or power steering hoses can make a drone or hum. Check for contact areas by looking for shiny spots where the hoses have been rubbing against something nearby.

Describing Sounds of Trouble

Your car can't talk about its problems. The engine can talk to you only by making noise. When your car starts sending you signals that something is wrong, you should take heed. The following chart lists sounds that you can describe to your mechanic to help him or her diagnose your problem.

Describing Trouble Sounds to Your Mechanic

Sounds Like	What to Call It
Continuous bass drum roll, distant thunder	Boom
Door buzzer, buzz saw far away	Buzz
Camera shutter, retractable ballpoint pen	Click
Heavy door closing	Clunk

Sounds Like	What to Call It
Sharpening an ax on a grinder, garbage disposal	Grind
Air escaping from a tire, steam from a radiator	Hiss
Someone knocking on your door	Knock
Marbles rattling inside a can, popcorn popping	Ping
Champagne bottle cork popping	Pop
Baby's rattle, stone bouncing around in a can	Rattle
Lion roaring, waterfall	Roar
Bowling ball rolling down an alley, distant thunder	Rumble
Screaming on an amusement park ride	Screech
Drop of water on a hot skillet	Spit
Branch breaking	Snap
Tennis shoes on a wooden court, door hinge needing oil	Squeak
Silverware being hit together	Tap
Bowling ball being dropped	Thud or thunk
Fan rubbing against its cage	Whir
Electric drill motor, mosquito	Whine

Explaining Car Problems

Often, the description of an automotive problem gets lost in translation. Communication is vital if you want to have the problem corrected the first time. The following chart lists some new vocabulary you can use when describing a problem to your mechanic. Study this list so that you'll be able to speak your mechanic's language.

Describing Automotive Problems to Your Mechanic

Problem	What to Call It
Pressing the brake pedal produces less and less braking.	Brake fade
The brake pedal moves when you apply the brakes.	Brake pulsation
The suspension runs out of travel and the body hits the rubber stop with a heavy thud.	Bottoming (also called bottoming out). This is like there are no shock absorbers and the chassis is hitting the frame with a thud.

Problem	**What to Call It**
You use the starter to turn the engine a slight amount without actually starting it.	Bumping the engine
A job done incorrectly has "come back" to be done again. A bad word to a mechanic.	Comeback
The engine is being turned by the starter but is not starting. The engine just turns over.	Cranking
Your car experiences a temporary or complete loss of power. The engine quits at sharp intervals. The problem may be intermittent or repetitive, and it may happen during acceleration or deceleration. It's like someone turning off the ignition.	Cuts out
The engine pings or pre-ignites. This problem can be mild or severe and is usually worse during acceleration. The engine makes sharp, metallic knocks that change with the rpms.	Detonation
The engine keeps running after you turn the key off.	Dieseling (named after diesel engines, which don't need ignition power to run)
The brakes apply too much with too little effort; they're overly sensitive.	Grabby brakes
You get a momentary lack of response as you press the accelerator. This condition occurs at all speeds but is most apparent when first starting. Severe cases can cause the engine to stall.	Hesitate (see also "Sag")
There is unwanted harshness, looseness, or reverse feedback in the steering wheel.	Kickback
The engine gives a sharp jerk or pulses. This problem is most noticeable at idle or low speeds and disappears at higher speeds.	Miss (also known as a misfire)
The car steers left or right by itself, either while you're driving or when you apply the brakes.	Pull
The engine runs unevenly at idle, sometimes making the car shake.	Rough idle

Problem	What to Call It
The vehicle doesn't respond immediately when you press the gas pedal.	Sag
A mechanic has done an incomplete alignment job without checking or setting the camber and caster angles.	Set the toe and let it go
The steering wheel moves rapidly from side to side or shakes when you hit a bump or use the brakes.	Shimmy
The engine delivers limited power when accelerating, under load, or at high speeds.	Sluggish
Your car gives less than anticipated response. With accelerating, refers to little or no increase in speed when depressing the gas pedal. With braking, refers to a soft or mushy brake pedal when stopping.	Spongy
The action of the engine coming to life. Firing up. Igniting.	Starting
The steering wheel is hard to turn first thing in the morning but is OK the rest of the day.	Steering morning sickness
The steering wheel must be turned farther than normal to make the car change direction; looseness in the steering wheel.	Steering play
The vehicle speeds up and slows down without your moving the gas pedal.	Surge
The steering wheel and the whole car shake, due to an out-of-round/imbalanced tire. This happens all the time, regardless of stopping or starting.	Tire tramp
The steering wheel pulls during acceleration or deceleration; this is typical of FWD cars.	Torque steer
You feel that you are pulling a trailer behind you; sudden or sharp onset/release; bucking.	Trailer hitching
The vehicle requires frequent steering corrections to keep on a straight course.	Wander

Dog-Tracking Blues: Rear-Wheel Misalignment

Have you ever noticed the car or truck in front of you *dog-tracking*? That's when the rear tires don't line up with the front ones. The term comes from observing how dogs' rear legs go off to the side when they run. Dog-tracking is a symptom of a rear-wheel misalignment problem.

If you draw a line from one rear tire to the other and make a perpendicular line forward from the center of that line, it should pass exactly between the center of the front tires. If the rear tires are not pointing exactly to the front, the line will be off center. This is called the *rear thrust line*, and when it isn't exactly in the middle of the front tires, the car dog-tracks down the road. The figure here shows an out-of-alignment vehicle and a properly aligned one.

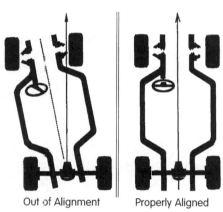

Out of Alignment   Properly Aligned

Dog-tracking usually goes unnoticed by the driver of the vehicle because it is impossible for that person to see what the rear wheels are doing. What the driver can notice is that the steering wheel is not centered or the vehicle pulls to one side. Careful examination of the front and rear tires may reveal uneven wear on one side.

Bad alignment can shorten the life of a tire by one-third. It also causes a small loss of fuel economy. Of the more than 170 million passenger cars and trucks on the road, some estimates say that 30 million could use a good four-wheel alignment.

Four-wheel alignments can find dog-tracking problems by measuring the thrust line of the rear wheels in comparison to the front wheels. The alignment mechanic can then make adjustments to the rear wheels to solve the dog-tracking problem. When having your car aligned, ask whether the shop offers four-wheel alignment.

Even shops that have four-wheel alignment equipment often don't check the rear wheels for thrust line problems. An estimated 59 percent of wheel alignment jobs done at dealerships are performed only on the front wheels.

To ensure that you get a real four-wheel alignment, ask the mechanic to print out the specifications for all four wheels before and after the alignment. Ask to have the readings explained in terms of which angles were out of spec and how the changes were accomplished. Some corrections are adjustable right on the car; some require special shims or correction kits.

If you suspect your car has a rear-wheel alignment problem, here are a couple of easy ways to find out:

Visual test: Have someone follow your car while you drive down a straight road. That person should look along the outside edges of both left tires as if sighting down a fence. Does the rear tire line up with the front along the left edges?

Tracking test: Find a flat, smooth driveway and hose down a 10-foot patch with water. Drive slowly in a straight line across the wet area. The wheels will then leave wet tracks on the adjacent dry area. Stop the car and slowly back up about six feet without moving the steering wheel. If your car is dog-tracking, the rear tire tracks will not match up when you back over the tracks that your car made while going forward.

12

Finding a Good Mechanic

Remember *The Andy Griffith Show*, in which everyone lived in the mythical town of Mayberry? Their cars all ran great, thanks to Goober, the world's best auto mechanic. Good ol' Goober. He could just pop a car's hood, listen for a moment, and identify the problem without the aid of computer diagnostic machines. Using only a screwdriver, he would dive under the hood, make a tiny adjustment to the engine, and—poof—the car was fixed.

Does such a person exist in the real world of auto repair? Are there still places where you can count on the best treatment, the lowest prices, and most important, honest service? The answer is yes . . . provided that you know where and how to look.

Understanding Shop Typology

As any experienced diner knows, you don't order burgers in a Chinese restaurant. The same holds true for repair shops: Going to a discount tire store for tires may be OK, but going there for transmission service may be a bad idea.

There are four basic types of repair shops: dealerships, specialty shops, independent general repair shops, and mass merchandisers. I'll compare them in the following paragraphs.

The *dealership* is where cars are first introduced to the motoring world. Dealerships usually have the best equipment and mechanics available—and sometimes the highest prices. When other mechanics give up on a problem, the car usually ends up at the dealership.

Dealerships are the place of choice for warranty repairs, extended service contracts, and emission repairs. Car owners who insist on factory-trained mechanics and original equipment parts typically take their vehicles to dealerships.

A popular misconception is that all repair and service work must be done at the dealership or the vehicle factory warranty is voided. In fact, anyone can do the work, provided that he or she performs all the necessary adjustments and services detailed in the owner's manual.

Specialty shops were born when the first factory-trained mechanics left dealerships to work on their own. These shops are generally a good bet. They offer service equal to the dealership at a lower cost. But they usually concentrate on just a few specific makes or models.

Independent general repair shops are as much an American tradition as apple pie. These shops handle all types of services and repairs on a wide variety of vehicles. Often, the owner is on the premises (one sign of a good shop), and the mechanics who work at a given independent shop are usually specialists for one type or make of vehicle. Independent shops tend to specialize in only one or two makes. Good independent shops develop a following of satisfied customers and generally provide the best service for the best price.

Mass merchandisers, or chain stores, offer bargains galore. But, to the unwary, they can also prove to be the most costly repair option because they may have quotas and use high-pressure sales tactics. (See Chapter 13, which discusses rip-offs in detail.) These places may be staffed by poorly trained, entry-level employees. In some cases, low-quality repairs can cause expensive damage to other parts—which you won't discover until much too late to do anything about it.

Example: David wants his Mercedes battery replaced. The dealer wants almost $200 for a battery, so David decides to have a department (chain) store auto shop install a new battery. While there is no installation charge, it takes almost two hours to complete the job. When David examines the car after paying the bill, he finds spilled battery acid in the battery tray, a loosely mounted battery, and grease prints on the white fender.

S hop chain stores for good prices on tires, batteries, and accessories, but don't take your difficult drivability problems to them. If you decide to go to a chain store repair shop, be sure that the repair is done properly and that other items are not damaged in the process. If possible, don't leave until you check the work.

Been Here Long, Neighbor?

If a shop isn't any good, it will soon be put out of business by either a bad reputation or the state's attorney general. The bad guys don't stay in one place very long. Typically, after a couple of years in a location, the shop closes and reopens under another name. As soon as word to stay away from the place gets out in the new neighborhood, the shop moves on to yet another location.

Ask how many years a shop has been in its location. A smart shop advertises its longevity. In many of the best independent and specialty shops, the name of the shop reflects the name of the owner or someone in his or her family.

Example: Mr. Ripp U. Off opened a shop on a busy street in town and advertised heavily in the newspaper. His gimmick was a two-year, 24,000-mile warranty on all repairs. Ripp had a big sign hung along the highway proclaiming his marvelous guarantee.

People came from all over to take advantage of Ripp's incredible warranty (incredible because most repairs are warrantied only as long as the parts, typically 90 days). Some parts carry a one-year warranty, but labor is extra. In other words, the part is replaced free, but you must pay for the labor to replace it.

How could Ripp make such an offer? Maybe he was counting on people moving too far away to take advantage of the warranty. Or perhaps he hoped they would lose their receipts or forget that the repair was still covered when it failed again. Could Ripp really believe that his parts and workmanship could outlast the warranty? Or did he secretly plan on moving before all those people came back for free replacements?

That's exactly what happened. Complaints started to mount. People became disgusted with Ripp's repair shop. The parking lot emptied out. Finally, he closed the doors and moved to another town, presumably to open again under another name.

Look It Over

Give the shop a good once-over. Is it well lit and properly ventilated, or is the air foul and junk piled to the ceiling? Take a good look at the shop floor. Is it covered with a decade's worth of grease and grime? That muck and mire will eventually wind up inside your car, probably on the carpet.

Conversely, if the shop seems more like an operating room than a garage, look out. The mechanics may not have anything to do but clean floors all day. A busy and efficient shop will be somewhat messy, especially by the end of the day—but not festooned with junk and old, worn-out parts.

Example: I once worked briefly in a shop owned by an alcoholic who, at one time, had been a good mechanic. But now he didn't care about anything but beer, which he consumed by the six-pack. The place was a mess. The parking lot was completely full of junked cars left behind because they were not worth fixing.

The lifts were old and rickety. They leaked hydraulic fluids and dropped cars without warning. Old driveshafts were used to prop them up so they wouldn't fall on us when we were working under them. The floors were so covered with filth that it was impossible to tell where the dirt parking lot ended and the shop floor began. If you dropped a small car part on the floor, it was lost forever.

Ask About Membership Affiliations

A good repair shop is involved in its community. Look for signs of involvement, such as photos, plaques, and trophies. Look for membership in groups like the Lions Club, Rotary, Better Business Bureau, Little League, Boy Scouts, and so on. A shop owner who cares about the community usually takes extra measures.

Professional and trade organization memberships are also a plus. Look for signs that acknowledge the shop's affiliation with groups such as AAA (American Automobile Association), ASE (National Institute for Automotive Service Excellence), ATRA (Automatic Transmission Rebuilders Association), ASA (Automotive Service Association), and ASC (Automotive Service Council).

Take the Diagnostic Test

Equipment is an important measure of any service facility. Does the shop have modern diagnostic machines? Do the machines appear to be in good working order? Does the equipment look as if it is in use, or is it shoved into a corner and out of the way?

Look around the write-up area for the credentials of the mechanic staff. Ideally, you should see certificates that match the brand names of the diagnostic equipment. For example, if the shop has an Allen Smart Engine Analyzer, at least one mechanic should have a training degree from Allen. Also, make sure that the certified mechanic listed on the certificate still works there.

Inspect the Cars in the Lot

One way to tell whether a shop is the right place for your car is to check out the other cars parked in the lot. Are there any cars like yours, or does your car stand out like a horse among donkeys? Is yours the only imported car in a lot full of domestics, or vice versa? Is your car the only new one while the rest look ready for the boneyard? Is the lot fairly deserted? What chased all the other customers away? Is the place about to go out of business? These signs are not good.

While you are looking around the lot, check the dust level on the parked cars. Do they look as if they have been there a long time? Does it look as though your car might join their ranks of the living dead? Maybe you should escape while you still can.

Size Up the Staff

Check out the staff and get a feel for their attitude. Do they seem helpful? Ask a few simple questions: How much is an oil change? What about a tune-up? How much time does a simple repair take? If the person waiting on you barks at you, acts angry, seems upset, or gives you an uneasy feeling, take your business elsewhere.

Determine Whether the Shop Wants Your Business

Is the shop booked for days or even weeks? Some shops really don't want any more business, so they treat regular customers with respect but treat newcomers so badly that they don't come back. You may be told that your car can't be worked on for an unreasonable period of time, or you may be quoted an unusually high price because the staff is trying to chase you away.

Example: Hojo John's repair shop had been in the same location for many years. Everything about the place was right. The owner was on the premises, the shop had been in the family for two generations, and it was located on a busy highway. The shop was always so loaded with work that it was difficult to find a place to park.

The shop's reputation in the community was great, but new customers were treated rudely and were often quoted very high prices. One man was told to get rid of his car because it was going to be very hard to fix, even though there was nothing wrong with it in the first place. Another person was told that the catalytic converter was cracked (a very expensive repair) when, in fact, the muffler had cracked open again. The reason? This new customer had recently purchased a muffler with a lifetime warranty from Hojo, who didn't want to replace the muffler and was trying to get rid of him.

Get to Know Shop Procedures

Before choosing a repair shop, check the length of the guarantee on the parts as well as labor. Some shops give the standard 90-day guarantee. Others offer guarantees for six months or even a year. Be sure to ask, or you may find out that you paid for a "taillight guarantee." This means they guarantee the job for only as long as they can see your tailights as you leave (about five minutes).

Talking to the customers sitting in the waiting room on a busy Monday morning is a good idea. Candidly ask how fairly they have been treated. Explain that you are considering the shop for your own car and that you'd like to know what they think about the shop. If people jump up and start yelling and shaking their fists, you'd better skip this one.

Ask about the parts the shop intends to use. Does it use original equipment parts, rebuilt or remanufactured parts, or name brands? What brands does it install? If you aren't sure about the quality of the brand, check with several parts stores and ask how good that particular brand is.

How Much Is This Going to Cost?

In these days of stretching a dollar, many people are looking around for a less expensive or more reliable repair shop. Hard times are also forcing people to wait until it is absolutely necessary before repairing their vehicles. Repair shops are noticing that customers are bringing their vehicles in with huge lists of work to be done all at once or waiting until the vehicle won't run at all before fixing it. In fact, more vehicles are being towed in than ever before.

When shopping around for a repair shop, you need to know some important things about how repair shops operate. If you understand the advantages and disadvantages of the different pricing systems, you are in a better position to choose which type of shop will best meet your needs for a particular type of repair. Here are the relative advantages and disadvantages of pricing by hourly clock rate, menu of prices, flat rate or commissions, variable flat rate, and flat rate plus parts commissions.

Hourly Clock Rate

In this system, you pay the posted garage labor rate per hour multiplied by the clock time necessary to complete the job.

Advantages

- It's easy to understand how the cost of each job is calculated.

- Calculating the cost of each repair is simple.

- It promotes quality work because the mechanic is paid to be on the job, not to hurry and finish as fast as possible.

Disadvantages

- Poor (slow) work habits can add to labor time.

- Technical problems encountered during the job can increase the hourly time needed to complete the job and end up costing you more than preset prices.

- Accurate estimates are impossible because the shop has no way of knowing how long a particular mechanic will take to complete a particular job.

Menu of Prices

Some shops have a preset price list for all jobs that they perform. These prices are usually set to compete with other shops in the area. Repair jobs are sometimes lumped together into a package (such as shocks, struts, tire rotation, and alignment).

Advantages

- It's easy to understand costs up front, before the job is started.

- The system is simple to implement, involving no variation from customer to customer.

- Customers are not penalized for poor (slow) work habits of the mechanic.

- The system is good for selling the total preventive maintenance job.

Disadvantages

- This system is not as profitable for the shop—an incentive to oversell.

- The shop must continually survey the local marketplace for competitive pricing.

- Package pricing can irritate customers who want only one particular job and not the whole package of items that the shop wants to sell.

Flat Rate or Commissions

The job cost is based on a published flat-rate manual, which lists the time it should take to complete every type of repair possible on every make, model, and year of vehicle.

Advantages

- The shop can control its job profits by adjusting its rates for labor.

- Cost estimating is simple.

- Customers are not penalized by poor (slow) work habits of the mechanic.

- The system encourages high mechanic productivity.

Disadvantages

- Problems with the job (frozen or rusted bolts, parts that don't fit right or are defective) can cause headaches for the mechanic, who is not paid for the time they take. He or she then tries to make up time and winds up cutting corners on the rest of the repair.

- Flat-rate manuals can be inaccurate, either undercharging or overcharging. Some flat-rate manuals published in the after-market give the mechanic the most time for a given job. The manuals published by the carmakers list the least amount of time for the job. This standard encourages mechanics to try to get back at management and beat the system. The result is shoddy repairs.

- Mechanics may skimp and cut corners to beat the flat rate, not carrying out all the job functions called for in the job description. You wind up with an improper, incomplete, or shoddy repair.

Variable Flat Rate

The job is priced not only by following the flat-rate manual but also by taking into account the skill level required to achieve it. A tire balance or oil change is a low-skill-level job and is priced at a much lower per hour rate than a job repairing a fuel-injection problem.

Advantages

- Mechanics will look for more problems and try to sell more work so that the shop can make more money. So the mechanic will take the time to go over your car and tell you about the things you need.

- The labor talent is maximized, so the mechanics with more skill receive more compensation than mechanics with less skill. This arrangement makes for a happier work environment and better job performance.

- The system encourages high productivity by creating a productive environment and happy workers.

- Customers don't pay high labor rates for unskilled work such as changing tires and mufflers.

- The shop can control job profits by adjusting labor rates.

- Cost estimating is simple; the shop can offer competitive pricing.

- Customers are not penalized by poor (slow) work habits of the mechanic.

- Customers can still question the skill level required to carry out a particular task.

Disadvantages

- Problems with the job (frozen or rusted bolts, parts that don't fit right or are defective) can cause headaches for the mechanic, who is not paid for the time they take. Job price estimating becomes more difficult. Also, flat-rate manuals can be inaccurate, either undercharging or overcharging. Mechanics may skimp and cut corners to beat the flat rate, not carrying out all the functions called for in the job description.

- Mechanics resent being paid at lower pay scales when called to do repair jobs below their functional level.

Flat Rate Plus Parts Commissions

In this system, the mechanic shares in the profits of parts sales as well as labor. The more parts sold, the more the mechanic makes on the job.

Advantage

- Mechanics will look for more problems to sell more work so that the shop can make more money. This pricing structure means your car will be carefully looked over and any impending problems will be brought to your attention.

Disadvantages

- Mechanics will be less likely to fix a problem part and will call for a replacement instead, making more money for the shop and themselves.

- Customers may be sold parts they don't need or sold new parts when the old ones can easily be repaired.

The following table tells where you are most likely to encounter which type of repair billing system.

Where You'll Find the Different Types of Billing

Billing Type	Where You'll Find It
Hourly clock rate	Specialists, dealerships, and family-run independent repair shops; example: automotive electrical repairs
Menu of prices	Specialty shops like brake, muffler, and transmission repair shops
Flat rate or commissions	The most common method used today by all types of shops
Variable flat rate	Dealerships
Flat rate plus parts commissions	Chain stores and mass outlets; examples: tire and department stores

Fixing It "Write" the First Time

When you take your car to a repair shop, you have less than a 50/50 chance of getting the problem fixed the first time. Communication is a major problem. You ask for one thing to be looked at or repaired and wind up having something different done, maybe something you didn't even know was necessary.

You'll be ahead of the game if you go to the repair shop equipped with a complete, written description of the problem (typed neatly if possible). Here are some questions the mechanic may ask when doing the vehicle prewrite-up:

- When does the problem occur: hot, cold, or while warming?

- Does it happen when you first start the car or after you have been driving? How far do you have to drive before it happens?

- Is the problem intermittent? Can it be duplicated so that the mechanic can witness it?

- What is the engine speed when the problem occurs? Does it happen at road speed? At idle?

- Does it occur on the highway?

- Does it happen during acceleration, deceleration, steady speeds, or braking?

- Does the grade of the road have anything to do with it?

- Does turning the car cause the problem to happen or stop?

- When did it first start happening? Did it begin after the car had been worked on?

- Does running the defroster, air conditioner, or other accessories have anything to do with the problem?

- If your car has power steering, does turning the wheel change anything?

- Does hot, cold, rainy, snowy, or damp weather have any bearing on the problem?

  Also be prepared to provide the following:

- The car's basic statistics: whether it has automatic transmission, power steering, A/C

- The size of the engine

- A history of the problem: when it began and what has been done to fix it

If you are not sure what has been done, bring copies of repair orders to help identify previous repairs.

13

Meeting Mr. Ripp U. Off

Disreputable Mechanics and Other Rip-Off Artists

Automobile service and repair can be cash cows for rip-off artists. Anyone can rent a garage, don some overalls, put out a sign that says "Mechanic on duty," and start fixing cars. In most states, licensing of mechanics is not a requirement and probably never will be. Meanwhile, scams and flimflams abound.

Recognizing Mr. Ripp U. Off's Trademarks

When visiting a repair shop for the first time, keep an eye out for Mr. Ripp U. Off's trademarks. Look for one or more of the following indicators:

• The shop does a diagnostic on your car and charges you for the work even though you didn't request it. When you ask why a diagnostic was ordered, Ripp tells you something like, "We have to do this to establish a baseline for your car," or "We do this to all first-time customers."

• The shop doesn't offer a written diagnosis of the problem. Ripp tells you only *what* your car needs. He never bothers to tell you *why* your car needs it.

• Ripp tells you that it is impossible to give you a written estimate before starting to work on your car. He says, "I have no way of knowing how much your transmission problem is going to cost until I take it apart." By then, it's too late to leave.

• You don't see any mechanics' credentials posted (Ripp doesn't have any).

- The atmosphere makes you uneasy, and your intuition tells you to stay away. Maybe it's the 13 junked cars out back.

- Ripp tries to scare you with statements like, "I wouldn't trust my family in that car anywhere. You could be stranded at any time."

- You see Ripp's favorite signs posted: Cash only. No checks. No credit cards.

Protecting Yourself

Here are some general tips for protecting yourself from being ripped off:

- Communication is the key to getting a successful repair. Find a shop where you can talk with the mechanic directly. If you can't, prepare a neatly printed or typed page describing *exactly* what is wrong with and/or what you want done to the car. Attach the note to the dash.

- Ask for an estimate written on shop stationery or a work order. Scribbled numbers on a notepad are useless in court. Many states require shops to provide a written estimate, but *you must ask for it.*

- Shop around for the best hourly rates and job costs. Hourly rates vary, as do parts markups. Ask how much the *total* job will cost—including incidentals like solvents, shop rags, environmental fees, and surcharges.

- Ask how long the work is guaranteed and how long the parts are warrantied. Ask who pays for the labor if the part fails. Get a written guarantee.

- Write on the repair order near the bottom, "No other work is authorized without owner's consent." Point this statement out to the service advisor.

- If the job involves interior work, paint, body work, and frame work, ask whether the shop plans to subcontract the work. Go to the shop and talk with the subcontractor. Tell him or her that you will not settle for anything less than top-quality work.

- If the shop tells you that providing a realistic estimate for the entire job is impossible, get costs for teardown and reassembly alone. Doing so provides you with a ballpark estimate *and* a built-in escape hatch if you decide you don't want to go through with it.

     Example: Billy had 140,000 miles on his car when he started to hear a knocking from his engine. The shop diagnosed the

sound as a rod bearing but said that it couldn't give him an estimate until a mechanic tore down the engine and looked inside.
He asked for a teardown estimate. The shop estimated $485 to
remove the engine, open it up, and determine the cause of the
knock. Additional costs would crop up, depending on the actual
problem and the cost of reassembly. Instead, Billy decided to
have a used engine with low mileage installed for $800. By know-
ing the cost of the teardown before he told the shop to do it, he
was able to avoid spending money on an engine too old to be
repaired easily. He saved over $300.

- When signing the repair order, write neatly across the bottom,
"Save replaced parts for customer inspection." The mechanic
doesn't know whether you are from the consumer protection
division of the state's attorney's office, the Better Business
Bureau, or what. This statement alerts the mechanic that he or
she had better be careful.

- Women, no matter how knowledgeable you are, take a man along
when you go in for the write-up. Find a male friend who looks
like Mr. Clean to go along and watch. He doesn't have to say a
thing. In fact, if he says something, he may tip off the mechanic
to his lack of knowledge. If your friend remains silent, however,
the mechanic has no way of knowing what Mr. Clean knows.
Unscrupulous service people still see women as an easy mark.
Having a male observer can make a big difference in how you
are treated.

- Place several quarters in plain sight on the dash, console, or
floor. If any are missing when you pick up the car, look out. You
are in the clutches of Ripp. Anyone who will steal change will
also cheat you on repairs.

Avoid Disreputable Shops

If you don't take your car to Mr. Ripp U. Off's shop, the chances
of his chiseling you are zero. Do a little homework. Never
mind the Yellow Pages ads. Whom do your friends and co-work-
ers recommend? Whom do they say to avoid? You may not escape
Ripp altogether this way, but you'll narrow your exposure
considerably.

Pay with Plastic

Whenever possible, pay with a credit card or gas company charge
card. Your credit card is the best defense if a dispute arises, because
federal law allows you to refuse to pay the charge. Phone calls are
a waste of time. Write a letter stating why you are unhappy with
the work for which you were charged. Send a copy to the charge
card company and the shop. The charge card company will charge

the bill back to the shop, forcing it to sue if it wants your money. Courtrooms give Ripp headaches because all the dirty facts of his bad job will come out.

That's why Ripp posts a sign saying, "No credit cards, no checks. Cash only." If you see this sign, leave!

Understanding the Rip-Off Doctrine

Sometimes it would be good to have a lawyer in your back pocket, especially when it comes to dealing with unscrupulous repair establishments. Lawyers can see the earmarks of a swindle in progress and can carefully take the right legal steps to prepare for the possibility of future litigation. Wouldn't it be great to be able to spot the makings of a rip-off beforehand?

If you know the signs of a scam in the making, you may be able to avoid the situation in the first place or at least engage in *damage control* to minimize your losses. If you suspect that something is amiss after work has begun, it is vital to carefully document the exact process. Make notes as you go along. Write down the names, dates, and people you deal with. This will help you prevail in litigation if it becomes a necessity.

The following sections give you a short field guide to the different types of rip-offs you might encounter.

Parts? What Parts?

You ask for the return of replaced parts (a law in most states) but the repair shop fails to return them or returns only some of them. When pressed about where the remaining parts are, the shop representative or service advisor is unable to offer an adequate explanation.

Example: When asking for the return of his parts, a customer noticed that there were only six items returned when the bill listed eight. He asked why there was a difference; the shop could not offer any reason for the discrepancy.

Write in bold capital letters on the repair order: "Keep replaced parts for customer's inspection."

Value Added

When you ask for a certain type of repair to the vehicle, the rep or service advisor automatically adds another type of service or labor operation. Or after you leave, additional repairs are added to the work order.

Example: When you ask for a tune-up, the shop charges an additional $75 for a diagnostic analysis that you "have to have."

Authorize only those repairs necessary to cure the problem. Ask, "Is this repair going to cure the problem?"

Example: You bring the vehicle to the shop for a brake special. You sign the repair order and leave, thinking the brake pads will be replaced for $39.95. When you return, the bill is almost $600. In addition to the brake special, the repair order lists new calipers, rotors, wheel cylinders, and shoes.

Always ask for a copy of the repair order after you sign it. Sometimes a rep will be in a hurry and forget to get your signature. Remember, the document is not legal until you sign it.

The shop is doing routine scheduled maintenance and calls with terrible news about the vehicle. It was in perfect condition but suddenly needs a high-ticket item. It's entirely possible that a mechanic made a mistake and destroyed the part, creating the problem. You are told that the problem "definitely" existed before the vehicle arrived at the shop for the routine service.

Example: Your vehicle is undergoing routine maintenance. You receive a call from the mechanic, who tells you that the engine is in terrible shape and will not last much longer. The shop pressures you to have another engine installed immediately. The *real* story is that the mechanic changing the oil didn't tighten the oil filter when he installed it during routine maintenance, and all the oil leaked out. Now the engine has a bad rod knock.

Have the vehicle inspected by a different shop before authorizing anything further.

Invoice Shock

A relatively minor electrical repair is being performed and suddenly the shop calls to say that the car has *major* electrical problems. The shop tries to scare you into having several items replaced because the charging system is "too weak to keep the new battery charged." The vehicle didn't exhibit these problems when it was brought in, but now the shop "discovers" that several expensive items need to be installed.

Example: You are having your battery replaced because it is nearing the end of its five-year warranty and you don't want to be stranded. The service advisor calls you to the counter and says that the alternator and voltage regulator are faulty and need to be replaced as well. Those items were functioning when the vehicle was brought into the shop. In reality, no one ever opened the hood or performed any diagnostics on the vehicle. The shop is just trying to sell additional parts and labor without ever properly checking the system.

Authorize only replacement of the item that you agreed on and ask for proof that the other electrical items are faulty. If necessary, get a second opinion.

Milking the Cow

Your car won't start and is towed to a garage for starter problems. The garage lists several items that need to be repaired. In fact, only one item involved in the starting system is needed to repair the vehicle, but the shop says other items are also defective.

Example: The vehicle fails to turn over one very cold morning. You have it towed to a garage and are told that the car needs a starter, alternator, and battery. In reality, the starter and alternator are perfectly good; only the battery needs replacing.

Have the vehicle inspected by a different shop. Make this a rule for any repair costing more than $100.

The Big Con

Replacing a clutch or transmission is often used as an opportunity to sell a new engine even if the current engine is in perfect working order.

Authorize only those repairs necessary to cure the problem. Be on the alert for "snowballing" repairs. Get a second opinion.

Example: The clutch is being replaced because it is slipping. The shop calls you and says that the engine will need replacement in the very near future. The shop encourages you to replace the engine now, while the vehicle is already apart.

Warranty Wringer

A repair is covered under warranty, so you don't expect any cost. But warranty repairs are sometimes viewed as an opportunity to gouge the owner for other, nonwarranty items. The shop insists that the other repairs are necessary to carry out the warranty work.

Example: Your car is towed to the dealer because it won't start. You are told that the computer was bad and is covered under warranty. But when you pick up the car, you are presented with a bill for a major tune-up, including a new distributor and ignition coil. You are told that the other work was necessary because those things caused the computer to go bad.

When warranty repairs are made, write on the bottom line of the repair order, "Only warranty repairs are authorized."

Line Up the Loot

Alignments are one of the biggest scams in the industry. You may be told that an alignment was performed, but the steering still pulls or the tires wear out quickly. In truth, no standard exists for what items are to be adjusted or corrected in an alignment.

Example: You are buying a new set of tires because the original ones wore out quickly. You purchase an expensive set of tires and have the vehicle aligned. The new tires wear out prematurely. The shop blames it on you and says you must have hit a pothole or curb. In reality, it never did a proper alignment on the front end

Ask for a printout of the vehicle's alignment specifications before and after the alignment is performed. The printout will show the normal readings and the current readings. If something is still wrong with the alignment, you have printed evidence of it, especially if the alignment wasn't carried out properly and some alignment angle wasn't adjusted. Also, you now have a document showing the alignment angles were correct when the car was given back to you.

of the vehicle. (The factory alignment may have been thrown off when the car was unloaded from the truck.)

Missing Pieces

The vehicle is dropped off without any body damage or missing parts. When you pick it up, there is a missing hubcap or a new dent in the door. The shop claims that the problem was there before you left the vehicle.

Example: You drop off your car before the shop opens, using the early-bird key drop. When you pick up the car, the expensive wire wheel covers are missing. The shop claims that the covers were never there.

Bring the vehicle in during working hours. Walk around it and point out to the service advisor that there are no physical problems (scratches, dents, and so on) and that all the wheel covers are present. For example, say, "Look, there are no missing hubcaps. My car has no dents in the doors and there are no grease prints on the fenders. I would like it returned that way."

Automatic Dollars

Be careful when getting your automatic transmission serviced. Shops often scare owners by showing them the drain pan and claiming that the material in the pan is reason to rebuild the transmission. Remember that it is normal to find solid material (clutch pieces and metal shavings) in the drain pan.

Example: You take your vehicle to a transmission repair chain for a $19.95 service special. You are told that the transmission is in horrible shape and is about to fail. The drain pan is offered as testimony to the problem. The pieces of material in the pan are said to be evidence of impending doom.

Chain Store Shuffle

Chain stores often use alignments to produce additional revenues. Customers are told that additional items are required so that the alignment can be done.

Tell the repair shop that you are going to have the transmission inspected by a different shop.

Example: You bring the vehicle to an auto repair chain for an alignment special. You are told that the vehicle's springs are sagging and that the shop will need to install spring inserts between the coil springs to correct the sag so it can perform the alignment. You are charged $10 to $20 for the inserts. In reality, spring inserts cost less than a dollar—and you don't need them in the first place.

I f it sounds fishy, get a second opinion. **Never** let anyone install spring inserts. They are a rip-off.

Disreputable, or Just Plain Dumb?

Some situations aren't really an intentional rip-off but rather the product of employee stupidity. Nevertheless, you're the victim, so watch out. Dealing with fly-by-night operations or places known to employ many novices, such as discount department store chains, chain auto stores, or parts stores with repair facilities, is just asking for trouble. Here are two examples.

High-Tech Hassles

Routine service is performed, and not long afterward a major electrical fault occurs. The repair shop denies any responsibility. In reality, its carelessness inadvertently caused an expensive high-tech solid-state item to fail, even though the failure didn't occur immediately.

Example: The vehicle is tuned up, battery cables are cleaned, and the oil is changed. A few days later, the digital dashboard or the on-board computer fails. Why? A novice mechanic left the ignition key in the On position when the battery cables were disconnected to be cleaned. This weakened the transistors, which failed within a few days.

Losing Your Cool

You are having your car's cooling system worked on. Afterward, the engine overheats and is damaged. The shop is sympathetic, but the repairs will be very expensive.

Example: You take the vehicle in to have the coolant flushed and replaced. A routine maintenance to the cooling system is carried out. Suddenly the mechanic discovers major problems with the cooling system: The head gasket is leaking, and the vehicle will overheat unless repaired immediately. There was no coolant loss before the vehicle was brought in for the routine maintenance.

As you drive away, the engine overheats almost immediately. You return to the shop and are told that additional items, including a new head gasket, are needed to repair the problem. The vehicle wasn't overheating initially, but now it needs a major repair. Why? When the mechanic drained and refilled the radiator, air bubbles were trapped inside the engine and the mechanic didn't properly purge the air. The engine overheated and blew the head gasket.

Have the vehicle serviced only by a trained, veteran mechanic. Ask how long the mechanic assigned to your job has been working as a mechanic. Ask to see credentials, certificates, and anything else that shows his or her qualifications.

Complaining Effectively

What do you do if you get the car back and it's not fixed? Or they broke something else? Or you're not satisfied for some other reason?

Your first response may be to run right down there and throttle somebody. Well, not really throttle, but . . . holler a little. The trouble is that service managers and shop owners get this treatment all the time. Most have developed a callus on the conflict resolution area of their brains. They may even see your ranting and raving as justification for ripping you off. So save your shouting for the ballpark. If you want satisfaction, you need to use calculated diplomacy.

Call first. Alert the shop that you're coming in. Just showing up with the problem will generate animosity. Worse yet, the mechanics may be so busy that they either can't get to your problem immediately or they do a quick fix with no lasting results. A phone call paves the way.

Be calm. Determine in advance to be calm. After all, you may be mistaken. Even if you're right, the best way to get your car fixed is to deal person-to-person in a rational manner. Statements like "I'll sue you for every penny you've got" are much more effective on subsequent visits. Keep in mind that you may have to stage a blowup at some later point; it will mean more if you've previously been calm and cool.

State the problem. Do not attempt to diagnose what has gone wrong. The problem may or may not be related to the repairs. Don't blame the shop until it is apparent that the shop caused the problem. If the problem persists from a previous visit, make it very clear that you want your money back or the problem fixed.

Get a second opinion. You may want to have a different shop look at the car before you return it to the first shop. Have them examine the suspect repairs and generate a work order spelling out what was done wrong.

Example: You have a clutch installed. Now your car lacks power. You have a second shop look over the work done by the first shop. The second shop finds loose vacuum hoses, missing bolts, and so on. If you had returned to the first shop, it would have covered up the sloppy work and you would never have known.

Go to the top. Don't waste your time arguing with someone who likes to argue with customers. Ask to speak to someone in the next management level. Be prepared to go all the way to the top of the organization, if necessary. It may take some time before you reach someone who actually cares if you are satisfied. Persist. Don't waste your time with people who have neither the power nor the authority to help you.

Tell the boss. Always let someone in upper management, preferably the owner of the business, know about shoddy work. The employees aren't going to admit they messed up. If you don't complain, the owner will assume that everything is fine. Give him or her a chance to be involved and make it right.

Document everything. Always plan ahead for your day in court. Without a written record, it's your word against theirs. Not only do well-documented facts further your case, but producing them says you mean business and are determined to prevail. Keep all old repair orders.

Take notes on all telephone conversations and keep records of each visit. Write down the names of everyone you talked to, his or her position, what was said, and the date and time of the conversation. Put your complaint in a letter as soon as the problem begins, to document the event. Send a follow-up letter after each visit. Describe what transpired and what, if anything, has been done to rectify the problem.

Suggest a solution. How can the shop satisfy you? Suggest a way for the shop to make good, a solution that lets it off the hook. Be realistic about the remedy. If you don't know a good solution, have someone from another shop give you suggestions.

Get help. If you can't seem to get the problem resolved at the shop, try bringing in the big guns—the following powerful allies available in your own community:

- **Your state's attorney general:** Routing complaints through this office is typically a slow process but sometimes effective. At the very least, your complaint against that business will be registered and kept on record. If the shop receives enough complaints, its business practices may be investigated.

- **Autocap:** This arbitration board deals with problems with certain brands of new cars (Alfa Romeo, BMW, Honda, Isuzu, Jaguar, Mazda, Mitsubishi, Nissan, Rolls-Royce, Subaru, Toyota, and Volvo).

- **Better Business Bureau:** This agency deals with new car arbitration for certain brands only (Audi, GM, Honda, Nissan, Peugeot, Porsche, Saab, and Volkswagen).

- **Department of Motor Vehicles:** This agency can revoke the operational license of a car dealer. Now, there's power! The DMV deals with problems in warranty coverage and abatement.

- **Media:** Your local TV stations, radio stations, and newspapers may have consumer action services that could help resolve the problem.

If you are complaining to more than one community resource, it's better not to mention the others that you've contacted. Each agency has its own system of operation. Some can take months to respond to your complaint, and if it appears that other agencies are involved, some will drop your case in deference to the others.

Example: If the local TV station's action line sees that you're taking your problem to the attorney general, it may ignore your case.

The best way to circumvent a problem with the repair shop is to have a good working relationship in the first place. Get to know your mechanic and stay with that person. Let him (or her) know how happy you are about his work, and don't forget him on the holidays. Also, send a thank-you note (and maybe doughnuts or cookies) after your car has been fixed.

Writing a Complaint Letter

Communication is crucial to having a satisfactory repair experience with a shop. First, communicate the exact state of the car. Second, communicate exactly the repairs you expect to receive or the result you want. And finally, communicate exactly why you are satisfied or dissatisfied with the results.

When the repair doesn't fix the problem, people often immediately assume that the shop is at fault. In some cases, the problem was never properly communicated in the first place. Then the shop was never informed that it did something wrong. Over 90 percent of the customers who stop doing business with a repair shop make no effort to tell the shop about their dissatisfaction. They simply don't go back.

About 70 percent of unhappy customers don't complain to the shop because they feel it's not worth their time and the shop probably won't be interested in what they have to say anyway. On average, an unhappy customer tells nine or ten other people, but a happy one tells only five. Nearly 95 percent of unhappy customers would come back again if the shop solved their problem quickly and satisfactorily.

Following is a list of tips and techniques for writing an effective complaint letter. This list is for both shop owners and the motoring public and is written to help improve people's satisfaction with the repair process. You can apply these letter-writing guidelines to any type of problem or service.

Document, document, document. Start by taking notes at the very first hint of a problem. Be sure to get the full names of those with whom you deal. Never trust your memory. Your emotions may cause you to jumble things together; some events may be forgotten completely and others may be colored by your frustration. Write down everything that comes to mind. Also, get the date, time, place, rank of management, and anything else that might prove valuable in writing an effective complaint letter. Months later you might be asking yourself, "Who was the gruff guy who was rude to me on the phone?"

If your car has been back more than once, or if other repair shops have attempted the same repair, include copies of the documents associated with those attempts. Never send the originals. Make sure that the copies are dark and legible. Be sure to keep the original of every receipt—even if you are satisfied with the repair.

State the problem clearly. Don't beat around the bush. State your problem with the shop as clearly and succinctly as possible. If your car still clunks on bumps, keep your discussion to that topic. Many people state the entire repair history of the vehicle before getting to the point and relating the current problem. Don't volunteer all the details of the car since you purchased it. Save it. If the need arises for a detailed chronological history of the vehicle, you will be asked. Don't waste time telling how your neighbor had a car with the same problem, and he had the widget sensor replaced and . . .

Get a second opinion. Have a family member, co-worker, or business associate read your letter before you mail it. You may not have stated something clearly. Sometimes a neutral third party will see other aspects of the problem that you haven't. If you have a difficult time composing the letter, spend the money to have an attorney do it on his or her letterhead. That action always gets immediate attention.

Paint the outcome. A letter that doesn't steer the shop in the direction of resolution isn't likely to produce the result you intend. If you come right out and state your desire for an amenable solution, you give the shop something to work toward. Tell it what you want it to do. At the same time, don't make unreasonable requests.

Share responsibility. Sometimes both you and the shop share responsibility for the problem. If this is true, say so in your letter. Offer to help with the resolution. This gesture will make you appear less of an enemy to the shop and will more likely resolve the problem.

Set a deadline. Your letter should have a timetable for resolution. Make it clear that if they don't meet the time limit, you will go to more drastic measures. Typically you should give the shop 10 working days to smooth out the problem before you "seek resolution with the courts."

Watch that attitude. Keep the tone slightly on the positive side of neutral. Name-calling and threatening will only alienate the shop further. Remember the saying, "You can catch more flies with honey than with vinegar." Your letter is not a place to vent your frustration, especially if you really want to motivate the shop to fix your problem. Remember, your letter may be the first time management becomes aware of your plight with their staff. They may be very grateful that you took the time to share your problem with them instead of just taking your business elsewhere.

Document pain and suffering. Keep careful records of all out-of-pocket expenses involved in your attempts to resolve the matter. Record the time you spend on the phone, trips back and forth, and time you spend talking with others as part of the resolution process. Did you lose time at work? Did the improper repair jeopardize your safety? Did you make any long-distance calls? Did you have to borrow or rent a car?

State the case. Tell the shop up front exactly what you plan to do if it fails to take care of the situation. Give the name of your attorney and your intention to litigate if the shop doesn't take care of you. Keep the tone of the letter as neutral as possible. Just make it clear you mean business.

Photocopy it. Be sure to list several other consumer agencies (either inside or outside the company) to which you are sending copies of the letter. When the shop sees the list, it will be motivated to solve the problem as quickly as possible. No one wants the Better Business Bureau or the Consumer Protection Agency breathing down his or her neck.

Look professional. Don't send a handwritten letter. If necessary, pay someone to type it for you. The more professional the letter looks, the more impact it will have. Be sure to keep a copy for your own records.

Use good grammar and make the letter simple, plain, and easy to read. Don't belabor the point. Don't repeat yourself. Summarize the letter in the opening paragraph, and reread it to make sure it is sensible and easy to understand. Ask a friend or co-worker to read it for clarity.

Be available. Make sure that the shop can contact you easily to resolve the problem. Give both work and home phone numbers or the phone number of someone with whom they can leave word. Forcing them to resort to answering your letter with another letter can really frustrate them and drag things out. If you are afraid to deal with them by phone, seek the help of a friend or family member.

If the matter involves a large amount of damages, you would be wise to seek the help of an attorney in the negotiation. If an attorney handles the letters and follow-up phone calls, the shop will likely resolve the problem quickly.

Targeting Insurance Fraud

Ripp is the modern equivalent of a carpetbagger. He and his cronies have bogus birth certificates and driver's licenses under fake names. They rent a cheap apartment and have a phone installed. Their only furnishings are an answering machine and a phone jack.

As Ripp and his cohorts set the stage for their scam, they buy cheap, older vehicles and insure them with the minimum required liability insurance. Next, they purchase a wrecked car from another state—a car that was totaled but is still drivable—making it almost impossible to track insurance records and vehicle identification numbers (vins). Now the final step: a staged accident between the older car and the out-of-state totaled (yet drivable) car. The accident scene is set in a parking lot or some other location, always on private property so that the police do not have to be involved. The older car is smashed badly enough to be totaled and the drivable total is totaled again. Then the insurance companies pay for it twice.

Insurance scams like this one are operating in all of America's major metropolitan areas and are driving insurance rates through the roof. These scams involve no personal injury, and because damages are purposely kept below $5,000, they easily escape notice. Insurance adjusters are quick to reimburse small claims of a few thousand dollars and don't play hardball when it comes to settling. They just want to move the claim through the system quickly and get on to more serious accidents.

In a recent fraud case, when the perpetrator was caught he had at least 15 aliases, four social security numbers, and nine different driver's licenses. He is believed to have fleeced insurance companies for more than $1 million in the past few years. Another fraud ring was caught after filing 11 different claims worth more than $45,000 while using the same car, a totaled BMW that was still drivable.

You can help fight the rising costs of car insurance. Fraud is a major component in insurance price escalation, and only consumers can really fight the battle. One of the best ways to fight insurance fraud is to avoid insurance scams. Common types of fraud include staged auto accidents, arson for profit, exaggerated injury claims, and phony or inflated theft claims. Here are some tips from the AAA to help fight this problem:

- Always have the police respond to the scene of an accident when there are any injuries. Be sure the police officer makes a complete list of the passengers in the other vehicle on the accident report and crosses out the spaces for additional names. Make your own list of all passengers in the other vehicle, noting their physical descriptions, names, and addresses. Be sure to get license and registration numbers. If possible, take pictures of the accident scene, including the injured victims.

- If you're injured, verify that the bills submitted by your doctor to your insurance company list only services that were actually performed. Never sign a blank medical form.

- If you suspect insurance fraud, check it out. Get involved. The end result will be lower premiums for you and everyone else. Call the insurance fraud hot line at 800-327-3202 for confidential help or to report suspicious activities. Or call the National Insurance Crime Bureau at 800-TEL-NICB.

Avoiding Rental Car Rip-Offs

When renting a car, pay attention as the final bill is being totaled. If you are entitled to a discount on the rental costs, be sure the discount is applied toward your final bill. Rental agents have been known to "forget" discounts. Once you sign the charge slip and leave the rental agency, you may have a difficult time recovering the discount due.

Whether on the phone or at the rental counter, get the name of the person assisting you. This information becomes especially important when questions arise about who quoted you a special price, authorized an upgrade, or gave you a discount.

Be sure to have your confirmation number handy; this may be the only way you can prove the rate you were quoted, especially when a discrepancy arises.

Dealing with Rental Car Gas Policies

Be aware of the gas policy when renting. Some rental companies require that the car be returned with the same amount of fuel it had when you picked it up. If you return the car and the rental company has to fill the tank, odds are you will pay much more than the current market rate for the gas. Rental agents don't have the time to fuel the car on the spot, so they rely on a chart that calculates mileage, approximate miles per gallon, and other factors (phases of the moon, perhaps?) to arrive at a dollar figure that no one in his or her right mind would pay.

You say you've fueled the car to the original level but the rental agency claims you haven't? The problem is that gas gauges can take several minutes to reflect the actual fuel level of the tank. When you first receive the car, take a moment to check the fuel level. Turn on the ignition for a few moments before loading your luggage to give the fuel gauge a chance to reach the correct reading. If this reading doesn't match the amount shown on the rental agreement, go back inside and request that the agreement be modified to reflect the real fuel level.

When filling the tank to a certain point, do not overfill. Fuel gauges respond slowly to change, making it easy to overshoot the mark. For example, if you need to return the car with three-fourths of a tank of fuel, leave the key turned on (engine off) when pumping. Set the filler nozzle latch on the slow-fill position and watch the fuel gauge as it goes up. When the needle shows half full, stop pumping. Usually the needle will continue to climb to the three-fourths mark. But if you have to return the car with a full tank, put the pump nozzle into the filler neck as far as possible and pump as fast as the equipment allows. When the pump nozzle clicks off, stop the process. This way, the gas gauge will read full, though you will save as much as two to three gallons of fuel.

Never buy the gas offered by the rental agents, even if they say they are selling it to you for less than the going rate. This claim is almost never true. The going rate will usually be at least 10 cents per gallon cheaper. Also, the rental company will assume that you will use the whole tank, which is almost never true.

Always decline the rental company's gas offer and fuel up the car yourself.

Sedating Rental Car Rip-Off Headaches

Check the car for any dents, scratches, missing hubcaps, or other damage and compare it to the damage report on the rental agreement before driving off the rental lot. You don't want to be held financially responsible for any damage done to the car before you rented it. If you find a scratch, a dent, or any damage on the rental car, make sure someone from the rental company signs a waiver absolving you of responsibility—before you leave the rental lot.

If you are renting at night or the rental garage has poor lighting, drive the car over to a well-lit area of the rental lot and examine the car in good light for damage that might not show up in the dim lights.

Check the car before leaving the parking lot. Make sure the tires are filled and have fairly new tire treads. They are your best protection against losing control and having an accident on slippery or wet roads. If the tires are low or in marginal condition, refuse the car and ask for another. Turn on the lights and make sure that all the bulbs work.

While the vehicle is warming up or cooling down, try every control in the cockpit. Take time to become familiar with the location of all the controls and make sure they operate correctly. Locate and check the operation of the horn, turn signals, wipers, locks, trunk release, and fuel door/gas cap. Adjust the seat to suit your driving comfort and adjust the rearview mirrors.

With the key on, engine off, check out the various dash warning lights. If you don't know what they mean, ask the attendant.

If the car doesn't work properly when you're driving away, go back. If there's a problem, you're better off turning around while you are still close than having to return after you have driven miles away. Also, remember to check the operation of the heating and air conditioning systems. A car with a broken heater, defroster, or air conditioner can be really uncomfortable and in some cases even dangerous.

As soon as you have the opportunity, take the vehicle up to the speed you intend to drive. Does the steering shake? Does it feel as if a tire is out of balance? Does the car seem to have square tires? Don't be afraid to go back and ask for another car.

Try several stops from highway speeds. Do the brakes work properly? Does the car pull one way or another? Does the steering wheel or brake pedal shake or vibrate when you forcefully apply the brake pedal to make quick stops? Wheel pull or pedal/steering wheel shake can mean the car needs brake service. If the brakes don't stop you in a panic situation and you have an accident, you will still be held responsible for the accident. Proving brake problems after the fact can be difficult, if not impossible.

Make sure you know whether the car is equipped with traction control and/or antilock brakes. How to tell? Turn on the ignition and look for the amber ABS warning light. All ABS illuminate this light. If the vehicle has traction control, there may be no way to know it, though some vehicles have a traction control disable button. If you have any questions, ask the attendant before you leave the lot.

If the vehicle has a problem and you are some distance from the rental company, ask that a replacement vehicle be delivered to you. Most rental companies will deliver a replacement and take the defective one.

When you turn in the rental car, make sure the attendant goes over the car while you are there and signs off that there is no damage on it. Otherwise, you can be charged for damage you were not aware of—damage that may have been already there or that occurred while the rental car was being serviced. Many rental companies do a final audit of the car's condition long after you are gone. By then, it is too late to disagree with their findings.

If you rent cars often, here are some rip-off prevention tips:

- Check ahead of time to find out whether your own car insurance will cover rental cars, too. If not, you may want to pay a few dollars more and have your own policy amended.

- The medical insurance offered by the rental agency for coverage may not be valid if you are found guilty of DWI (driving while intoxicated). The fine print may also reveal that the coverage is only supplemental to your own medical and life insurance.

- The special insurance that covers the contents of the car is duplicate coverage, too. Your homeowner's or renter's insurance probably already covers your personal property while you travel.

- Some policies contain clauses denying coverage if the car is broken into.

- Many companies tack on a mandatory fuel charge, even though the gas tank is half empty. This practice means that you are charged a set amount for fuel, whether you like it or not. Be sure to ask, "How much fuel is there supposed to be in the car for this charge?" Check the rental car for the proper allotment of gas. If you are supposed to get a full tank, make sure that you do.

- If you are told to take a cab to a hotel to pick up the car, find out who is paying the cab fare, who pays the tip, and who will get you back to the airport when you return the car. Many expenses may be hidden here.

- Find out whether there are any discounts and if they apply only on weekend or weekly rentals. The fine print may have many exclusion clauses. You might be surprised to find out that an insurance policy pays off only if you die standing up in the car on the last Monday before the spring equinox.

And what if your rental car is stolen? You could become really stranded without a rental car and without the means to rent another. Theft is a growing problem because car thieves know that rental cars are easy pickings that often have valuable luggage in the trunk. Rental cars are never equipped with car alarms or antitheft devices. They're easy to spot, too. Rentals may have special license plates, decals, and bumper stickers.

Depending on the rental company and the terms of the agreement, you may be held responsible for the entire cost of the car if it is stolen. Since most rental cars are sedans with low mileage, you may be responsible for a $12,000 to $20,000 car. To add insult to injury, the rental company may refuse to rent another car to you until they complete their investigation. It may also tie up all the credit available on your credit card, making it impossible for you to rent a car from anyone else.

Use a separate credit card for renting a car to prevent your credit from being tied up.

Check your driving record before renting. If you have three or more traffic violations in the past five years, even parking violations, you may be denied a rental car when you try to pick it up. Many of the bigger rental companies have gained access to driving records and are denying rental cars to drivers who have bad driving records or outstanding parking tickets.

The Foreign Shortchange

If you haven't been out of the United States and are planning a road trip, you may need a primer on how to deal with foreign gas station attendants. Even if you aren't going north or south of the border, some of these tips are useful in avoiding automotive rip-offs everywhere.

One complaint of many visitors to other countries who drive recreational vehicles (RVs) is having to deal with service station attendants. It seems that many of them attempt to shortchange tourists, one way or another.

Before your first refueling experience, ascertain the price per liter of the type of fuel you intend to purchase. It is usually listed on the pump. If you cannot find it, ask someone. Have a calculator in your possession to figure the total.

Here is a list of guidelines for RVers:

- Always get out of your vehicle and monitor the entire fueling procedure. Never just sit in your rig and trust that everything will be done for you.

- Always check that both the "cost of fuel" and "liters" meters on the pump read zero before the attendant begins to pump.

- When the attendant finishes pumping your fuel, immediately write down the cost of fuel and number of liters shown on the pump's meter. Occasionally, you will find a pump that has an inoperable cost meter. In this case, you will need your calculator to multiply the number of liters pumped times the price per liter. (The attendant may have a calculator, too, but don't take his or her word for it.)

- Ask the attendant for a receipt. When you get it, check to see whether the numbers agree with those on the pump. If not, don't allow the attendant to ring off the figures on the pump (for the next customer) until you have pointed out the difference and settled the matter.

- Before you receive your change, figure out (on paper if necessary) how much change you are supposed to receive. When you are given your change, make sure you count it in front of the attendant. Don't walk away or turn away from the attendant, and don't let him or her walk away from you until you have counted your change and are satisfied that you have received the correct amount.

- Finally, check your fuel gauge to make sure that you really did receive the fuel you paid for.

If you follow these guidelines, you should not have problems with attendants at gas stations. And if an attendant does try to make a few dollars at your expense, he or she will end up with a little more respect for your savvy.

Driving in Mexico

With the signing of the North American Free Trade Agreement (NAFTA) and all the free trade that is going on between the United States and Mexico, many people have been heading south to check out our new trading partner. However, you need to know some things about driving etiquette when taking to the roads there. First, make sure that your insurance will cover your travel. Check with your agent, because you may have to purchase special insurance when you get there. Also, be prepared for road conditions much worse than you ever encountered when driving in the United States, despite the fact that Mexico has spent billions fixing up its highways. As for etiquette, here are some tips:

- In Mexico, a stop sign is often treated just like a yield sign is treated here. If you come to a complete stop and no one is coming, the driver behind you will either run into you or beep the horn in anger because you stopped for "no reason."

- "Right on red" is against the law unless a sign permitting it is placed at the intersection.

- You use left-turn signals to let the driver behind you know that it is OK to pass you, not to signal a left turn. You can cause a big problem if you signal a left, because the driver starts to pass you and then you turn left into his or her car. If you need to make a left turn, pull over to the right-hand lane or shoulder, wait for the road to clear, and then turn left.

- Avoid bus rides unless you want a real thrill. Bus drivers are among the most reckless drivers of all. If you see a bus coming, watch out. The drivers always go too fast and take chances that you would never consider.

- Green Angels are the Mexican equivalent of our motorist clubs' roadside assistance programs. More than a thousand Green Angels are employed by the Mexican government; they drive around in green trucks to help stranded motorists. If you break down, have someone call the Green Angels for help. Labor is free, but you have to pay for parts.

- Never take a rental car across the border without permission from the rental company. You may wind up in big trouble if you do.

14

Avoiding Car Theft and Other Disasters

Car thieves, like home burglars, generally have an easy time. Their thievery, unfortunately, is made simple by car owners who obligingly leave doors unlocked (four out of five cases) or leave keys in the ignition (one out of five cases).

Professional car thieves are entering the field in increasing numbers, yet most cars are stolen by amateurs who can be stopped fairly easily. You need all the self-defense you can get to fight both the amateurs and professional thieves who are out to get your car. This chapter outlines some ways to reduce your chances of becoming a victim.

> **F**irst and foremost, never leave your keys in an unattended car. It is an open invitation for an amateur thief to take a joyride.

Reducing the Risk

Clever thieves take note of the keyed-lock numbers printed on ignition keys and obtain duplicates by calling a car dealer with the number while posing as the car's owner. Parking lot attendants, hotel valets, and quick oil-change attendants, who have easy access to these numbers, sometimes double as car thieves. Have the dealer or locksmith remove the numbers to eliminate this problem. But first record these numbers in a safe place in case you ever need them to obtain a duplicate.

Writing your name, address, and phone number on a keytag is inviting trouble. If your keys are lost or stolen, the tag will lead the thief directly to your car—and your home. Never leave more than the ignition key with parking lot attendants, as they can have your keys duplicated while you're away.

Install personalized license plates. Thieves don't want to be identified and will avoid your car.

If your car has a halo light ring that lights up the hole for your
ignition key, look out. Because of the way your ignition lock is con-
structed, it can easily be jimmied, so your car has a higher risk of
being stolen. You should invest in a car alarm.

Park Carefully

Where you park and how you leave your car can directly reduce
its chances of becoming a thief's target. Keep these tips in mind
when you're parking:

- Avoid leaving your car in an unattended parking lot for an
  extended period of time. Statistics show that a car is five times
  as likely to be stolen from an unattended lot than from the street
  or from an attended lot.

- Park under a streetlight and/or near a busy entrance. You may
  have to park farther from your destination to obtain a well-lit
  parking spot, but the extra bit of walking is worth it.

- When staying in a hotel, ask the desk clerk for the safest place
  to park your car.

- Driver's or passenger's side vent windows and windows that are
  not rolled all the way to the top are a favorite means of entry
  for thieves. Always lock all doors, the rear hatch, and the vent
  windows and close all windows tightly when leaving the car
  unattended.

- Don't advertise—a desperate thief will find the temptation
  irresistible. Before leaving the car, remove valuables from
  view. Remove car phones, CB radios, tape decks, tapes, CDs,
  packages, and purses and lock them in the trunk. If possible,
  remove the car phone or CB antenna and lock it up in the trunk
  as well.

- You may neglect to lock your car because there is nothing in it
  to steal. But what about the car itself? Note that thieves also
  steal older cars to use in drug trafficking.

- Always remember to replace the cigarette lighter. A missing
  lighter may tip off a thief that you have a valuable car phone or
  radar detector.

- Replace your car stereo with a removable one. These units can
  easily be pulled out and stored safely out of sight in the trunk.

Even better are the types with removable faceplates. You can also place a dummy cover over your stereo, making it appear cheap and undesirable.

- Park with your front wheels turned sharply right or left to make the car difficult to tow away.

See the section "Staying Safe in Parking Lots" later in this chapter for further information about parking smart.

Operation Identification

For about $10, you can purchase an electric engraver and etch your vehicle identification number on the car phone, CB, tape deck, or CD player. Engrave the car's vehicle identification number (VIN) on the car in several places: on the underside of the hood, inside the trunk lid, and inside the door edges. This makes it easy to identify your car if it is recovered in a chop shop or if someone alters the VIN tag. Engraving the VIN someplace on the car may also deter the chop shop from stripping the vehicle.

These systems are simple, effective, and usually inexpensive. Some types of VIN applications can be done in the aftermarket or by the vehicle owner. Car dealers offer glass etching kits that can engrave these numbers on all the glass windows in the car.

Note that these devices do not deter thieves in the first place. In general, a thief is not on the lookout for VIN markings and will steal the car anyway. Auto manufacturers have been reluctant to mark parts with the VIN because of the costs involved. They are marking only the most likely theft targets, and the marking is in the form of peel-off labels.

Always carry your VIN, your license tag number, and a complete vehicle description in your wallet or purse. If your car is stolen, you will quickly be able to give the police the information they need to apprehend the thief.

Never leave your driver's license, registration, or any other form of ID in your car. If the thief is stopped by police, he or she can fool them by using your ID.

Use Antitheft Devices

You may want to purchase a security device to reduce the risk of someone stealing your car. The investment will be a wise one, especially if your car is at high risk of theft or you live or work in a high-risk area. Read on for details about the different types of security devices and their advantages and disadvantages.

Alarms

Function: When a thief enters the car, an alarm triggers a siren, horn, blinking lights, cellular phone, kill switch, or some other device. The alarm can also be triggered by an interior motion detector or similar device. Some alarms release smoke.

Cost: Moderate

Advantages: Designed to deter the theft of the vehicle, they can also deter theft of items inside the vehicle. Signs on the vehicle state that an alarm is present. These systems can qualify you for insurance discounts. They are usually passive.

Disadvantages: False alarms are a nuisance and can make your neighbors angry. They can also negate the effectiveness of the alarm when a thief is actually breaking into the vehicle; bystanders may not react when the alarm sounds. Some cities are fining car owners for frequent false alarms.

Auto alarm systems can tell a thief what type of alarm you have. This information may make it easier to disable the alarm. Use a generic sticker instead.

Locking Devices
Several types of locking devices are on the market today. They can be purchased at auto parts stores.

Manual Steering Wheel Locking Devices

Function: They lock the steering wheel or the brake pedal, making it impossible to drive the vehicle.

Cost: Low

Advantages: These devices are inexpensive and require no special installation. Their high visibility may encourage a would-be thief to look for another, easier target. The device can be removed as needed and moved to your next vehicle when you sell the car.

Disadvantages: A thief can remove this device in about 20 seconds by sawing the steering wheel. In some vehicles, the thief can simply bend open the steering wheel and remove the device. Because these devices require some effort to install, drivers don't always use them, especially when leaving the vehicle for a short time. Failure to remove the device can lead to a crash. Sometimes the presence of such a visible device is a signal to the thief that this car is worth stealing.

Ignition and Steering Column Locking Devices

Function: They encapsulate the steering column, preventing access to the ignition lock and switch mechanism. These devices are intended for use only on vehicles with the Saginaw steering column, which is very easy to force.

Cost: Low

Advantages: The high visibility of such devices may encourage a would-be thief to look for an easier target. These devices prevent thieves from breaking the lower outer steering column covering and working the lock.

Disadvantages: Permanently installed versions are unsightly and crude looking. They make it difficult for a mechanic to service the steering column. They can be removed in a few minutes using a hacksaw. The versions that must be attached before the driver leaves the vehicle require some effort to install, so drivers don't always use them.

Electronic Passkey Systems

Functions: Called resistant key systems or smart keys, electronic passkey systems come in two general classes:

- A passkey or embedded coded key requires a special key to be recognized by the car's computer before the engine will start.

- For an electronic lock or keyless device, a code is entered by a door-mounted keyboard, key switch, remote control, or similar device.

Cost: Moderate to high (in some cases very high), and system must be installed at the factory

Advantages: This passive device is the easiest of all antitheft devices to use. It is also by far the most effective in preventing theft.

Disadvantages: Failure of the device can render the car inoperative. Usually, these devices must be ordered with the car and are not installed in the aftermarket. An experienced thief can pry the door-mounted keyboard with a screwdriver, then short it out and open the door.

Tracking

When activated via radio frequency, these systems notify the police that the vehicle has been stolen and give the car's current location. There are three types in use today: triangulation, global positioning, and cellular phone alarm systems.

Triangulation

Function: The police department must be fitted with special direction finders to track down radio signals from the stolen vehicle. At least two police units are required. Currently, LoJack markets this system.

Cost: High

Advantages: Most vehicles fitted with this system are recovered. Thieves will shun the vehicle if they know it has such a system on board because they know the police will track them down. It can also aid in recovery of hijacked vehicles.

Disadvantages: Triangulation is currently available only in limited areas. The signal can be blocked by parking garages, tunnels, mountains, or buildings (canyon effect). Also, this system works only within the city. The owner must notify the police before the vehicle is driven out of town and can't be tracked. It is also costly and difficult to install.

Global Positioning Systems (GPS)

Function: The vehicle is fitted with a very small satellite transmitter that continually sends a microwave signal up to several satellite receivers in stationary orbit. The monitoring station can pinpoint the exact location of the vehicle at any time by satellite navigation triangulation.

Cost: High

Advantages: Most vehicles fitted with this system are recovered. Thieves will shun the vehicle if they know it has such a system on board because they know the police will track them down. It can also aid in recovery of hijacked vehicles. This system can be used to track the whereabouts of the vehicle at all times (trucking companies use them for this purpose).

Disadvantages: The signal can frequently be blocked by parking garages, tunnels, mountains, or buildings. If the thief disables the device before the owner notifies the police, the system can be defeated. High cost and difficulty of installation prohibit universal use.

Cellular Car Phone Alarm Systems

Function: The car is fitted with a combination car phone and alarm system that triggers the car phone when the car is broken into. The car phone can be set up to automatically dial the local police, informing the dispatcher that the car is being broken into and giving a complete description of the car. The car phone can also be programmed to call the owner or any other number desired. In some systems, the phone can be programmed to send the thief a message, scaring him off.

Cost: Moderate to high

Advantages: The unit is self-activating and does not require the owner to discover that the car is being stolen. It uses existing cellular technology, so it requires no satellite or triangulation.

Disadvantages: The unit depends on the existence of a cell-site to connect the call, as well as available lines during peak usage periods. The signal can be blocked by parking garages, tunnels, mountains, or buildings.

Kill Switches and Starter Interrupt

Function: These systems immobilize the vehicle unless the driver takes some specific action. They can be either passive or active and are most effective when used in conjunction with another antitheft device.

Cost: Low

Advantages: These devices are cheap and easy to purchase in the aftermarket or can be readily installed by the car dealer or car stereo shop. They are simple to operate and take precious time for the thief to locate and circumvent.

Disadvantages: They are not always active when the vehicle is unoccupied, especially when it is left briefly. A short or malfunction can prevent the vehicle from starting even for the owner or can cause the vehicle to quit running suddenly.

Phonies

Function: These fool would-be thieves into believing that there is an on-board alarm system, when in reality the sign is the only antitheft device. Phonies can be window stickers, blinking dash-mounted alarm lights, or alarm boxes.

Cost: Very low

Advantages: They are easy to install and very cheap. If you don't have a real alarm, installing one of these stickers on the window or adding the blinking box to the dash or console is a good idea.

Disadvantage: Professional thieves can readily distinguish the phony from the real thing and will ignore the phony deterrent.

Conventional Antitheft Devices

Function: Factory-supplied theft deterrent devices offer some protection right from the factory. These devices include tapered or hard-to-jimmy door locks, trunk locks, and hood locks.

Advantages: They are already installed in the vehicle. These factory devices can dramatically reduce the number of vehicle thefts by amateurs.

Disadvantages: Drivers become careless and forget to remove their keys and lock up every time they leave the vehicle.

Other Devices

I'll bet you didn't know there were so many different kinds of antitheft devices out there. Hang on—here are two more worth mentioning.

Automatic License Plate Readers

Function: Installed by police at strategic locations (such as the entrance of a tunnel or the beginning of a large bridge crossing), these automatically read license plates and check a computer file for stolen vehicles.

Cost: Extremely high

Advantages: The vehicle owner has to install nothing. Readers can apprehend vehicles that have been stolen for use in other criminal activities. Police can easily trap the criminal once the car has been identified by setting up a roadblock at the opposite end of the bridge or tunnel. This system can also be used to apprehend scofflaw drivers who are delinquent in paying parking fines.

Disadvantages: The system is extremely expensive and is only in the experimental stages of development. The stolen car must be reported in a timely manner and entered into the database fast enough for the license plate reader to acknowledge the stolen vehicle. Also, the stolen car must pass by a toll booth or go through a tunnel when the device is in use.

Vin Tracking

Function: This system apprehends vehicles stolen from other states by identifying the hidden VIN on the vehicle. Every vehicle has a hidden VIN that cannot be easily changed. When a valuable vehicle is bought or sold, the new owner checks for the hidden VIN to make sure it matches the registered VIN.

Cost: None

Advantages: It is extremely difficult for thieves to modify the hidden VIN because it is stamped right into the frame. Attempts to modify or grind away the numbers are futile; they can always be found with chemical metallurgy.

Disadvantages: The location of hidden numbers is not generally known, making this type of inspection difficult.

Avoiding Carjacking

Carjacking, or stealing cars by force, is one of the most hideous crimes to hit the nation in recent years. It is the modern equivalent of piracy. Expensive exotic cars are, understandably, the favorite targets of carjackers.

Today's cars are hard to steal—unless you have the keys. It's much simpler to stick a gun in someone's face and demand the keys than to disarm car alarms and ignition interlocks.

Unfortunately, most local and state criminal codes don't define carjacking. It is usually reported as auto theft or armed robbery, so there are no solid statistics to indicate times, places, or victims of this type of crime.

Background News

While it is unlikely that you will fall prey to this kind of crime, preventive actions on your part can further reduce the risk. Start by being aware of some common themes among carjackings:

- Carjacking isn't a problem just in large cities. It happens in suburbs, small towns, and rural areas as well. For some young people, carjacking may be a rite of passage, a way to achieve status, or just a thrill. Teens (and adults) are committing more crimes of violence than ever before.

- Carjacking is a crime of opportunity. The thief is searching for the most vulnerable prey without regard to sex, race, or age.

- Cars, especially luxury ones, provide quick cash for drug users and other criminals.

- Sophisticated alarms and improved locking devices make it harder for thieves to steal unoccupied cars.

Presenting an Opportunity for the Carjacker

Carjackers look for windows of opportunity. An example is a driver stopped at an intersection with the windows rolled down or the door obviously unlocked. Other places of opportunity include the following:

- Parking garages and mass-transit lots

- Shopping malls and grocery stores

- Self-service places like gas stations

- Car washes and bank ATMS

- Residential driveways and streets where you get into or out of your car

- Any place where drivers slow down or stop

Taking Precautions

An informed public is a good step toward thwarting criminals. Here is some information to help you avoid a carjacking:

- Don't pick up hitchhikers (and don't hitchhike yourself).

- Park near walkways and sidewalks. Avoid parking near Dumpsters, woods, large vans or trucks, or anything else that limits your visibility.

- Avoid parking where there is little foot or auto traffic.

- Avoid parking in secluded, poorly lit areas—especially late at night. Most carjackings occur between 9 P.M. and 3 A.M. The later in the day it is, the more likely you are to be carjacked. Be especially alert in unstaffed lots and enclosed parking garages.

- Keep doors locked and windows up while driving, especially when stopped in traffic. If someone approaches your car, don't open your window for any reason. Remember, you are not safe if you are not moving.

- Walk with purpose and stay alert. Don't walk to your car alone at night. Have someone accompany you. If you spot someone loitering nearby, don't go to your car. Turn around and go the other way. Call the police if the stranger lingers.

- Approach your car with your key in hand. You don't want to be fumbling around for keys while standing next to your car; that's a perfect time to get mugged. Be sure to look around and inside the vehicle before getting in.

When you're in your vehicle, your horn can serve as a good deterrent. If someone suspicious approaches your car, honk your horn and don't get out. Criminals don't like attention.

- Plan your trips carefully, especially in unknown areas. Don't get lost. If you do get lost, don't ask for directions from anyone standing around on the street. Go to a gas station or other well-lit area and ask for help. Also, be wary of anyone asking for directions or handing out fliers.

- Trust your instincts. If something makes you feel uneasy, get into the car quickly, lock the doors, and drive away. A man was driving in an unfamiliar area of a major city. When he stopped to ask for directions, he was robbed. The man was an easy mark since he appeared to be lost.

- Keep your doors locked and windows rolled up (at least partway if it's hot and you don't have air conditioning), no matter how short the distance or how "safe" the neighborhood.

- Drive in the center lane to make it harder for would-be carjackers to approach the car.

- When you're coming to a stop, leave enough room to maneuver around other cars, especially if you sense trouble and need to get away. Remember, you're not safe if you're not moving. When approaching a red light, leave space between your vehicle and the one in front of you. If someone approaches in a threatening manner, drive away. If someone tries to stop your car by blocking you, especially if there is a gun, get out of there fast.

- Avoid driving alone, especially at night.

- Don't stop to assist a stranger whose car is broken down. Drive to the nearest phone and call police to help.

- If you often drive at night or alone, consider a CB radio or cellular phone to make it easier to summon help in an emergency— especially if you have to travel in dangerous areas of town. Even a fake mobile phone will do. If you think you are in danger, pick up the phone and pretend to call for help. A would-be carjacker will shy away from someone who is in the process of reporting the crime that he or she is about to commit.

Never combine your car keys and house keys, and never attach a label with your home address to your keys.

Preventing Future Problems

Never leave your vehicle registration, insurance card, or driver's license in your car. If you do, the thief will know where you live and may burglarize your home. Remove any papers that have your home address on them. Put a copy of the registration and your business card under the back seat. If your car is found, this is one of the first places the police will look for identification. Also, drop business cards down inside the doors.

Take your garage-door opener with you when you leave your car. If your car is stolen with the opener left inside it, the thief may try to get into your house.

Reacting in a Threatening Situation

If someone suspicious runs into you, don't get out of your car. Roll up the windows, lock the doors, and motion for him or her to follow you. Drive to the nearest police or fire station. If none is available, drive to a fast-food restaurant drive-up window and summon help. Another option is to go to a well-lit place where there are plenty of people, such as a convenience store.

If you are threatened by an attacker wielding a club, pipe, or knife and your doors are locked and windows closed, remember that it will take time to break the glass and get inside. You have time to drive away. Don't panic, but get out of there fast!

A teenager kept her wits about her when a gang of men approached her car, blocked it, and demanded that she get out. Avoiding untold harm, she stepped on the gas and sped away, almost running them over. She might not be alive to tell her story if she had complied with their demands.

If an armed attacker demands your keys, turn them over. Resisting can get you hurt or even killed. Remain calm. Try not to scream or look nervous. Do whatever you are told. Be polite and tell the carjacker that you will do as you're told. If other people are in your car, instruct them to get out slowly when you do. Keep your hands high and visible. You *never* want to go for a drive with a carjacker, and neither do your passengers.

Identifying the Carjacker

Carjackers are often under the influence of drugs. Look for over-animated behavior or signs of intoxication. Pay attention to clothing; look for gold jewelry or clothing that seems out of place. Also, beware of anyone whose face is partially covered with a hood.

If you are alert, you may be able to spot a potential attacker before he spots you. If you see that you are about to become a target, take immediate evasive action before the attacker can get close. Awareness is your best defense. Keep your eyes open.

If you can't avoid being carjacked, try to get a description of the attacker. Note as many details as possible, such as tattoos, scars, or anything else unusual.

Wait until the attacker is out of sight before you go for help. Then call the police and give them a description of your car and tag number. The carjacker might come back to kill you if he thinks that you will identify him later.

Staying Safe in Parking Lots

Modern shopping malls are popular hunting grounds for thieves. Malls project a feeling of security when often just the opposite can be true. Even when the mall has security police and cameras, it is not as safe as you might think. The following sections provide some tips for problem-free parking, especially at malls.

Parking Your Car

- Park under or near a light if there is any chance that you will return after dark.

- Park in the major aisle areas in plain view of the entrance to your destination. You may walk a little farther, but it's worth the peace of mind.

- Don't park next to vans, the vehicle of choice for kidnappers and other criminals.

- If you see someone watching you from another vehicle as you pull up, park somewhere else. If you're particularly suspicious of the person, report him or her to police or mall security.

- Jot down your parking location as you leave your car. Include which building or store is nearest. This may save you a lot of time wandering around when you return hours later, arms loaded.

- If you keep valuables in your vehicle, stow them in the trunk before you leave home. Doing so when you park tells a watching thief, "Forget the door locks—the good stuff is in the trunk."

Facts About Car Theft

Most cars are recovered within a few weeks after they are stolen.

While a holdup can be a misdemeanor, carjacking is a federal crime. So is kidnapping.

Stolen cars equipped with homing or tracking devices can be recovered very quickly, sometimes within minutes. If you live in a large city, consider purchasing a tracing device such as LoJack.

Most exotic cars are stolen for parts and go to chop shops where they are dismantled; others are shipped to other countries. The chance of recovery in these cases is usually slim.

Cars of lesser value are often stolen for use as getaway cars in other crimes. These cars are usually recovered but are typically trashed inside.

Vehicles that are most likely to be stolen for parts are BMW, Mercedes-Benz, Lexus, Cadillac (full-size), Jeep Cherokee, and Corvette.

Returning to Your Car

Just dropping off packages so you can shop some more? Move your car to another part of the lot. It's worth losing your space.

Someone may be watching, ready to unburden your trunk of your packages when you leave.

As you come within sight of your car, glance beneath it and adjacent vehicles. Muggers have been known to hide under or between parked cars and grab victims by the ankles. This is especially true for vans or trucks, which usually have more clearance under them.

Have your key in your hand and ready to insert in the door lock. Fumbling for your keys is an invitation to be mugged.

Car keys can serve as weapons. Clench the key in your fist, with the biggest key sticking out between your index and middle fingers. Use it in a swiping motion across the attacker's face, aiming for the eyes. You can also use the key to punch at the bony parts of the attacker's face.

Take a moment to glance into the back seat of your car or rear area of your van as you get into your vehicle.

If you are seriously concerned about reaching your vehicle safely, ask a security officer to walk with you. They're there to make sure that you stay safe.

If your car won't start when you turn the key and someone walks up offering help, refuse. This may be the very person who disabled your car. Lock yourself in the car and ask the person to call the police or mall security.

Shop with others rather than alone. Be sure to leave word at home as to where you're going and when you expect to return. Running late? Call home.

The safest time to shop is early in the day, when the mall opens. Criminals prefer working under cover of darkness. Crowds are lighter in the morning too.

Spotting a Stolen Car

Every year, millions of cars are stolen and resold to unwary buyers who get burned when the stolen car is discovered and confiscated. Some $20 billion worth of insurance money annually goes toward paying fraudulent insurance claims. Some people even arrange to have their own cars stolen. It is estimated that 15 percent of all insurance claims are for fraudulently stolen cars. In major cities like New York, Miami, and Philadelphia, about one in five police reports for stolen cars is falsified. The theft is actually arranged and the stolen car goes to a chop shop where it is stripped for valuable parts or fitted with a phony VIN to be resold to an unsuspecting sucker.

I have compiled a checklist of some of the items that you might come across in a stolen vehicle. Take this list with you when checking out a used car. It may save you a great deal of trouble and money by helping you to avoid buying a stolen vehicle.

- Is the VIN plate loose or showing any signs of tampering? Are the rivets loose?

- Are the rivets holding the VIN plate original? All VIN plates since 1970 have rosette-style stainless-steel rivets with six "petals" and a hole in the middle.

- Has the VIN plate been repainted?

- Are the VIN plate numbers stamped as the original factory numbers? Do the numbers show any signs of tampering?

- Is the dashboard or instrument cluster loose or mispositioned?

- Are the keys originals or duplicates? If duplicates, where are the originals?

- Do both door locks and trunk lock work with the same key? In cars where the door key should fit the ignition, are the keys the same?

- Is the ignition switch loose? Does it show any signs of tampering or chisel marks?

- Is the steering column original, or does it look as if it was recently replaced?

- Does the driver's side door jamb still have the DOT sticker (a plastic-coated paper decal that lists the date of manufacture, VIN, GVWR, and other data) on it? Is the sticker firmly attached, or does it appear to have been tampered with?

- Does the VIN on the door-jamb sticker match the VIN on the title and VIN plate?

- Does the engine have its original ID numbers, or have they been removed?

- Does the license plate look brand new? Does it have new mounting bolts? Does it match the registration?

- Is the car from out of state? Was the registration issued recently in your state? Is the previous owner unknown?

How to Spot a Laundered Car

When considering the purchase of a used car, you should be aware that thieves often "launder" stolen cars or cars that insurance companies have declared totaled. If you wind up buying one, you will get ripped off in a big way. The car will continually have expensive problems. If it was stolen, it will be recovered by the police—and you will lose your investment. Be suspicious if:

- There is a discrepancy between the VIN on the title and the body, door, or other body part.

- The title is made out to a dealer and is in the dealer's name. This ploy is often used to alter a vehicle's identification.

- The vehicle is old but has low mileage. (Also suspect odometer tampering.)

- The vehicle is from the East Coast and is being sold on the West Coast. Also suspicious are Canadian vehicles brought here.

- The deal is too good to be true.

If you have any doubts, contact your local police and have the secretly located VIN checked by the authorities. If you suspect that the vehicle you have inspected is stolen, call the National Insurance Crime Bureau at 800-TEL-NICB. NICB offers rewards of up to $1,000 for information leading to the arrest and/or conviction of those involved in auto fraud.

Rip-Off Scams on the Road

Travelers are so busy attending to where they are going that they are perfect targets for Mr. Ripp U. Off. He lurks at rest stops, gas stations, service plazas, and roadside stands, waiting for the unwary, weary wayfarer to happen by. Long-distance driving can create a feeling not unlike jet lag; confusion, dizziness, and lack of mental awareness can set in. When you stop and get out of the car, you may not be paying attention because you're distracted by the unfamiliar surroundings.

This is the perfect setup for Ripp to get you. He knows that you're in a dazed and careless condition from all those road miles. He is watching. You forget to lock the rear hatch, vent window, or even the door. As soon as you turn the corner, pounce! You become another victim of travel crime. Here are some tips for beating Ripp on the road:

- Always empty the car when staying in a hotel. An innocent suitcase may entice Ripp to break your car window. Your belongings are safer with you in your room than in the trunk.

- When parking downtown, pay the extra money and park in an attended parking garage. Choose one that allows the attendant to see all the cars on the lot.

- When stopping for food, park the car where you can see it while you eat.

- Never leave the car unattended while buying gas. The perfect time for Ripp to strike is when you go to pay for the gas. Keys in the ignition, full tank of gas . . . what more could he want?

- Don't keep important papers all in one place. Make copies of registration documents, insurance data, credit-card numbers, and travelers' check ID numbers. Keep them in several safe places; you'll need those numbers if you get in trouble. They won't do you any good if they are in your car and the car is stolen.

- Use travelers' checks and credit cards, especially if you are going to be carrying large sums.

- If you are confused or lost, try not to show it. A lost traveler is a prime target for Ripp.

- Take along an inflatable dummy or Mr. Safe-T-Man so it looks as though you have a male passenger in the car.

Outsmarting Roadside Rogues

Throughout your travels, various Mr. Ripp U. Offs are waiting for you all along the way. The world is full of new victims for Ripp, and travelers are some of his favorites. Why? Because they are often confused and tired and aren't on the lookout. Businesspeople and vacationers alike are a criminal's bread and butter. Listen and learn as Ripp spills the beans.

The Front-Desk Eavesdropper

How I work: I hang around the front desk, usually pretending to read a newspaper. I wait for someone to check in. When the clerk hands you the key, I listen to hear if he tells you your room number. Now I have a juicy target to rob.

How to stop me: Don't accept that room key. Demand another, and tell the clerk not to announce your room number to the world. Bring all valuables into the room with you and be sure the deadbolt on your door is locked.

The Room-Key Cad

How I work: I check into a room at a motel and immediately make a copy of the key. Then I either switch to another room or check out altogether. Now I have a key to your room. I also know that a motel or hotel room key often opens several room doors. I walk the halls, trying each lock. If the key I have fits, I enter the room and rob it.

How to stop me: Stay at hotels and motels that offer coded electronic card keys, not actual keys.

The Next-Door Neighbor

How I work: I check into a room with interconnecting doors. These doors have the easiest locks to pick. While you are gone, I'll clean you out and be hundreds of miles down the road before you discover what I've done.

How to stop me: Ask for a room that does not have a connecting door.

The Special Delivery Specialist

How I work: I call you pretending to be the front desk. I tell you that I have a telegram, pizza, or some other made-up item that you are to come pick up. You step out, and I step in.

How to stop me: Always call back to the front desk for verification. If you're still suspicious, don't leave your room. Have the item brought to you.

The Safe Skimmer

How I work: My buddy works at the front desk, and when someone leaves a real juicy valuable, he tips me off. I come in, fake a holdup, and rob the safe. Surprise! The hotel is liable only for the first $50.

How to stop me: If you are staying in town for a while, rent a safe-deposit box from a nearby bank. If not, keep your valuables with you at all times.

The Credit Slip Scammer

How I work: I'm the janitor, and one of my jobs is to empty the trash. I spend a great deal of time going through the garbage from the front desk and restaurant. Why? Because I find the carbon strips from your credit-card transactions. I save them until I have enough. Then I quit my job and go on a spending spree using your card numbers.

How to stop me: Ask for the carbon to be returned to you and tear it up into tiny pieces.

The Photo Opportunist

How I work: I offer to take your picture. You give me your camera. Say cheese! I'm already halfway down the block, with your camera in my hand.

How to stop me: Don't let strangers use your camera.

The Accident Victim

How I work: I jump in front of your car and pretend that you hit me. When you stop, get out, and help me to my feet, I jump into your car and steal it.

How to stop me: Lock the car whenever you leave it, even if only for a moment.

The Locked-Out Lurker

How I work: I pretend to be locked out of my room and ask the maid to let me in. She happily complies, giving me access to your goodies.

How to stop me: Always take all your valuables with you. Never leave anything behind that you don't want to lose. When leaving, turn the TV on loud enough to be heard outside the room and hang the "Do Not Disturb" card on the door.

The Bump and Rob Driver

How I work: I drive a real junker. If I need quick cash, I drive around dark neighborhoods until I spot a likely victim. I follow until the time is just right and then I run into the back of your car. You get out to take a look at the damage, and I hold you up. Then I slash your tire so you can't follow me. Better yet, I steal your car.

How to stop me: Never get out of your car in a bad part of town. If the surroundings look scary, drive to the nearest public place, convenience store, fire department, or police station. Try to stop where there are people around.

The Spilling Scammer

How I work: While at a bar, I "accidentally" spill my beer or soda on you. The idea is to lavish you with apologies while I pick your pocket. I use other variations to distract you and steal your brief-case or luggage.

How to stop me: Always keep your wallet in a front pocket. Never let your luggage get out of sight. Even better, keep your luggage close to you or between your legs.

The Nothing Missing Scam

Your car has obviously been broken into, yet nothing appears to be missing. The ignition lock shows no signs of tampering, and the police are puzzled. You think that maybe the thief was frightened away while trying to steal the car. You thank your lucky stars and maybe even have a car alarm installed. Months go by and the event is completely forgotten.

When it comes time for your car insurance renewal, you are flabbergasted by the huge increase in the premium. "This can't be!" you exclaim and reach for the phone to complain to your agent. You are told the increase is the result of an accident you had a few months back. "What accident?" you ask. After much consternation and further checking, you realize that your insurance card was stolen and used to dupe the insurance company.

Here's how the scam works:

The thief looks for cars parked in places that signify that the owner is probably far away from home. Convention centers, hotels, and cars with out-of-state tags are targeted.

Once the thief has stolen your insurance card, he calls your insurance company, pretending to be you—the owner of the vehicle. The thief explains to the insurance agent that he (posing as you) was involved in an accident in which he was at fault. The "accident" took place in the city where the car has been broken into. The thief tells the agent that "John Doe's" car was hit by your car.

The thief, still posing as you, tells the insurance agent that you are out of town and won't be able to settle the claim in person. In fact, you can't be reached by phone for several days either. The agent is asked to settle the claim directly for repairing the car belonging to John Doe.

Later that same day, the thief calls the agent and identifies himself as John Doe. He wants your insurance company to make immediate arrangements to have his damaged car fixed. Your agent instructs him to take the car to the local claims office so that your insurance company can get an adjuster to examine the damage and settle the claim.

The thief shows up at the local insurance adjuster's claims office in the city you were visiting. He brings a stolen car with some believable damage done to it. The nature of the damage prevents the adjuster from determining how fresh it is. Also, the claim is small enough that no additional investigation by the insurance company is required.

The claims adjuster issues a check for the repair to the thief, who is now posing as John Doe. The thief uses a fake ID to cash the check and cannot be traced.

The thief repeats the process over and over again, moving from city to city and pocketing huge amounts of cash for his efforts.

This particular scam is so widespread that it has become a major concern for insurance companies. The lesson: Never leave your insurance card in your glove box. Instead, carry it in your wallet.

15

Your Emergency Road Kit

Something as simple as a can of gas might make the difference between an inconvenience and a real emergency. I have compiled a list of things that you should pack "just in case" any time you travel in your car. Any one of these items can make a life-saving difference if you get stuck.

Jumper Cables

Don't go cheap. Get cables with copper wire, not aluminum. Heavier is better. Many late-model GM cars are equipped with side battery terminals, so look for a set of cables with built-in side adapters or purchase a pair of these adapters separately. You never know when you'll need a jump from the General.

Flares

Sometimes called *fusees*, emergency flares can keep fast-moving traffic from running into your disabled car. Reflective triangles work too, but they are not as visible. Keep at least six flares in the trunk, packed in a waterproof plastic bag. A neat alternative is the Lightman emergency strobe device. This little strobe will make you and your vehicle very visible and can easily be carried on your person if you need to walk at night.

Flashlight

Because of the high humidity found in vehicles, a plastic flashlight is recommended—the larger, the better. Keep the batteries in a separate plastic bag so they stay fresh. The warning flashers that come mounted on larger flashlights are generally too dim for use with traffic. *Best*: A portable floodlight that has its own stand so you can set it up and aim it. *Don't* depend on a light that plugs into the cigarette lighter; your battery may be dead. In a pinch, light sticks are a good source. They produce light from a chemical reaction the same way that lightning bugs do. Simply break the inner part of the stick by bending it, and you've got at least 30 minutes of greenish-colored light.

Spares

Tires aren't the only spares to consider. Carry an assortment of fuses, lightbulbs, accessory drive belts, a spark plug, and windshield wiper blades for your car. Spare liquids to have on hand include water, coolant, washer fluid, motor oil, and gas (in a safe, approved gas can).

Fix-Its

Useful stopgap materials include radiator leak sealants, duct tape to seal up air leaks or patch radiator hoses, and a tarp to work under in a heavy rain or lie on top of when working in mud or snow. Two kinds of electrical tape are available; get the heavy-duty, rubber-impregnated cloth variety. A can of silicone spray will dry wet wires and distributor caps and thaw frozen locks.

Clean-Ups

Pack a tube of waterless hand cleaner, several rags, a can of carburetor cleaner, spray solvent (to remove big grease spots), and a roll of paper towels. You may also want to pack a stain-removal stick for your clothing.

Tool Kit

Even the best mechanic is helpless without tools. Pack a good Swiss Army knife with scissors. *Best*: Knives that have blade safety locks. You'll need a 12-volt test light or small multimeter. Also pack two pairs of pliers: one 8-inch standard pair (with built-in wire cutters) and one needlenose pair. A standard socket set works both standard (U.S.) and metric sizes, but add 10 mm and 12 mm sockets to make it complete. A multipurpose screwdriver with different blades stored in the handle is great. An adjustable wrench works for just about anything else.

Fire Extinguisher

Shop around for a fire extinguisher that fits your car's storage space. Too big and it will be in the way. Too small and it won't be much help when you need it. The best types are good for class A, B, and C fires. You may want to put the fire extinguisher in a protective pouch or plastic bag for safe storage.

Miscellaneous

A good road atlas is handy when you're lost. So are a compass and a pad of paper and pencil. Seal up a stash of chocolate, pudding, or granola bars for instant energy food in case you are stranded for some time. Five dollars in "mad money" and a CB radio or cellular phone are useful, too. Take one that has its own battery, since your battery may be the very reason that you're stuck.

A warm sleeping bag is great if you are stranded in the cold, as is an all-night candle to help produce some extra warmth. Don't forget a raincoat, though a plastic garbage bag will do in a pinch. Also, a combination sun visor and "Send Help!" sign for the windshield is useful. Finally, pack a good book to read while you wait. I recommend *The Grapes of Wrath* because no matter how bad your situation is, reading that book will make you realize things could be a whole lot worse!

Ten Smog Tricks

Getting a vehicle to pass the smog test can be a real chore. Most motorists aren't aware of all the factors that come into play when taking a smog test. The following tips will help you give your vehicle a better chance of passing. If your vehicle does fail, look at the reasons(s) listed in your smog test report and consult the next section, "What to Check If You Fail," for possible causes and fixes.

Ten Tips to Improve Your Smog Test Scores

Get It Hot

The hotter an engine runs, the cleaner it is. In many cases, the engine cools down while you're sitting in line waiting for your turn to be tested. This is typically caused by a defective radiator thermostat, which allows the coolant to circulate even when the engine is not at operating temperature. Go to the test station during the warmest part of the day; cold weather makes emissions systems work less effectively. Make sure your engine oil is hot before entering the test lane. It will have to be operating for at least 30 minutes before the test. Do not let the engine idle for more than a few minutes. If the line is long, shut off your motor and wait before starting it. Just before your turn, rev the engine at 2,000 rpm for at least two minutes to precondition it for the test.

Raise Your Idle

Engines are less efficient when running at idle. Any problems with low compression, vacuum leaks, leaking injectors, or dirty carburetor jets show up at idle. Holding the gas pedal a small amount (to around 1,200 rpm) when the idle portion of the test is being run helps overcome these kinds of problems.

Add Alcohol

The air-fuel mixture has a great deal to do with the tailpipe emissions. Alcohol burns much cleaner than gasoline. If the fuel level gets to empty and alcohol is added to the gas tank, the emission levels will drop. There are a number of products currently on the market designed for this purpose; simply follow the instructions on the container.

Replace the Air Filter

The more air the engine gets, the cleaner it burns. If your air filter is dirty, even slightly, replacing it can reduce emission levels even more.

Change Oil

Old oil causes crankcase emissions to contribute to the air-fuel mixture. Have the oil changed just before you go for the test. Old oil can cause CO failures at 2,500 rpm, putting CO at 1 to 1.5 percent over the limit. Simply changing the oil can reduce emissions enough to make the car pass. Synthetic oil does a better job of reducing emissions because synthetics burn cleaner.

Install Hotter Spark Plugs

In some cases, the air-fuel mixture is not burned completely. Installing spark plugs one heat range hotter can further reduce emissions. **Note:** If the hotter spark plugs cause the engine to ping, do not continue using them.

Check for Exhaust Leaks

Repair any exhaust leaks. Small exhaust leaks allow exhaust to escape and oxygen to be drawn in. Every puff of exhaust leaking out is followed by a vacuum pulse, which draws in outside air. The introduction of air into the exhaust system can prevent the catalytic converter from properly treating nitrates of oxygen (NOx) emissions. Exhaust leaks can also reduce back pressure, preventing the EGR system from working properly and raising NOx.

Set the Timing

Over time the ignition timing tends to change, usually becoming too far retarded. Setting it to specifications will help reduce HC emissions. Maintain your engine—have it tuned up and keep it running in the best shape.

Gas It Up

Use the correct-octane gasoline specified in the owner's manual. Don't use high test if your engine requires regular, and vice versa. In general, using high test in an engine designed for regular will increase HC emissions. Use the freshest gasoline with the most detergents you can find. Buy gas at the busiest station in town. A full fuel tank will help pass the evaporative emissions portion of the test—but don't overfill. Shut the pump off when the nozzle clicks. Don't top off the tank. Inspect your gas-cap seal. If it is torn or damaged in any way, you will fail the test. Buy another cap in advance before taking the test.

Clean Injectors

If you own an older multiport fuel-injected vehicle, consider having the injectors cleaned before taking the test. While injector cleaning really does little to clean the injectors, it does a world of good for the smog test results. Injector cleaner helps remove carbon buildup in the combustion chamber as well as on the intake valves. This usually has a drastic effect on emissions.

What to Check If You Fail

If your vehicle failed the test because of excessive exhaust emissions, the most likely cause is that the engine needs a tune-up. If you just had a minor tune-up, consider a new set of spark plug wires. If they are fairly new, try installing a new oxygen sensor. If these items are all new and functioning, your vehicle may need a new catalytic converter.

Hydrocarbon (HC) emissions are a result of a mixture that is too rich or too lean. *Lean*: combustion of the mixture didn't reach all the hydrocarbon molecules and some are exiting out the exhaust unburned. *Rich*: the mixture is so rich that the fuel cannot be burned because of the lack of oxygen. High HC also happens when there is an ignition problem such as a bad spark plug.

If your smog test showed a failure of hydrocarbon emissions, look for high HC for any of the following reasons:

- Engine not at normal operating temperature. Cool cylinder walls tend to "quench" the flame front and "put out the fire"

- Vacuum hose(s) disconnected or leaking, causing a very lean mixture or preventing the proper operation of emission components

- Exhaust leaks in front of the oxygen sensor, causing high HC and high CO

- Faulty spark timing, spark advance

- Faulty spark plugs, wiring, coil, distributor, or ignition system—low spark strength

- Engine idle speed too high or too low

- Carburetor set too lean or plugged fuel injector

- Internal engine problems such as worn rings or burned valves, which cause low compression. A worn intake cam lobe will cause high HC emissions at idle. A worn exhaust cam lobe will cause high HC emissions both at idle and just above idle.

Carbon monoxide (CO) emissions are caused by a rich air-fuel mixture. This is the result of incomplete combustion of the hydrocarbon molecules causing the mixture not to be burned properly. CO has only one oxygen atom because there wasn't enough oxygen available during the combustion process. There was too much fuel present for the available oxygen.

Look for high CO for any of the following reasons:

- CO failures at 2,500 rpm with CO at 1 to 1.5 percent over the limit can come from old oil

- Rich mixture due to rich settings/high float level, choke, or carburetor malfunction

- Improper fuel injector operation, dirty/sticking fuel injector

- Stuck PCV valve, allowing raw oil or an oil mist and blowby gases to be drawn into the engine through the air-intake system

- Worn internal oil seals, valve guides, piston rings, allowing oil to be burned—low compression

- Plugged air filter, starving the engine of oxygen

Nitrates of oxygen (NOx) come from excessively high combustion temperatures or an excessively lean mixture. NOx is created when combustion temperatures are over $2,500°F$. This condition occurs only when the engine is under load—not at idle.

Look for high NOx from any of the following reasons:

- Engine overheating or cooling-system restrictions. Beware of blockages inside the cooling jacket surrounding the combustion chamber. Check for a stuck thermostat—EGR system malfunctions. EGR introduces inert exhaust gases back into the engine, which lowers combustion temperatures and reduces NOx. Leaking EGR values cause deficiency misfires, which appear similar to a lean misfire. To pinpoint which type you have, adding propane to the intake will correct only a lean misfire problem.

- Lean fuel mixture. Look for vacuum hose(s) disconnected or air leaks into the intake manifold or vacuum leaks. Check for a proper float level—improper operation of emission components.

- Carbon deposits in the combustion chamber prevent proper heat transfer into the cooling system. Carbon deposits can also raise compression.

- Dirty injectors cause a slightly lean mixture and more NOx.

- Timing advancing too far. This can be caused by (a) a faulty coolant sensor, telling the computer the engine is cold; (b) a knock sensor problem; (c) a Baro sensor reading high altitudes; (d) a faulty computer; (e) Ford's EVP (EGR value position sensor) reading that there's lots of EGR activation when, in fact, there is not lots of EGR. Timing not advancing enough causes the engine to run hot.

- Stuck engine preheat system. Look for a stuck preheater door or an EFE that is keeping hot air going into the engine after it has warmed up.

- If the air pump switching mechanism fails to switch the air from upstream to downstream, the NOx section of the three-way catalyst will not be able to operate efficiently because NOx catalytic converters are very efficient when oxygen levels are low. Remember: the oxygen needed for proper HC/CO conversion will reduce NOx conversion.

- If there is a problem with too much oxygen in the exhaust system, the NOx section of the catalyst will not be able to operate correctly in converting NOx. Or one section of the catalytic converter can be bad while the other section is OK. Replacement is necessary to lower NOx levels.

Flowchart 1: Vehicle Won't Start

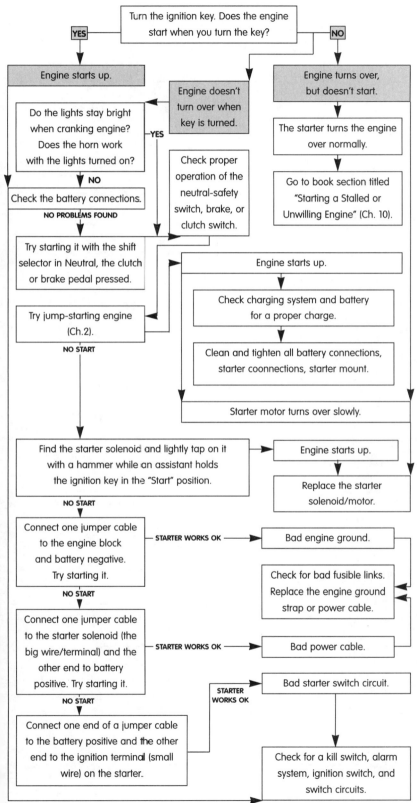

Flowchart 2: Vehicle Pulls

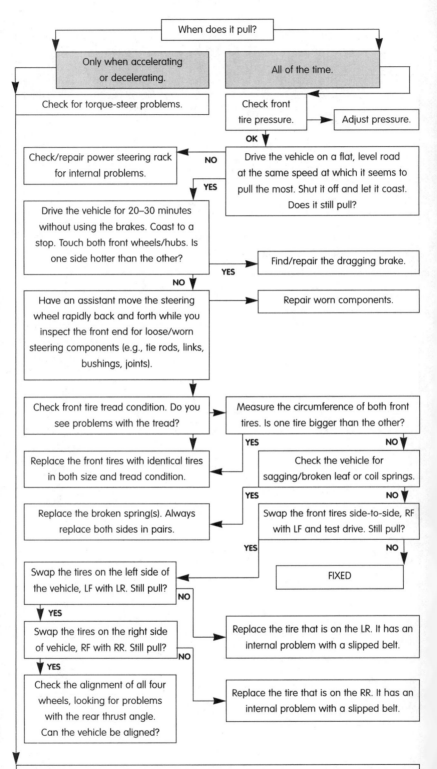

Flowchart 3: Vehicle Overheats

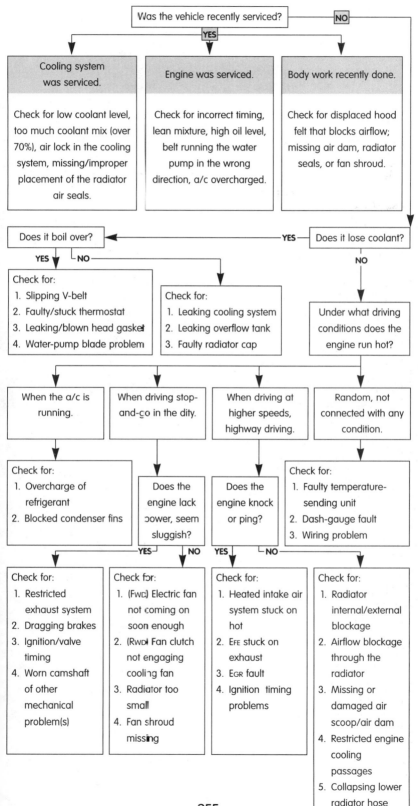

Was the vehicle recently serviced?

NO

YES

Cooling system was serviced.

Check for low coolant level, too much coolant mix (over 70%), air lock in the cooling system, missing/improper placement of the radiator air seals.

Engine was serviced.

Check for incorrect timing, lean mixture, high oil level, belt running the water pump in the wrong direction, a/c overcharged.

Body work recently done.

Check for displaced hood felt that blocks airflow; missing air dam, radiator seals, or fan shroud.

Does it boil over? ← **YES** — Does it lose coolant?

YES ⌐**NO**

NO

Check for:
1. Slipping V-belt
2. Faulty/stuck thermostat
3. Leaking/blown head gasket
4. Water-pump blade problem

Check for:
1. Leaking cooling system
2. Leaking overflow tank
3. Faulty radiator cap

Under what driving conditions does the engine run hot?

When the a/c is running.

When driving stop-and-go in the city.

When driving at higher speeds, highway driving.

Random, not connected with any condition.

Check for:
1. Overcharge of refrigerant
2. Blocked condenser fins

Does the engine lack power, seem sluggish?

Does the engine knock or ping?

Check for:
1. Faulty temperature-sending unit
2. Dash-gauge fault
3. Wiring problem

YES⌐ **NO** **YES**⌐ **NO**

Check for:
1. Restricted exhaust system
2. Dragging brakes
3. Ignition/valve timing
4. Worn camshaft of other mechanical problem(s)

Check for:
1. (Fwd) Electric fan not coming on soon enough
2. (Rwd) Fan clutch not engaging cooling fan
3. Radiator too small
4. Fan shroud missing

Check for:
1. Heated intake air system stuck on hot
2. Efe stuck on exhaust
3. Egr fault
4. Ignition timing problems

Check for:
1. Radiator internal/external blockage
2. Airflow blockage through the radiator
3. Missing or damaged air scoop/air dam
4. Restricted engine cooling passages
5. Collapsing lower radiator hose

Index

About the Author

An automotive technician since 1964, David "Dré" Solomon is a Service Technician Society member and is the society's technical services manager. He is certified by the National Institute of Automobile Service Excellence as a Master Automobile, Master Heavy Duty Truck, Master Auto Body, Paint, and Advanced Engine Performance Technician. Solomon has taught high-tech automotive computer diagnostics coast to coast since 1986, participates in the National Train the Trainer Works for the U.S. EPA, and is a Certified Fluke Scopemeter trainer. A contributing editor for numerous periodicals, including *Trailer Life*, *Women's First*, *Import Service*, *Emissions Monthly*, *Bottom Line Personal*, *Boardroom Reports*, and *Moneysworth*, Solomon is the author of *Hints and Tips to Make Life Easier* (Reader's Digest) as well as an acclaimed book on Bosch fuel injection and is a contributor to the book *Beat the System* (Rodale Press). For more than a decade, he has published the *Nutz & Boltz* newsletter. Solomon has been inducted by the Society of Automotive Engineers as a full member and is also a member of the North Atlantic Council of Automotive Instructors. He is listed as a World Class Automobile Technician in the Automotive Hall of Fame.